KIDS' HOLIDAY FUN

Great Family Activities Every Month of the Year

By Penny Warner

Illustrated by Kathy Rogers

 **Meadowbrook Press**
Distributed by Simon & Schuster
New York

Library of Congress Cataloging-in-Publication Data
Warner, Penny.
    Kids' holiday fun : great family activities every month of the year / Penny Warner ; illustrated by
Kathy Rogers.
                  p.   cm.
    Includes index.
    1. Holidays—Juvenile literature. 2. Special days—Juvenile literature. [1. Holidays.
2. Handicraft.] I. Rogers, Kathy, ill. II. Title.
    GT3933.W36 1994
    393.2' 6—dc20

                                    94-28477
                                       CIP
                                     AC

ISBN 0-88166-214-3
Simon & Schuster Ordering # 0-671-89981-3

Creative Advisor: Bruce Lansky
Editor: Cathy Broberg
Managing Editor: Dale E. Howard
Production Manager: Amy Unger
Art Director: Erik Broberg
Desktop Publishing Coordinator: Patrick Gross
Illustrator: Kathy Rogers

Published by Meadowbrook Press, 18318 Minnetonka Boulevard, Deephaven, MN 55391.

BOOK TRADE DISTRIBUTION by Simon & Schuster, a division of Simon and Schuster, Inc.,
1230 Avenue of the Americas, New York, NY 10020.

99 98 97 96   6 5 4 3

Printed in the United States of America.

DEDICATION

To my family, Tom, Matthew, and Rebecca, the ones who
make every day a holiday and every moment a celebration.

ACKNOWLEDGMENTS

I'd like to thank the following kids for sharing the holidays with us: Chad Anderson, Brenton Burpo, Craig Clemetson, Jason Cosetti, Tara Cubel, Jonathan Ellington, Steven Ellington, Brian Hurley, Geoffrey Pike, Brie Saunders, Brooke Saunders, Kelli Saunders, Kristin Saunders, Sean Saunders, Jana Swec, Joseph Swec, Tim Swec, Mia Thiele, Heather Thornton, Holly Valdez, Samuel Valdez, Zachary Valdez, Jennifer Ware, Alexander Warner, Nicholas Warner, and Simonie Webster.

Thanks to my Early Childhood Education and Special Education students at Diablo Valley College, Chabot College, and Ohlone College for sharing their wonderful ideas. Thanks especially to students Marianne Mendonsa, Stacey Norris, James Rudder, and professors Dr. Linda Barde, Deya Brashears, Barbara Burri, Norma Meyerholtz, and Peyton Nattinger.

Thanks to Jonnie Jacobs, Margaret Lucke, Lynn MacDonald, and Sally Richards, my inspirational writing group.

Thanks to Sonja Brown, Laurie Erickson, Ann Fate, Irma Kelley, Deb Sieber, Gail Sorenson, Lisa Steinman, and Beth Thompson for reviewing the manuscript.

And a special thanks to Bruce Lansky and my wonderful editor at Meadowbrook Press, Cathy Broberg.

CONTENTS

INTRODUCTION

The holidays around my house have always been a time for family gatherings, festivities, food, and fun. Anytime we can celebrate a special day, we do—all year-round from New Year's Eve to Christmas Day. Every month offers more opportunities for merriment!

After years of hosting family holiday celebrations and collecting great ideas for things to do, play, eat, and enjoy, I've put together all the best ideas in this easy-to-follow, how-to book called *Kids' Holiday Fun*. Its thirty-four popular holidays feature lots of favorite traditional ideas you may recognize, with many new ideas added for today's new interests. I've provided a wide range of activities that families can do together, or that older kids can do by themselves. The book contains suggestions for decorations, activities, arts & crafts, recipes, and party ideas, along with practical tips, variations, and more—all with an emphasis on fun!

So check the date on your calendar, flip open the book to the appropriate month, and find a special day to celebrate with your family.

Happy Holidays!

Penny Warner

January

NEW YEAR'S EVE & NEW YEAR'S DAY
December 31 & January 1

New Year's Day is one of our oldest holidays, but it hasn't always been celebrated on January 1. In fact, January wasn't even a month until the first century B.C., when Roman Dictator Julius Caesar created a new calendar. Most of the world now uses the Gregorian calendar, a revision of Caesar's calendar that Pope Gregory XIII introduced in 1582.

The New Year prompts people to look back over the year past and forward to what the future may hold. Some people take time to make resolutions to improve their lives. Many others set aside New Year's Eve for parties, celebrating with confetti and noise-makers and singing "Auld Lang Syne" at midnight, when the New Year officially begins. New Year's Day, a national holiday, is a day to watch football games and parades and to gather with family and friends. It is also a holy day for many religions.

Confetti Bags

5, 4, 3, 2, 1. . . Celebrate! Preparing for the big countdown is half the fun of New Year's Eve. And smashing these confetti-filled bags will be a favorite part of the celebration. It's messy, but lots of fun.

Time: 30 minutes

Complexity: Easy

What to Do:

1. Use the markers to draw festive designs on the paper bags.
2. Cut the crepe paper up into tiny pieces to use as the confetti.
3. Put the confetti into the bags.

Materials:
- Markers (all colors)
- Paper bags (lunch-size)
- Crepe paper (all colors)
- Scissors
- String

4. Blow the bags up and tie them shut with the string.
5. Pop the bags when the clock strikes twelve.

Variation: Use balloons instead of bags. Be careful not to inhale when blowing up the balloons, and be sure to pick up all the balloon pieces after the party so toddlers won't swallow them.

Practical Tip: Have a clean-up race after the confetti explosion.

Party Hats

Have a blast creating these wacky party hats! They're a must for New Year's Eve.

Time: 30 minutes

Complexity: Easy

What to Do:

1. Cut the construction paper into 4-inch-wide strips, long enough to wrap around your head with a little extra to overlap.
2. Cut a zigzag design along one side of each strip.
3. Decorate with the glitter, sequins, ribbons, and crayons or markers.

Materials:
- Construction paper
- Scissors
- Glitter, sequins, and ribbons
- Glue
- Crayons or markers
- Tape

4. Measure the strip to fit your head and then tape it together.

Variation: Make a cone-shaped hat or any other shape you want.

Noisemakers

Strike up the band, the New Year is here! These kazoo noisemakers are a great way to celebrate the New Year.

Time: 30 minutes

Complexity: Easy

What to Do:

1. Decorate the toilet-paper tubes with the glitter, sequins, ribbons, and crayons or markers.
2. Cut one saucer-size circle out of the cellophane for each tube.
3. Wrap a cellophane circle over one end of each tube and secure with rubber bands.

Materials:
- Toilet-paper tubes
- Glitter, sequins, and ribbons
- Glue
- Crayons or markers
- Cellophane
- Scissors
- Rubber bands
- Tape

4. Hold the open end of a tube up to your mouth, and then hum or make other noises.

Variation: Make other noisemakers by placing candies, popcorn kernels, or beans in small metal boxes or paper plates folded in half and stapled shut.

Resolution Book

Say good-bye to the past and hello to the future. This activity is a good way for your family to share feelings and find solutions to problems.

Time: 30–60 minutes

Complexity: Easy

What to Do:

1. Using the ruler and pencil, draw vertical lines down a piece of light-colored construction paper, creating a column for each family member.

2. Have the family members write their names on the top of the columns.

3. Discuss resolutions, and then have the family members write their resolutions under their names with pens. The parents' resolutions could parallel the children's.

4. Fill the other pages of the book with drawings or pictures, cut from old magazines or catalogs, that illustrate the resolutions. For example, a picture of a couple waltzing will encourage parents to learn how to dance and a picture of a child playing a piano will stimulate children to practice.

Materials:
- Construction paper (light-colored)
- Ruler
- Pencil
- Pens (all colors)
- Paper punch
- String or notebook binder
- Scissors
- **Optional:** old magazines or catalogs

5. Use the paper punch to punch three holes along the left side of the pages, and then bind the pages together with string or put in a notebook binder.

Variation: Do this activity using a video camera or tape recorder. Just record your family members talking about their resolutions. Pull the tapes out whenever you need a reminder.

Practical Tip: Keep the resolutions simple so there will be little pressure. For example: "Keep room clean" or "Start a new hobby."

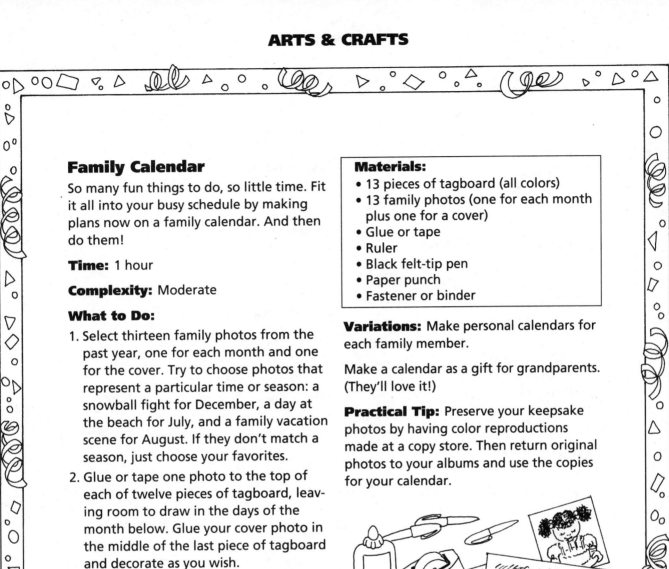

Family Calendar

So many fun things to do, so little time. Fit it all into your busy schedule by making plans now on a family calendar. And then do them!

Time: 1 hour

Complexity: Moderate

What to Do:

1. Select thirteen family photos from the past year, one for each month and one for the cover. Try to choose photos that represent a particular time or season: a snowball fight for December, a day at the beach for July, and a family vacation scene for August. If they don't match a season, just choose your favorites.

2. Glue or tape one photo to the top of each of twelve pieces of tagboard, leaving room to draw in the days of the month below. Glue your cover photo in the middle of the last piece of tagboard and decorate as you wish.

3. Label each month, and then use the ruler and felt-tip pen to draw in a grid for the dates. Fill in the appropriate dates for the upcoming calendar year.

4. Mark special family dates like birthdays, anniversaries, family vacations, and anything else family members want to remember.

5. Punch holes in the top of the tagboard and bind together.

6. Hang the calendar up in a central location for your family to use and enjoy throughout the year.

Materials:

- 13 pieces of tagboard (all colors)
- 13 family photos (one for each month plus one for a cover)
- Glue or tape
- Ruler
- Black felt-tip pen
- Paper punch
- Fastener or binder

Variations: Make personal calendars for each family member.

Make a calendar as a gift for grandparents. (They'll love it!)

Practical Tip: Preserve your keepsake photos by having color reproductions made at a copy store. Then return original photos to your albums and use the copies for your calendar.

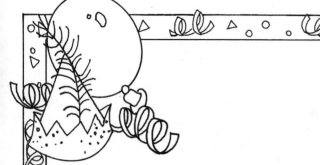

BUNCH OF BEVERAGES

This special night calls for extra-special refreshments. Everyone will love toasting in the New Year with these yummy drinks.

Cherry Sparkler

Here's a traditional favorite also known as a "Shirley Temple."

Ingredients:
- 1 32-ounce bottle ginger ale
- 1 6-ounce bottle cherry juice
- 4 maraschino cherries
- **Optional:** ice

Materials:
- Large spoon
- Pitcher
- 4 tall glasses
- Straws

Serves: 4

Time: 5 minutes

Complexity: Easy

What to Do:

1. Pour the ginger ale and cherry juice into the pitcher and stir well.
2. Pour the mixture into four tall glasses.
3. Drop a cherry into each glass.
4. Serve with a straw and ice, if desired.

New Year's Frost

Mmmm! This delicious drink tastes like apple pie à la mode.

Serves: 4–6

Time: 5 minutes

Complexity: Easy

Ingredients:
- 1 16-ounce can applesauce
- 1/4 teaspoon cinnamon
- 1 pint frozen vanilla yogurt
- 1-1/2 cups milk

Materials:
- Blender
- Glasses
- Straws
- Spoons

What to Do:

1. Put half of the ingredients into the blender, cover, and blend until smooth.
2. Pour the blended mixture into glasses, and then blend the second half.
3. Serve in glasses with straws and spoons.

Hot Chocolate Mint

Here's a warm, creamy drink with a hint of mint.

Serves: 4

Time: 5 minutes

Complexity: Easy

Ingredients:
- 4 cups milk
- 8 tablespoons cocoa mix
- 4 drops peppermint flavoring

Materials:
- Spoon
- Saucepan
- Stove
- Mugs

What to Do:
1. Combine the ingredients in the saucepan and warm over low heat, stirring occasionally.
2. Pour into mugs and serve.

Winter Warmer

Brrrr . . . this warm berry drink is sure to warm you up on this frozen and frigid night.

Serves: 6

Time: 10 minutes

Complexity: Easy

Ingredients:
- 1 32-ounce bottle cranberry-juice cocktail
- 1 16-ounce bottle apple juice
- 3 cinnamon sticks

Materials:
- Large spoon
- Saucepan
- Stove
- Mugs

What to Do:
1. Combine the ingredients in the saucepan and warm over low heat, stirring occasionally.
2. Pour into mugs and serve.

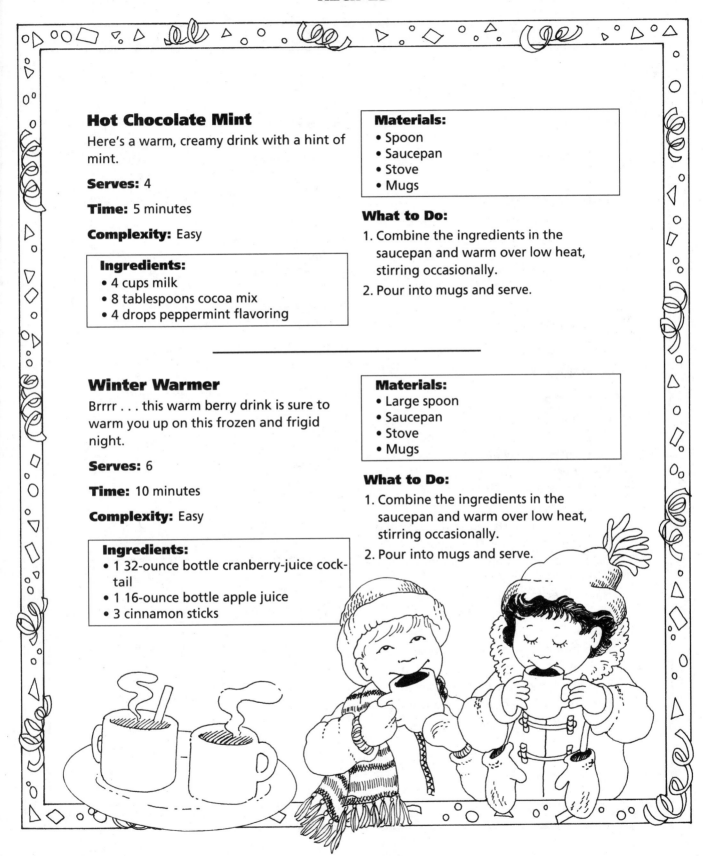

Time Capsule

Here's a great way to capture time in a bottle—or rather a box. This activity helps the whole family remember fun times over the last year, and the capsule becomes a cherished collection of childhood treasure in years to come. Make it a yearly tradition.

Time: 30–45 minutes

Complexity: Easy

What to Do:

1. Collect memorabilia from the past year's events such as a vacation, birthday party, moving day, last day of school, Halloween, visit to the hospital, trip to the zoo, and Valentine's Day.

2. Make an inventory list of all the items you want to include in the time capsule for future reference. For example: postcard from June family vacation to Yellowstone, program from Susan's first clarinet recital, balloons from David's fifth birthday party, and so on.

3. Talk about each item and the event it's from before placing it in the box.

4. Store the box in the attic or another safe place. Look through the box at the beginning of the next year before creating a new time capsule.

Materials:
- Memorabilia from the year's events, such as photos, ticket stubs, vacation postcards, programs from plays or school recitals, letters, invitations, party favors, Halloween masks, and so on
- Dress or shoe box
- Paper
- Pen or pencil

Variations: Make a family scrapbook or yearbook out of the year's memorabilia.

Make a collage out of memorabilia to hang up and enjoy.

Practical Tip: Decorate the box with construction paper, markers or crayons, glitter, and so on.

Memory Clock

Tick-tock, tick-tock. Watching the clock on New Year's Eve can make kids restless and wild. Here's a good party activity to settle things down a little. It's also a good way to reminisce about the fading year.

Time: 30 minutes

Complexity: Easy

What to Do:

1. Cover the table with the paper tablecloth or piece of tagboard.

2. Using a dark-colored felt-tip pen, draw a large clock on the tablecloth or tagboard. Fill in the hour markers with both numbers and months. For example, write "1" and "January" at the first spot, "2" and "February" at the second, and so on.

3. Using a felt-tip pen, draw Mickey Mouse–style hands (one short and one long) on the construction paper. Cut the hands out and either glue them onto the clock pointing to the "12" or attach them to the center of the clock with a brass fastener.

4. Outside of the clock face and next to the corresponding month, have the guests take turns writing in memorable events that happened over the year. Include both personal events, such as "Jackie made the soccer team," and news events, such as "Earthquake."

5. Continue taking turns adding memories until the tablecloth is filled with the past.

Materials:
- Table
- Paper tablecloth or large piece of tagboard
- Felt-tip pens (all colors)
- Construction paper
- Scissors
- Glue or brass fastener

Variation: Fill the clock with events your guests are looking forward to in the upcoming year, such as a summer vacation, an upcoming birthday, or the day when the braces will come off.

Practical Tips: Make sure your table is protected if pens are permanent and could soak through.

Use heavy-duty paper so it won't tear.

Save the memory clock to show the next year.

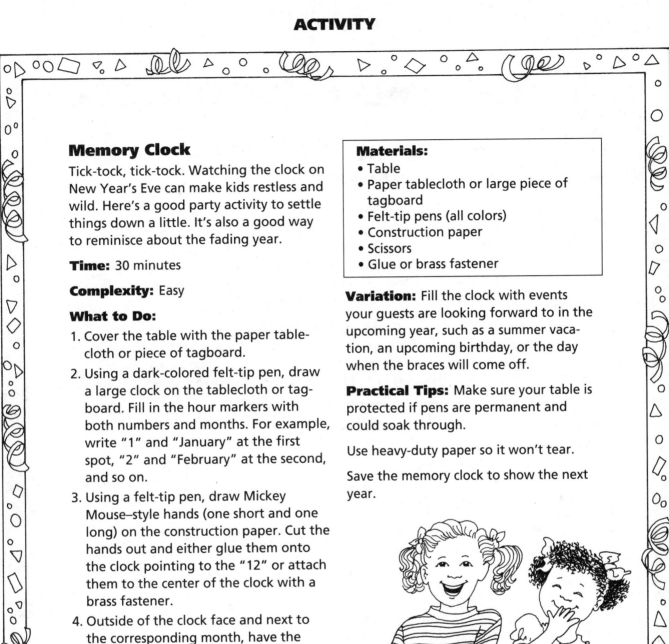

MARTIN LUTHER KING DAY
January 15

Martin Luther King Jr. was born in Atlanta, Georgia, on January 15, 1929. A Baptist minister, he led the American civil rights movement in the late '50s and '60s, believing that equality could be achieved through nonviolent action. His dream of equality and brotherhood became a vision for the nation. King received the Nobel Peace Prize in 1964. On April 4, 1968, he was assassinated in Memphis, Tennessee. His birthday was designated as a national public holiday in 1986.

This is a day to remember a great civil rights leader. It's also a day to recognize the rights and freedom we have in this country and to continue the fight for true equality. On this day many communities hold programs to honor King, and individuals participate in various marches and prayers in an effort to bring King's dream closer to reality.

Singing "We Shall Overcome"

Honor Martin Luther King by learning this song that was a major anthem of the civil rights movement. It's a good way to focus on civil rights and equality

We Shall Overcome

We shall overcome, we shall overcome,
We shall overcome someday.
Oh, deep in my heart, I do believe
We shall overcome someday.

We are not afraid, we are not afraid,
We are not afraid today.
Oh, deep in my heart, I do believe
We shall overcome someday.

We are not alone, . . . (today)

The truth will make us free, . . .

We'll walk hand in hand, . . .

Black and white together, . . . (now)

We shall all be free, . . .

Flag of Freedom

Flag-tastic! Make a colorful flag to carry in a Martin Luther King Day march or to display year-round. It's easy, and it will remind all who see it what this holiday means.

Time: 30 minutes

Complexity: Easy

What to Do:

1. Using the markers, draw a design on the fabric. Try to reflect the themes of equality and fellowship in the design. For example, draw two members of different races holding hands, a profile of Martin Luther King, or the slogan "We Shall Overcome." (You can make your design as elaborate or as simple as you desire.)

2. Glue the fabric to the wooden dowel or pole. Allow to dry.

3. Hang the flag outside your house or bring it to a parade.

Materials:
- Fabric (muslin works well)
- Wooden dowel or pole
- Markers (all colors)
- Glue

Variation: Make a poster instead of a flag. Hang it up at home or bring it to school to share.

Practical Tip: Read information on Martin Luther King to inspire ideas for the flag.

Portrait Studio

Martin Luther King stressed that all people should be accepted and loved no matter what their differences. This fun activity helps kids understand how unique each one is and yet how much alike we all are.

Time: 45–60 minutes

Complexity: Easy

What to Do:

1. Have one person lie down on a large sheet of paper and have someone else draw the outline of the person. Take turns until all have been outlined.

2. Draw in features, such as clothes, facial features, and hair styles. Have the artists look in the mirror if they forget to add ears, freckles, fingernails, and so on.

3. Cut the portraits out and tape them to the wall, with each one holding the hand of another one.

4. Talk about how all of the portraits are similar and how they are all different.

Materials:
- Sheets of white paper as large as a child's body (available at arts-and-crafts stores and stationers)
- Crayons or felt-tip pens
- Scissors
- Mirror
- Tape

Variations: Have everyone draw in someone else's portrait so they can notice the similarities and differences firsthand.

Draw portraits of famous figures in history or fantasy, such as Martin Luther King, Abe Lincoln, or Superman.

Draw costumes from other countries.

Practical Tip: If you can't find large enough paper, tape together several small sheets.

February

CHINESE NEW YEAR
(Date Varies)

Gung Hei Fat Choy! That means "Good Luck" in Chinese and is the usual Chinese New Year's greeting. The New Year is the biggest celebration for the Chinese—the festivities go on for fifteen days. This lunar holiday begins at sunset on the day of the second new moon following the winter solstice (usually between January 21 and February 20).

As the Chinese New Year approaches, families clean their homes to escape bad luck in the upcoming year. Feasts are held on New Year's Eve, and all stay up late, believing that doing so brings a longer life to parents. People dress in their best clothes and new shoes on New Year's Day and give small gifts to each other. The celebration continues until the first full moon is celebrated with the great Feast of the Lanterns. Carrying homemade lanterns, people fill the streets, joining a great parade led by an enormous dragon, which closes this grand holiday.

Chinese Wand

Bright colors are a favorite part of the Chinese New Year celebration. Join in the festivities by waving these colorful Chinese wands, made out of ribbon or crepe paper, at a Chinese New Year parade or just at home.

Time: 10 minutes

Complexity: Easy

What to Do:

1. Cut a piece of ribbon or crepe paper as long as each person is tall.
2. Securely tape the ribbon to a pencil or chopstick.
3. Wave the wand in the air, making different patterns, shapes, and movements. Write names or make circles, figure eights, and other designs.

Materials:
- Ribbon or crepe paper
- Scissors
- Pencil or chopstick
- Tape

Variation: Have several friends over to make the wands and to develop a group "drill" to perform for family or neighbors.

Practical Tip: Trim the ribbons if their length is troublesome.

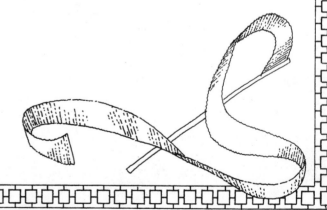

Paper Lantern

Red, a lucky color in China, is the predominant color in all New Year's decorations. The Chinese believe that red not only conveys wishes of a great start to the New Year but also brings good will, harmony, and beauty. Trim your party room in red and make these Chinese paper lanterns to hang from the ceiling.

Time: 45 minutes

Complexity: Moderate

What to Do:

1. Fold a piece of red construction paper in half, lengthwise.

2. Use the pencil and ruler to draw lines every 1/2 inch along the folded edge. Cut on these lines from the fold to within 1/2 to 1 inch from the edge of the paper.

3. Open the paper. Curl it into a cylinder with the short ends at the top and the bottom.

4. Glue or staple the edges of the paper lantern together.

5. Draw four rectangles 1-1/4 inches by 3-1/2 inches on the blue construction paper. Cut these out for your candles.

6. Draw and cut out from the construction paper eight large yellow flames and eight small red flames.

7. Glue a yellow flame on both sides of the blue candles; then glue a red flame in the center of each yellow flame.

8. Glue the paper candles to the inside of the lantern.

Materials:
- Construction paper (red, yellow, and blue)
- Pencil
- Ruler
- Scissors
- Glue or stapler

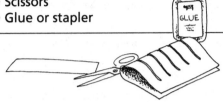

9. Cut a piece of construction paper into a strip about 1 to 2 inches wide by 8 to 10 inches long. Glue or staple the strip to the top of the lantern for a handle.

Variations: Use tissue paper instead of construction paper.

Instead of candles cut out traditional Chinese animal shapes like the rat, ox, or dog.

Practical Tip: For smaller children, pre-cut the paper for easier handling.

Chinese New Year Masks

Put on a happy face, or a sad one, or a scary one—the possibilities are endless with homemade masks. Masks are a playful part of Chinese New Year parades, and making these festive disguises lets you stretch your imagination.

Time: 45–60 minutes

Complexity: Easy—Adult assistance recommended.

What to Do:

1. Prepare the stiff paper plates ahead of time by cutting them into interesting shapes and cutting out eyeholes with the scissors or Exacto knife.

2. Cut the soft paper plates into large shapes; then staple, glue, or tape these pieces to the outside of the foundation (stiff paper plate) to make the mask larger and more interesting.

3. Decorate the masks with the materials listed above to create bright, scary, or crazy faces.

4. Glue or tape pieces of ribbon or yarn (about 6 inches long) to the base and sides of the masks.

5. Staple or glue a wooden dowel, ruler, tongue depressor, or Popsicle stick to the side of each mask.

6. Hold a mask in front of your face and have a parade.

Materials:
- Stiff white paper plates
- Soft white paper plates
- Construction paper (all colors)
- Decorations, such as sequins, glitter, stars, ribbons, stickers, confetti, and puffy paints
- Poster paints, felt-tip pens, or crayons
- Paint brushes
- Stapler, glue, or tape
- Scissors or Exacto knife
- Ribbon or yarn
- Wooden dowels, rulers, tongue depressors, or Popsicle sticks

Variation: Use pieces of cardboard or tagboard instead of paper plates.

Practical Tips: Provide lots of arts-and-crafts materials.

Cut out different shapes from the colored construction paper that the artists can use on their masks.

Chinese New Year Firecrackers

These Chinese New Year Firecrackers don't explode, but they're great for party-room decorations or for just playing with.

Time: 15–30 minutes

Complexity: Easy–Moderate

What to Do:

1. Tie a piece of string around a small gift, such as a Chinese finger trap, a Chinese fan, or some rice-paper candy.

2. Insert the gift into a toilet-paper tube. Be sure the free end of the string is long enough to dangle out from one end of the tube.

3. Cover the tube with red crepe paper, leaving 2 inches extra at each end and still allowing the string to dangle out.

4. Twist the ends of the "firecracker," still leaving the string dangling out.

5. Use the felt-tip pen to write a name on each "firecracker" or hang them up in a party room and let the guests choose one; then have them pull the string to pull out the gift.

Materials:
- String
- Small gifts
- Toilet-paper tubes
- Red crepe paper
- Felt-tip pen

Variations: Put New Year's fortunes inside the firecrackers instead of gifts.

Use cellophane instead of crepe paper for a crackly effect.

Decorate the firecrackers with stickers.

Practical Tip: Make sure all of the gifts are of equal value.

Almond Cookies

A Chinese dessert tradition that kids of all ages like indulging in, these almond cookies will melt in your mouth. They're also perfect for dipping in tea or milk.

Yields: 4 dozen cookies

Time: 30 minutes

Complexity: Challenging—Adult assistance recommended

Ingredients:
- 3-1/2 cups flour
- 2 cups sugar
- 1 teaspoon baking powder
- 2 cups margarine
- 1 egg, beaten
- 2 teaspoons almond extract
- 1 teaspoon vanilla
- 2–3 tablespoons whole blanched almonds

What to Do:

1. Sift the flour, sugar, and baking powder together in the medium bowl.
2. Add the margarine, egg, almond extract, and vanilla.
3. Mix the dough with your hands until smooth and blended.

Materials:
- Medium bowl
- Rolling pin
- Floured board
- 2" round cookie cutter
- Cookie sheet
- Oven, preheated to 375°

4. Roll the dough until it's 1/4-inch thick on the floured board.
5. Cut with the cookie cutter.
6. Place one almond in the center of each cookie.
7. Place the cookies 1-1/2 inches apart on the ungreased cookie sheet.
8. Bake until lightly browned (about 12 minutes).

Practical Tip: Use caution around heat.

Homemade Fortune Cookies

Will the new year bring riches to your family and friends? Only time will tell. In the meantime, write your own predictions to put in these homemade fortune cookies. They're sure to supply smiles.

Serves: 8

Time: 30 minutes

Complexity: Challenging— Adult assistance recommended

Materials:
- 8-1/4" x 1" slips of paper
- Pen or pencil
- Medium bowl
- Frying pan, lightly greased
- Spatula
- Large spoon
- Pot holder
- Muffin pan
- Stove
- **Optional:** electric mixer

Ingredients:
- 1/4 cup cake flour
- 2 tablespoons sugar
- 1 tablespoon cornstarch
- Dash of salt
- 2 tablespoons oil
- 1 egg white
- 1 tablespoon water

What to Do:

1. Write fortunes on the slips of paper. Set aside.

2. In the medium bowl sift together the cake flour, sugar, cornstarch, and salt.

3. Add the oil and egg white, and stir until smooth.

4. Add the water and mix well with an electric mixer or by hand.

5. Make one cookie at a time by pouring 1 tablespoon of the batter on a lightly greased frying pan. Spread to a 3-1/2-inch circle.

6. Cook over low heat until lightly browned (about 4 minutes).

7. Turn with the spatula and cook for 1 more minute.

8. Quickly place the cookie on the pot holder.

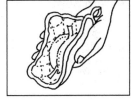

9. Put a paper fortune in the center of the cookie and fold the cookie in half.

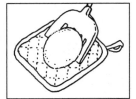

10. Fold the cookie again over the edge of the bowl to make a crescent shape.

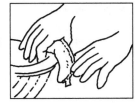

11. Place the cookie in the muffin pan to cool.

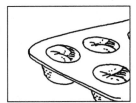

VALENTINE'S DAY
February 14

Though it's believed to be the day birds choose their mates, nobody knows for sure how Valentine's Day came into being. Some say it's been celebrated since the Middle Ages, and most agree it's celebrated in honor of St. Valentine, but *which* Valentine? As many as eight St. Valentines have been identified! According to one popular story, a jailed Valentine fell in love with the jailer's daughter and sent her letters signed, "From Your Valentine." Commercial valentines appeared about 1800.

Cards, kisses, and, yes, chocolates are popular gifts to give to your loved ones on this day, but you can express your love in many ways—hugs, kisses, and just sharing your time. Gift or no gift, Valentine's Day is the perfect time to tell your family and friends how much you love them.

Heart Mobile

Hearts galore! Here's the perfect decoration to get everyone in the mood for this loving holiday.

Time: 30–60 minutes

Complexity: Easy–Moderate

What to Do:

1. Cut billions and billions (well, a lot!) of hearts out of the construction paper in all different sizes.
2. Lay out a piece of the ribbon, and glue the paper hearts to both sides of it to make a long valentine mobile.

Materials:
- Construction paper (red, pink, and white)
- Scissors
- Ribbon (red, pink, or white)
- Glue

3. Make as many of these ribbon-heart mobiles as you like, then hang them from the ceiling to create a magical, romantic room of hearts.

Variation: Use fabric scraps instead of construction paper.

Practical Tip: For smaller children, pre-cut the hearts and let them glue them together.

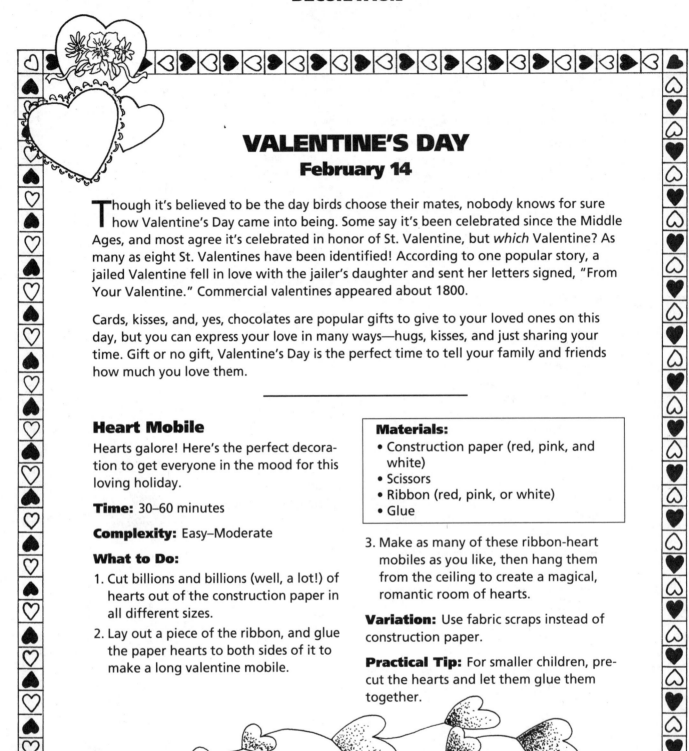

Heart Pin

If you can't afford anything from a jewelry store, here's an inexpensive way for you to make jewelry you'll be proud to give to your valentines.

Time: 60 minutes (plus baking time)

Complexity: Moderate—Adult assistance recommended

Ingredients:
- 4 cups flour
- 1 cup salt
- 1-3/4 cups water
- Red food coloring

What to Do:

1. Make up a batch of baker's clay by combining the flour, salt, and water and kneading it until well mixed.

2. Add a few drops of the red food coloring and mix well.

3. Roll the dough out and cut it into heart shapes, using a cookie cutter or cardboard pattern.

4. Insert a safety pin in the back of each heart and bake 2 to 3 hours (until firm). Allow to cool completely.

Materials:
- Heart-shaped cookie cutter or cardboard pattern
- Oven, preheated to 250°
- Acrylic paint and paint brush or permanent felt-tip pens
- Safety pins
- Varnish (such as Verathane)

5. Use acrylic paint or permanent felt-tip pens to personalize or add designs to the pins.

6. Varnish the pins and allow to dry.

Variations: Instead of coloring the dough with food coloring, just paint the hearts after they're baked.

Use your imagination and make anything you want, such as letters of a loved one's name, a reproduction of a loved one, a special message spelled out, or game pieces for chess or checkers.

Practical Tip: Work the dough on foil so you won't have to transfer it to the cookie sheet. Foil peels off nicely.

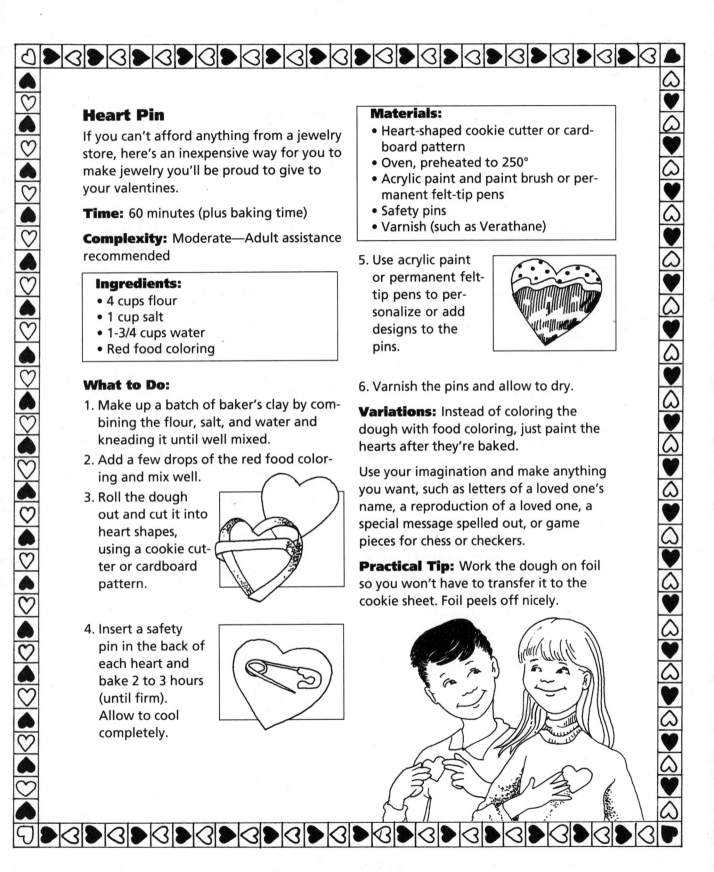

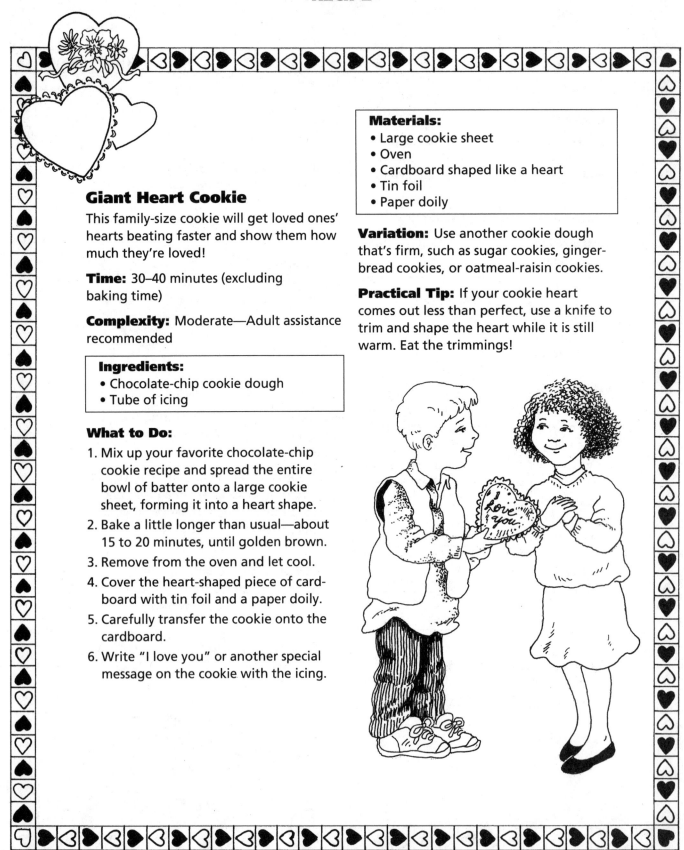

Giant Heart Cookie

This family-size cookie will get loved ones' hearts beating faster and show them how much they're loved!

Time: 30–40 minutes (excluding baking time)

Complexity: Moderate—Adult assistance recommended

Ingredients:
• Chocolate-chip cookie dough
• Tube of icing

What to Do:

1. Mix up your favorite chocolate-chip cookie recipe and spread the entire bowl of batter onto a large cookie sheet, forming it into a heart shape.
2. Bake a little longer than usual—about 15 to 20 minutes, until golden brown.
3. Remove from the oven and let cool.
4. Cover the heart-shaped piece of cardboard with tin foil and a paper doily.
5. Carefully transfer the cookie onto the cardboard.
6. Write "I love you" or another special message on the cookie with the icing.

Materials:
• Large cookie sheet
• Oven
• Cardboard shaped like a heart
• Tin foil
• Paper doily

Variation: Use another cookie dough that's firm, such as sugar cookies, gingerbread cookies, or oatmeal-raisin cookies.

Practical Tip: If your cookie heart comes out less than perfect, use a knife to trim and shape the heart while it is still warm. Eat the trimmings!

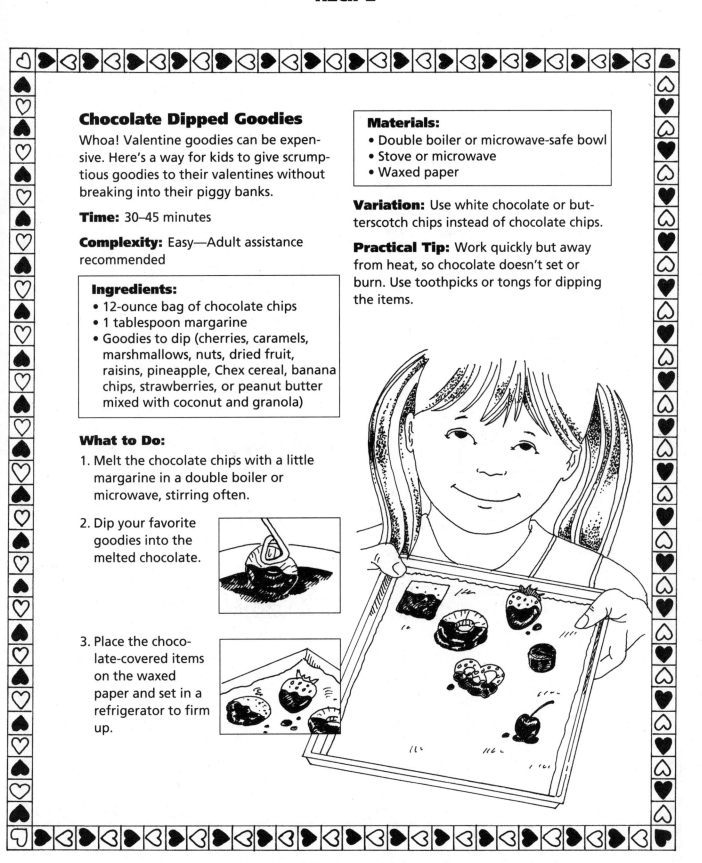

Chocolate Dipped Goodies

Whoa! Valentine goodies can be expensive. Here's a way for kids to give scrumptious goodies to their valentines without breaking into their piggy banks.

Time: 30–45 minutes

Complexity: Easy—Adult assistance recommended

Ingredients:
- 12-ounce bag of chocolate chips
- 1 tablespoon margarine
- Goodies to dip (cherries, caramels, marshmallows, nuts, dried fruit, raisins, pineapple, Chex cereal, banana chips, strawberries, or peanut butter mixed with coconut and granola)

What to Do:

1. Melt the chocolate chips with a little margarine in a double boiler or microwave, stirring often.

2. Dip your favorite goodies into the melted chocolate.

3. Place the chocolate-covered items on the waxed paper and set in a refrigerator to firm up.

Materials:
- Double boiler or microwave-safe bowl
- Stove or microwave
- Waxed paper

Variation: Use white chocolate or butterscotch chips instead of chocolate chips.

Practical Tip: Work quickly but away from heat, so chocolate doesn't set or burn. Use toothpicks or tongs for dipping the items.

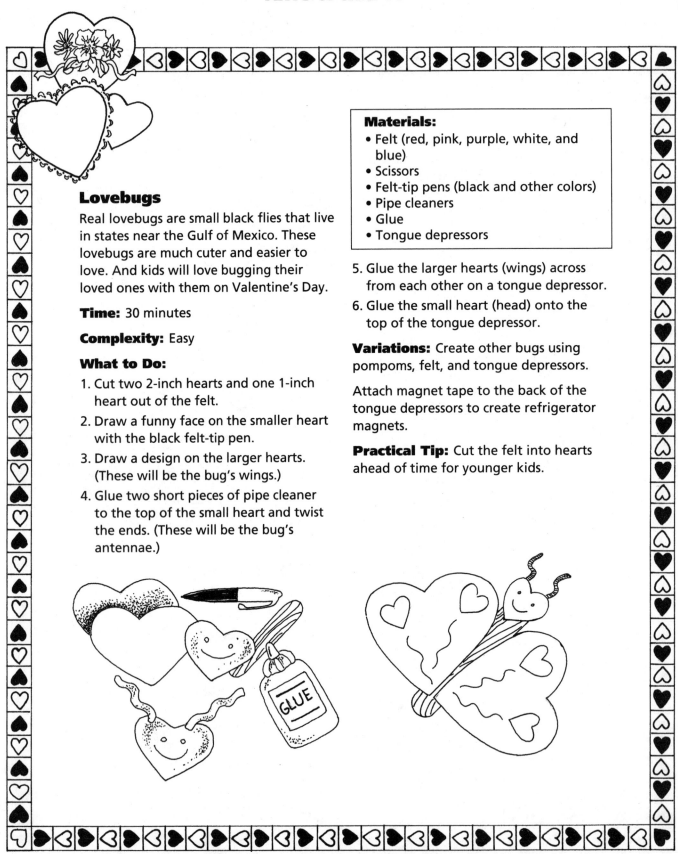

Lovebugs

Real lovebugs are small black flies that live in states near the Gulf of Mexico. These lovebugs are much cuter and easier to love. And kids will love bugging their loved ones with them on Valentine's Day.

Time: 30 minutes

Complexity: Easy

What to Do:

1. Cut two 2-inch hearts and one 1-inch heart out of the felt.
2. Draw a funny face on the smaller heart with the black felt-tip pen.
3. Draw a design on the larger hearts. (These will be the bug's wings.)
4. Glue two short pieces of pipe cleaner to the top of the small heart and twist the ends. (These will be the bug's antennae.)

Materials:
- Felt (red, pink, purple, white, and blue)
- Scissors
- Felt-tip pens (black and other colors)
- Pipe cleaners
- Glue
- Tongue depressors

5. Glue the larger hearts (wings) across from each other on a tongue depressor.
6. Glue the small heart (head) onto the top of the tongue depressor.

Variations: Create other bugs using pompoms, felt, and tongue depressors.

Attach magnet tape to the back of the tongue depressors to create refrigerator magnets.

Practical Tip: Cut the felt into hearts ahead of time for younger kids.

"I Love You" Coupons

Here's a great way to give yourself as Valentine gifts. A coupon book full of proposals and promises, written on heart-shaped pieces of paper, is endearing and lasts a lot longer than a box of candy.

Time: 30–45 minutes

Complexity: Easy

What to Do:

1. Cut 3-by-3-inch hearts out of the construction paper.
2. On the hearts write things to do for loved ones. A parent might include such things as "Good for one batch of favorite cookies," "Good for ten readings of your favorite story," and "Good

Materials:
- Scissors
- Construction paper (all colors)
- Felt-tip pens (all colors)
- Stapler or decorated envelope

for one full lunch box of favorites." A child's coupons might include: "Good for one car-washing," "Good for one week's menu-planning of healthy stuff I'll eat," and "Good for one poem or song written by me just for you."

3. Staple the coupons together into a coupon book or simply put them into a decorated envelope marked "Valentine Coupons."

Practical Tip: When presented with a coupon, perform the requested activity with good humor.

Treasure Hunt

Make your family work for their Valentine gifts—send them on a treasure hunt. They'll feel like secret agents as they decode the clues and discover the hidden treasure.

Time: 30 minutes

Complexity: Easy

What to Do:

1. Use inexpensive valentines or cut hearts out of construction paper.
2. Write instructions on the valentines like those on candy conversation hearts, such as "Be Mine . . . On Time" to get the hunters headed toward the clock,

Materials:
- Kid valentines or construction paper (red, pink, and purple)
- Pen
- Special Valentine gift

where you've hidden the next clue, "I'm True . . . In a Shoe," to get them to look in shoes, or "Hug Me . . . By the Tree," to have them look outside.

3. Hide the gift in the designated spot.

Practical Tip: Write puzzling notes for older family members and draw pictures for younger children who can't read.

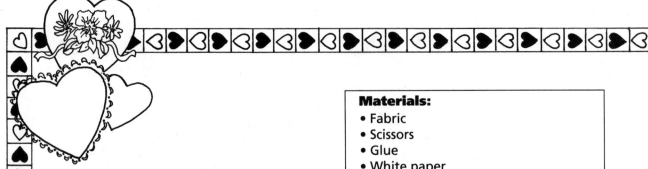

ASSORTMENT OF HEARTS AND CRAFTS

Have a make-your-own valentine marathon session with these fun-to-do arts and crafts. Just pile the materials up and let young artists create their own masterpieces.

Patchwork Heart

What to Do:

1. Cut a large heart out of the fabric.
2. Cut the heart into large pieces.

Materials:
• Fabric
• Scissors
• Glue
• White paper

3. Mix the pieces up.
4. Glue the heart back together on a large sheet of white paper.

Valentine Collage

What to Do:

1. Cut large hearts out of the red construction paper.
2. Glue a variety of the craft items onto the paper hearts.
3. Glue each heart onto a paper doily.

Materials:
• Red construction paper
• Scissors
• Craft items, such as rickrack, sequins, glitter, lace, ribbon, yarn, fabric, stickers, and paper
• Glue
• Paper doilies

Heart Prints

What to Do:

1. Cut a heart shape out of a sponge or potato.
2. Stamp the heart into the ink pad and then onto the white paper.
3. Cut the paper into a Valentine's Day card and write a poem or special message inside.

Materials:
• Sponge or potato
• Pink or red stamp pad
• White paper
• Scissors
• **Optional:** paring knife

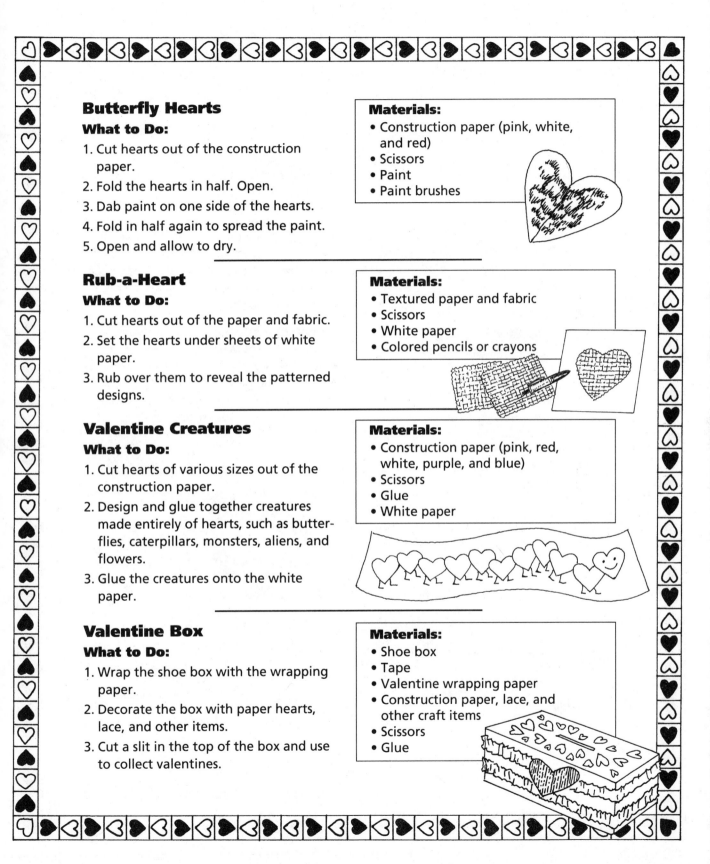

Butterfly Hearts
What to Do:

1. Cut hearts out of the construction paper.
2. Fold the hearts in half. Open.
3. Dab paint on one side of the hearts.
4. Fold in half again to spread the paint.
5. Open and allow to dry.

Materials:
- Construction paper (pink, white, and red)
- Scissors
- Paint
- Paint brushes

Rub-a-Heart
What to Do:

1. Cut hearts out of the paper and fabric.
2. Set the hearts under sheets of white paper.
3. Rub over them to reveal the patterned designs.

Materials:
- Textured paper and fabric
- Scissors
- White paper
- Colored pencils or crayons

Valentine Creatures
What to Do:

1. Cut hearts of various sizes out of the construction paper.
2. Design and glue together creatures made entirely of hearts, such as butterflies, caterpillars, monsters, aliens, and flowers.
3. Glue the creatures onto the white paper.

Materials:
- Construction paper (pink, red, white, purple, and blue)
- Scissors
- Glue
- White paper

Valentine Box
What to Do:

1. Wrap the shoe box with the wrapping paper.
2. Decorate the box with paper hearts, lace, and other items.
3. Cut a slit in the top of the box and use to collect valentines.

Materials:
- Shoe box
- Tape
- Valentine wrapping paper
- Construction paper, lace, and other craft items
- Scissors
- Glue

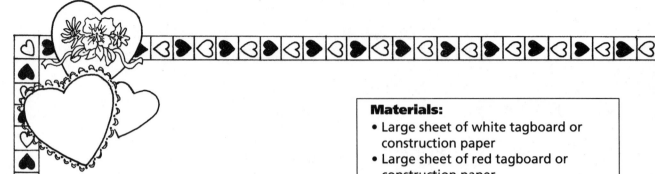

Puzzle Card

Love can be very puzzling. Here's a Valentine puzzle with a secret message that's easy to put together—kids will love making and solving it.

Time: 30 minutes

Complexity: Easy

What to Do:

1. Cut a large heart out of the white tagboard or construction paper.

2. Cut a heart out of the red tagboard or construction paper about an inch larger than the white one.

3. Glue the white heart onto the center of the red heart.

4. Write a Valentine message on the heart with the white candle or crayon. You won't be able to see what you're writing, so plan ahead carefully.

5. Cut the heart into puzzle pieces and slip them into the envelope with instructions to put the heart together and color over the white paper lightly with a dark crayon or paint to read the surprise message.

6. Deliver the valentine to someone special.

Materials:
- Large sheet of white tagboard or construction paper
- Large sheet of red tagboard or construction paper
- Scissors
- Glue or spray adhesive
- White candle or crayon
- Large envelope

Variation: Use just a red sheet of paper and write the messages with a red crayon or candle.

Practical Tip: Using spray adhesive ensures that the white paper will be completely secured to the red paper. If you use glue or paste, be sure to cover the back of the white heart completely so the pieces will not come off when you cut it up.

Heart Bingo

Here's a game of matching hearts for this heartfelt day. Reward the winner with a jar of heart-shaped candies.

Time: 30–45 minutes

Complexity: Easy

What to Do:

1. To prepare a game board for each player, cut one heart out of each piece of fabric for each board plus one extra set for the caller.

2. Glue the ten different hearts in two rows of five on each board.

3. Place the last ten hearts in a small bowl or box.

4. Give each player a game board.

5. Have someone pull a heart from the bowl or box and show it to the players.

6. Players must look at their cards and point to the hearts on their boards that match the heart that was drawn. Whoever points to the right spot first gets to place the drawn heart over the matching board heart.

7. Continue playing until all of the hearts have been drawn. Whoever collects the most hearts, wins.

Materials:
- 10 fabric scraps
- Tagboard, about 8-1/2" x 11" (one sheet for each player)
- Glue
- Scissors
- Heart-shaped cookie cutter
- Small bowl or box

Variations: If you have enough fabric scraps, cut out different hearts for each player's board. Then when hearts are drawn from the bowl, they will only match one card.

Instead of using fabric, color hearts on the game boards in all different ways and have matching ones to draw from the bowl.

Practical Tip: Make the game boards well in advance of the time you plan to play the game.

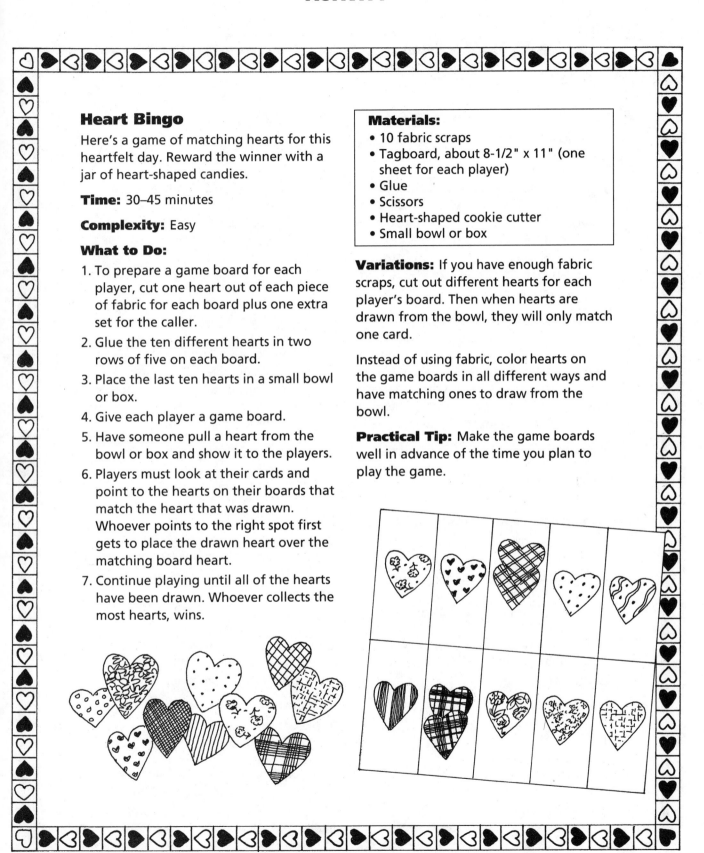

PRESIDENTS' DAY
Third Monday in February

Presidents' Day began as a day to honor George Washington and Abraham Lincoln. George Washington (1732–99) became the father of our country by leading the American army in revolution against the British. Sometimes it seemed that only his courage, faith, and strong will kept the ragtag army together. After winning the war, Washington presided over the Constitutional Convention in 1787. He then became our first president. After two terms he retired to his estate, Mt. Vernon, Virginia, where he died on December 14, 1799.

People called Abraham Lincoln (1809–65) "Honest Abe." He once walked through a snowstorm to return change to a customer of his store. He later became a lawyer in Illinois and was respected for his integrity. As our sixteenth president, Lincoln guided our country through its bitter Civil War. He is especially remembered for issuing the Emancipation Proclamation that freed slaves in the rebellious states. His Gettysburg Address clearly and simply stated the major goal of the war—to preserve the union and democratic government "of the people, by the people, for the people."

These two great presidents are still the main focus of this holiday, but it has also become a time to honor all presidents of the United States.

Singing "Yankee Doodle"

"Yankee Doodle Dandy!" This song, written during the American Revolution, was intended to ridicule the soldiers' uniforms. "Macaroni" does not refer to pasta but instead to an overdressed "dandy" (someone who pays a lot of attention to how he dresses). For whatever reason this folk song came into being, it is still fun to sing today. Give it a try!

Yankee Doodle
Yankee Doodle went to town
A-riding on a pony,
Stuck a feather in his cap
And called it macaroni.

Fath'r and I went down to camp
Along with Captain Goodwin.
There we saw the men and boys
As thick as hasty puddin'.

There was Captain Washington
Upon a slapping stallion,
Giving orders to his men;
I guess there were a million.

Refrain:
Yankee Doodle keep it up,
Yankee Doodle dandy.
Mind the music and the step
And with the girls be handy.

Papier Mâché Piggy Bank

Here's a safe place for kids to put their Washington dollars and nickels so they won't disappear so fast. It's a messy but fun project.

Time: 30–45 minutes

Complexity: Moderate—Adult assistance recommended

What to Do:

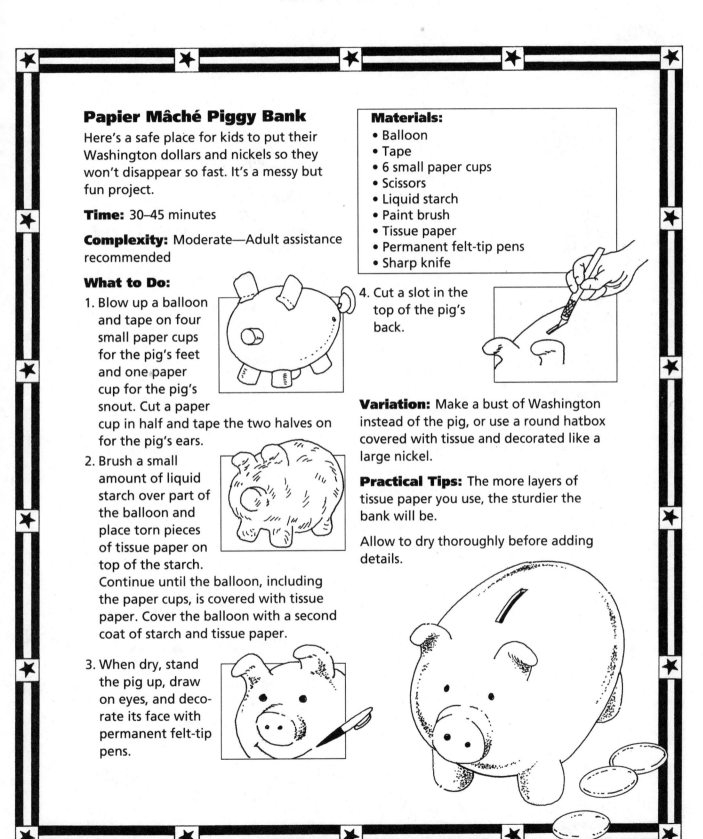

1. Blow up a balloon and tape on four small paper cups for the pig's feet and one paper cup for the pig's snout. Cut a paper cup in half and tape the two halves on for the pig's ears.

2. Brush a small amount of liquid starch over part of the balloon and place torn pieces of tissue paper on top of the starch. Continue until the balloon, including the paper cups, is covered with tissue paper. Cover the balloon with a second coat of starch and tissue paper.

3. When dry, stand the pig up, draw on eyes, and decorate its face with permanent felt-tip pens.

Materials:
- Balloon
- Tape
- 6 small paper cups
- Scissors
- Liquid starch
- Paint brush
- Tissue paper
- Permanent felt-tip pens
- Sharp knife

4. Cut a slot in the top of the pig's back.

Variation: Make a bust of Washington instead of the pig, or use a round hatbox covered with tissue and decorated like a large nickel.

Practical Tips: The more layers of tissue paper you use, the sturdier the bank will be.

Allow to dry thoroughly before adding details.

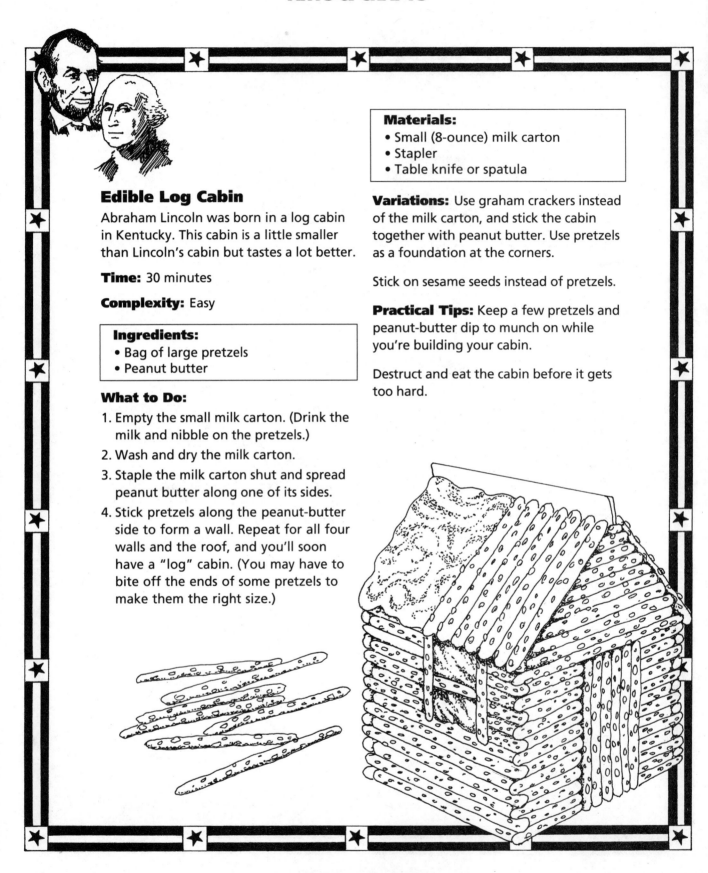

Edible Log Cabin

Abraham Lincoln was born in a log cabin in Kentucky. This cabin is a little smaller than Lincoln's cabin but tastes a lot better.

Time: 30 minutes

Complexity: Easy

Ingredients:
- Bag of large pretzels
- Peanut butter

What to Do:

1. Empty the small milk carton. (Drink the milk and nibble on the pretzels.)
2. Wash and dry the milk carton.
3. Staple the milk carton shut and spread peanut butter along one of its sides.
4. Stick pretzels along the peanut-butter side to form a wall. Repeat for all four walls and the roof, and you'll soon have a "log" cabin. (You may have to bite off the ends of some pretzels to make them the right size.)

Materials:
- Small (8-ounce) milk carton
- Stapler
- Table knife or spatula

Variations: Use graham crackers instead of the milk carton, and stick the cabin together with peanut butter. Use pretzels as a foundation at the corners.

Stick on sesame seeds instead of pretzels.

Practical Tips: Keep a few pretzels and peanut-butter dip to munch on while you're building your cabin.

Destruct and eat the cabin before it gets too hard.

If I Were President— Hat and Speech

Roll out the red carpets! This activity offers kids a chance to wear a different hat—that of President of the United States.

Time: 30 minutes

Complexity: Easy

What to Do:

1. First, make a presidential stovepipe hat. Roll a large sheet of construction paper into a cylinder that will fit head securely and tape it closed.

2. Set the cylinder on another sheet of paper and draw an outline of the circle.

3. Draw another circle about 2 inches wider than the first to make a ring that will form the base of the hat.

4. Cut 1/2-inch slits all the way around the bottom and top of the cylinder.

5. Fold the bottom slits outward.

6. Glue the ring on top of the slits to make the base.

7. Cut another circle to fit the top of the cylinder, fold the slits inward, and glue the circle to the slits to close off the top of the hat.

8. Cut a 2-inch band to wrap around the bottom of the cylinder and glue it on.

9. Cut out a 3-inch square, cut the center out of it, and glue it to the front of the hat to form a decorative buckle.

10. Put the stovepipe hat on and make a campaign speech for the presidency.

Materials:
- Construction paper (red, white, and blue)
- Tape
- Scissors
- Pencil
- Glue

Variations: Vote for the best campaign speech and elect a new president.

Put democracy to the test with a mock election. Your family can vote for anything and everything, such as where to go on your next vacation, what to have for Sunday dinner, who has which chores, and so on.

Practical Tips: Make the hat out of stiff paper so it will hold up longer and be easier to work with.

Make hats whatever colors you like—they don't have to be black like the original.

Cherry Cake

The name Washington reminds people of the word "cherries." Legend has it that Washington chopped down a cherry tree and when his father asked him who did it, he replied, "I cannot tell I lie. It was me, Father." Here's a tasty recipe you can whip up for your Presidents' Day celebration.

Time: 45 minutes (including baking time)

Complexity: Easy—Adult assistance recommended

Ingredients:
- Chocolate cake mix
- 1 can cherry pie filling
- Frosting
- Cherries
- Tube of icing

What to Do:

1. Mix up the package of chocolate cake mix and pour into the rectangular pan. Pour the can of cherry pie filling on top and swirl it into the batter with the spoon.

2. Bake cake according to package directions and let cool.

3. Frost cake and top with icing and cherries arranged in the shape of a tree. Your guests will love the surprise filling that keeps the cake moist and flavorful!

Materials:
- 9" x 12" cake pan
- Spoon
- Oven

Variation: Use other cake-top decorations.

Practical Tips: Don't swirl the cherry pie filling too much or you'll lose the pretty design.

Be sure the cake is fully baked by using a toothpick to test. The cake is done if the inserted toothpick comes out clean.

March

ST. PATRICK'S DAY
March 17

It's time to watch out for wee folk—Irish leprechauns, that is! It's also time for "the wearing o' the green" as we honor the patron saint of Ireland, Bishop Patrick, and everything Irish. St. Patrick introduced Christianity into Ireland during the fifth century. According to legend, he used the shamrock, or three-leaf clover, to teach his converts about the Holy Trinity. Legend also tells that St. Patrick performed many miracles, including chasing snakes out of Ireland.

In Ireland they honor St. Patrick with a national holiday and a week of religious festivities. Celebrations in the U.S. include parades and parties with green food and drink. People who are Irish (and most other folk) wear green clothes to get into the holiday spirit. Almost everyone claims to have a little Irish in them on this special day.

Shamrock Shake

This thick, mint-flavored shake is cool and refreshing. It's a St. Patrick's Day tradition worth repeating.

Serves: 1

Time: 5 minutes

Complexity: Easy

Ingredients:
- 2 cups milk
- 1 banana
- 1/2 cup mint ice cream

Materials:
- Blender
- Large glass
- Spoon or straw

What to Do:

1. Put all ingredients into the blender and cover.

2. Blend until smooth and creamy, about 30 to 45 seconds.

3. Pour into the large glass and serve immediately.

Variation: Tint light-colored ice cream or frozen yogurt green. Or substitute pistachio ice cream for mint.

Practical Tip: For a thicker shake, use 1 cup of ice cream and 1 cup of milk.

Magic Green Crystal Garden

Abracadabra! Here's an activity that magicians young and old find amazing. And it's the perfect way to turn your world green on St. Paddy's Day.

Time: 30 minutes (plus hours to grow crystals)

Complexity: Challenging—Adult assistance recommended

What to Do:

1. Dampen the pieces of brick, clay-pot chips, and sponge. Place them in the large glass jar, fishbowl, or terrarium.

2. Pour a few drops of the green food coloring over the broken bricks, clay pieces, and sponge.

3. In the small bowl, combine the ammonia, liquid bluing, and water. Slowly pour over bricks, clay pieces, and sponge.

4. Sprinkle salt over the top of the liquid. The garden will begin to grow in the next few hours, so check back every now and then to see how it's coming along.

5. While you wait, make some leprechauns to hide in the magic garden. Cut pictures of leprechauns out of coloring books or draw your own. Color them, and set them carefully in the garden so they can hide among the strange-looking crystals.

Materials:

- Large glass jar, fishbowl, or terrarium
- Pieces of brick
- Clay-pot chips
- Sponge
- Green food coloring
- Small bowl
- 4 tablespoons ammonia
- 4 tablespoons liquid bluing (available in laundry section of grocery stores)
- 4 tablespoons water
- Salt
- Paper or coloring books with leprechauns
- Crayons

Variation: Use different colors of food coloring.

Warning: Do not sniff the ammonia!

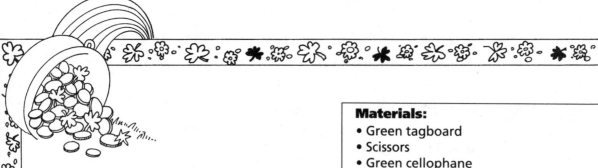

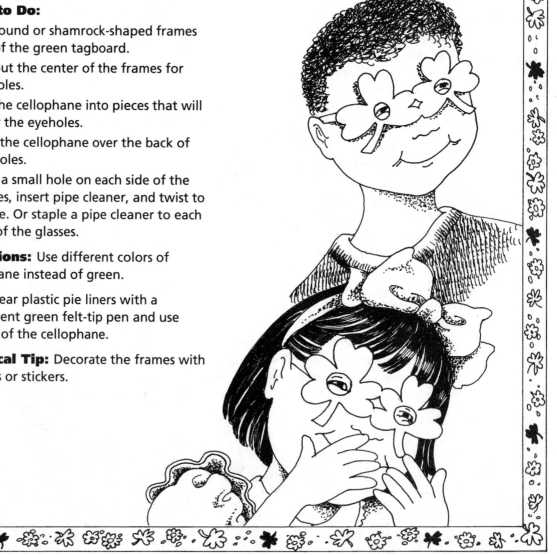

Materials:
- Green tagboard
- Scissors
- Green cellophane
- Glue
- Pipe cleaners
- **Optional:** stapler

Leprechaun Glasses

Put these glasses on and suddenly the whole world looks green.

Time: 20 minutes

Complexity: Easy

What to Do:

1. Cut round or shamrock-shaped frames out of the green tagboard.
2. Cut out the center of the frames for eyeholes.
3. Cut the cellophane into pieces that will cover the eyeholes.
4. Glue the cellophane over the back of the holes.
5. Poke a small hole on each side of the glasses, insert pipe cleaner, and twist to secure. Or staple a pipe cleaner to each side of the glasses.

Variations: Use different colors of cellophane instead of green.

Color clear plastic pie liners with a permanent green felt-tip pen and use instead of the cellophane.

Practical Tip: Decorate the frames with markers or stickers.

SHAMROCK PARTY

Here are some fun ideas for making your St. Patrick's Day party extra special.

Shamrock Cake

- Bake three heart-shaped cakes and join them together at their tips to form a shamrock. Or bake four cakes to make a lucky four-leaf clover.
- Frost with green-tinted icing and top with gold coins or use a decorator tube and create tiny shamrocks all over the cake.

Shamrock Decorations

- Cut out oodles of giant shamrocks from green construction paper.
- Tape the shamrocks to the walls, use them as place mats, or hang little ones from the ceiling.
- Make a shamrock mobile instead of the heart mobile described for Valentine's Day (page 20).

Rainbow Wall

- Cut out rainbow colors from construction paper or use a large sheet of white paper and color a rainbow with felt-tip pens or crayons.
- Tape your creation to the wall to form a giant rainbow wall.

Pot o' Gold

- Set a small table at the end of the rainbow with a large pot full of gold-coin candies or other treats.
- Pick some clovers and sprinkle them onto the tablecloth, with handfuls of gold coins here and there on the table.

Extra Touches

- Play Irish music in the background, something from the Irish Rover Boys or another group.
- Dress up as a leprechaun and have your guests do the same.
- Request that everyone wear as many green articles of clothing as possible. Award a (green) prize to the one who wears the most green.

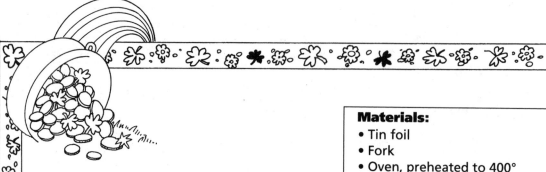

Stuffed Potatoes

St. Patrick's Day is the perfect time to serve traditional Irish favorites, such as corned beef and cabbage, and lots of potatoes. These potatoes will add a little pizzazz to your St. Patrick's Day dinner.

Time: About 1-1/2 hours

Complexity: Moderate—Adult assistance recommended

Ingredients:
- Potatoes (1 for each person)
- Cheddar, jack, and/or jalapeño cheese
- Bacon bits, ground beef, and/or cubed ham
- Green onions, cooked peas, and/or broccoli florets
- Chili or beef stroganoff
- Salt, pepper, Mexican seasoning, and/or Cajun seasoning

What to Do:

1. Wash and prick the potatoes with the fork, then wrap them in tin foil and pop

Materials:
- Tin foil
- Fork
- Oven, preheated to 400°
- Bowls

them into the oven for about an hour (check to see if done by inserting fork).

2. While the potatoes bake, prepare your stuffings. Shred, cut, and cook each ingredient as desired. Put each ingredient in a separate bowl.

3. Serve each guest one potato on a plate or in a bowl, then let them help themselves to their choice of stuffings!

Variations: Use just the potato skins instead of the whole potatoes. Fill with taco stuffings, pizza toppings, or hamburger fixings.

Practical Tip: Offer the potato stuffings "cafeteria" style or put everything on the table and have a "pass-around."

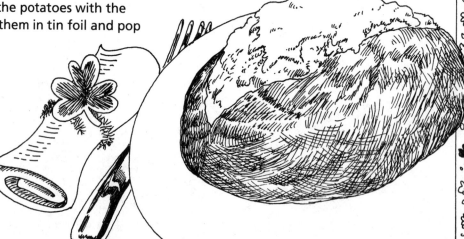

Leprechaun Detector

Worried about sneaky little leprechauns creeping up and surprising you? Afraid they'll steal away all your gold candy? Here's a way to keep the wee folk away!

Time: 20 minutes

Complexity: Easy

What to Do:

1. Buy some little bells at a hobby store or collect several small metal objects, like keys.
2. Tie the objects together with yarn.

Materials:
- Bells or several small objects, like keys
- Yarn
- Tack or ceiling hook

3. Attach the yarn to the ceiling so the door will brush against the objects when it opens. When a leprechaun (or anyone) enters, the objects will rattle and warn you that someone is there.

Variation: Tie the bells around door knobs instead of hanging them from the ceiling.

Practical Tip: Don't let the bells hang down too far or they'll catch in the door as it closes.

Hot Potato

Ouch! This fast-moving game is a great party activity. And you don't really have to use a hot potato, any potato will do—as long as it's not a mashed potato!

Time: 20–30 minutes

Complexity: Easy

What to Do:

1. Have the players stand in a circle about an arm's length from each other.
2. Give the "hot" potato to one player with instructions to toss it to any other player as quickly as possible because it's "hot."
3. Continue playing. Players are out of the game if they drop the potato or hold it more than 3 seconds.

Materials:
- Potato

4. The last player left is the winner.

Variations: Wrap the potato in tin foil so it looks like it just came out of the oven.

Have the players take a step back each time the potato hits the ground.

Have the players try to catch the potato one-handed to make the game more challenging.

Practical Tip: Use a softball or Nerf ball instead of a potato.

FIRST DAY OF SPRING
March 21

Spring has sprung! The first day of spring arrives on the vernal equinox, when the sun, heading north, crosses the plane of the earth's equator. Day and night are approximately equal in length on this day.

Spring officially arrives before the weather actually changes in many areas of the country. March winds can blow your hair, snap your flags, and fly your kites! People welcome spring by preparing their gardens, cleaning their windows, and starting new projects.

Homemade Bubbles

Welcome spring by filling the air with soap bubbles. All you need is a nice day and a few household items to blow these bubbles.

Time: 30 minutes or more

Complexity: Easy—Adult assistance recommended

What to Do:

1. In the small bowl or container mix the water, glycerin, dish detergent, and sugar or Karo syrup (makes the bubbles last longer).

2. Make a blower by one of the following methods: bend a wire into a circle, allowing part of it to be the stem; use a plastic straw or several straws taped together; punch a hole in the bottom of a paper cup and blow into the cup; or save a plastic six-pack holder and staple a dowel or stick to the holder.

Materials:
- Bowl or other small container
- 2 cups warm water
- 6 tablespoons glycerin (available at drugstores)
- 6 tablespoons liquid dish soap
- Dash of sugar or Karo syrup
- Blower (wire; plastic straw and tape; paper cup; plastic six-pack holder, stapler, and dowel or stick)

3. Dip the blower in the bubble liquid and blow, blow, blow!

Variation: Add food coloring to the mixture to make colorful bubbles.

Practical Tip: Blow or move blower slowly to make the best bubbles.

Popcorn Flowers

These fun-to-create popcorn flowers make beautiful spring bouquets! Have a little extra popcorn for your gardeners to munch on after the project is complete.

Time: 30 minutes

Complexity: Easy

What to Do:

1. Pop the popcorn, reserving some to eat after the flowers are completed.
2. Put handfuls of the popcorn in plastic baggies and add powdered tempura paint to each one.
3. Shake well to distribute paint all over the popcorn for a colorful blossom effect.
4. Cut stems and leaves out of the green construction paper and glue them to the tagboard.
5. Glue on the colored popcorn to make spring flowers.

Variations: Instead of coloring the popcorn with tempura paint, buy already colored popcorn, usually available at candy stores, gourmet food stores, and variety stores.

Materials:
- Popcorn
- Popcorn popper
- Plastic baggies
- Powdered tempura paint
- Tagboard, 8-1/2" x 11"
- Green construction paper
- Glue
- Scissors

Use cotton balls instead of popcorn. Color them the same way as described here for the popcorn.

Practical Tips: Be sure not to eat the paint-colored popcorn, even though it is nontoxic and very tempting.

Keep paper towels handy in case the powdered paint comes off on hands.

MAKING KITES

Go, fly a kite! After a long winter it's fun to get outside and run around. Kids can make their own kites out of many different papers and fabrics. Just keep in mind that kites should be strong yet lightweight.

Suggested Kite Coverings: Old sheets, fabric remnants, newspaper, brown package wrap, Christmas paper or gift wrap, plastic garbage bags, "Rip-stop fabric" (available at fabric stores), cellophane, tissue or crepe paper, department store bags, Mylar or other plastic sold by the yard, lining material, or construction paper

Practical Tip: Make sure that you have a large-enough piece before you begin cutting your kite. You can seam pieces together, if necessary.

Materials for Decorating: Felt-tip pens, watercolors, crayons, poster paints, construction paper cut-outs, posters, tie-dyed fabric, glitter, sequins, stickers, or rickrack

Practical Tip: Draw, paint, or glue on decorations, but don't overload it with excess weight or it won't fly well.

What to Draw: Superheroes, geometric designs, flowers, hearts, rainbows, clouds, birds, planes, monsters, dragons, names, messages, people, faces, or animals

Practical Tip: Be sure to make big, bold, bright designs, filling in with lots of color, so you can see the artwork from a distance.

Frame: Kite frames can either be made from wood or plastic. Wooden dowels or bamboo will work, as will plastic rods that may be found at plastics or hardware stores. The dowels should be about 1/4 inch in diameter, and if they are wooden, should be soaked for a few hours to allow for more flexibility. You'll need two dowels, 30-inches and 24-inches long, for the common diamond kite.

Tails: Most kites will spin if they don't have a tail. A tail keeps the kite balanced and upright. It's important to remember that wind resistance is the purpose of the tail, not weight. The friction of the wind blowing over the tail helps keep the kite upright.

Suggestions for Tails: Ribbons, rosettes, paper cups, fabric swatches, tissue paper, paper fans, or construction paper designs

Attach the tails with staples, safety pins, paper clips, tape, or small rings; or sew them on if you like. Make sure the tail is long—at least six times the width of the kite. Most mistakes are made by trying to use tails that are not long enough for the kite. It's better to have one too long than too short.

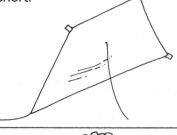

Diamond Kite

Get ready for kite-flying season. Construct this easy-to-make kite ahead of time so it'll be ready to fly on the first windy spring day.

Time: 1 hour

Complexity: Challenging—Adult assistance recommended

What to Do:

1. Notch the two wooden dowels at each end with the scissors or knife. Or buy pre-notched dowels.

2. Measure down the 30-inch dowel and mark off 8 inches. Measure down the 24-inch dowel and mark off 12 inches.

3. Cross the pieces at right angles to form a "+" shape at the two marks. Tie or tape the dowels together. Add some glue for strength and let it dry completely.

4. Run a string around the outside of the dowels, through their notched ends, to form a frame. Tape around the ends to keep the string secure.

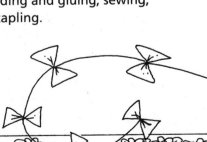

5. Measure and cut the fabric, allowing a seam for folding and gluing, sewing, taping, or stapling.

Materials:

- 1 30-inch wooden dowel
- 1 24-inch wooden dowel
- Scissors or knife
- Ruler or tape measure
- String or yarn
- Tape (masking or duct)
- Glue
- Fabric
- Kite string
- Kite tail

6. Poke two holes in the center of the kite and tie a string loosely through the holes, coming back out the back of the kite.

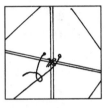

7. Attach another string to this loop, add the tail, and you're ready to fly.

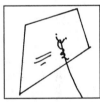

Variation: Cut all materials in half and make a mini-kite.

Practical Tip: Use lightweight materials for better aerodynamics.

Spring Butterflies

Butterflies are a sure sign of spring. Make these butterflies out of craft materials to keep inside.

Time: 30 minutes

Complexity: Easy–Moderate

What to Do:

1. Color small bowls of water with the food coloring.

2. Using the eye dropper, scatter drops of colored water onto the round coffee filters and watch the colors bleed and blend.

3. While the filters dry, draw eyes and body details on the wooden clothes pins.

4. Gather each coffee filter up in the center and clip with a clothespin.

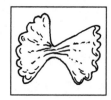

5. Make antennae for each butterfly by inserting a pipe cleaner into the end of the clothes pin and twisting it secure.

Materials:
- Food coloring
- Small bowls
- Water
- Coffee filters
- Eye dropper
- Wooden clothes pins (the pinching kind with the hinge)
- Pipe cleaners
- Felt-tip pens (all colors)

6. Bend the ends of the pipe cleaner.

Variations: Use tissue paper instead of coffee filters and use several sheets in different colors for a multilayered, translucent effect.

Decorate the butterfly body with sequins, glitter, and other decorations.

Make caterpillars from green pompoms glued to a large real or paper leaf (with a "bite" taken out) for a before-and-after exhibit.

Practical Tip: Be sure the coffee filter is dry before you gather it up or it may tear.

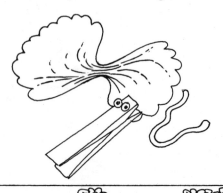

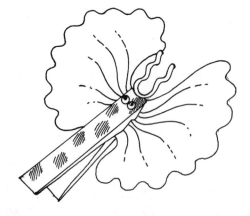

April

APRIL FOOLS' DAY
April 1

April Fools' Day may have originated in festivals celebrating the return of spring, when people feel silly and full of fun. Ancient celebrations seem to have lasted from the vernal equinox (about March 21) until April 1. However the practice of playing pranks on April 1 began, they're a fun way to celebrate the return of spring.

Celebrate April Fools' Day by playing lots of tricks and jokes on friends and family. It's the one day we can make fools of ourselves by becoming tricksters, jokers, and magicians. Just remember, though, that what goes around comes around, so don't do anything mean or hurtful. It's all just for fun!

___

Pig Snout

Soo-ee, pig, pig, pig! April Fools' Day is the perfect day to act a little "foolish." It's a hoot to wear a fake nose while pretending that nothing's different.

Time: 15 minutes

Complexity: Easy

What to Do:

1. Cut the cardboard egg carton apart into individual egg holders.
2. Use the felt-tip pens to color an egg holder (pig snout) pink or another color or design.
3. Poke or draw two nostril holes in the end of the snout.
4. Staple a rubber band or piece of elastic to the sides of the snout to hold the snout in place around your head.

Materials:
- Cardboard egg carton (with flat bottom)
- Scissors
- Felt-tip pens
- Large rubber band or piece of elastic
- Stapler

Variations: Use dixie cups instead of an egg carton.

Make other animals' noses, such as an elephant's trunk out of a toilet-paper or paper-towel tube.

Practical Tip: Make sure the rubber band or elastic is not too tight.

BACKWARDS PARTY

Everyone feels a little backwards once in a while—some people even put their clothes on backwards from time to time by mistake. April Fools' Day gives people a chance to act backwards and goofy on purpose! Celebrate this day with a "Sdrawkcab Ytrap" (that's "Backwards Party" spelled backwards!).

Invitations

Invite your friends to your Backwards Party by writing the invitations backwards. For example: "Emoc ot ym Sdrawkcab Ytrap!" Or write the information the opposite of what you really mean: "I'm not having a party. You're not invited! It's not at my house. And it's not a Backwards Party!" Tell them to dress backwards or to wear the opposite of what they normally wear.

Decorations

Decorate your party room upside down and backwards. Turn the chairs facing the wrong way or set them upside down. Place the tablecloth wrong side up and the plates, cups, and silverware upside down. Hang streamers from the ceiling and tape the balloons at the bottom of the streamers. Hang posters upside down, welcome guests with "Good-bye" instead of "Hello," and walk backwards when showing your guests to the party room.

Games

Play all your favorite games, but play them backwards or the opposite way. For example, instead of playing "Musical Chairs," play "Quiet Chairs." Tell the players to find a chair when the music begins, not when it stops. Instead of playing "Pin the Tail on the Donkey," play "Pin the Donkey on the Tail." Give the winner a booby prize and the loser the real prize.

Activities

Make T-shirts with puffy paints, backwards, so they can only be read in the mirror. Or write to each other in code with the alphabet letters written backwards as the code.

Food

Serve an upside-down cake. Offer ice-cream cones with the cone on top (served in a bowl). Serve drinks in bowls, cake in cups, and ice cream on plates.

Party Favors

Send the guests home with prizes wrapped inside-out. Make sure there are lots of funny booby prizes, like a bag of dog treats, a giant pair of underwear, a record by an old musical group, or a hideous statue of Elvis.

Goofy Grab Bag

Oooh, what's that? Here's a goofy guessing game to play at your April Fools' party.

Time: 45 minutes

Complexity: Easy–Moderate

What to Do:

1. Place the goofy items in the large paper bag.

2. Have one player reach in and feel an object without looking at it. Blindfold the player, if desired.

3. Have the player describe the object and guess what it is. If right, the player gets to keep the item. If wrong, the player selects another player who must keep the item.

4. Have the next player take a turn. Continue playing until all the players have guessed an item.

Variations: Place different kinds of candy bars in the bag. Have the players reach in, grab a candy, and try to guess what it is.

Materials:
- Large paper bag
- 6 or more small goofy items such as: giant underwear, gummy worm candy, already chewed gum in a pouch, dog biscuit, hair net, toy false teeth, rubber snake, slice of frozen pizza sealed in a bag, diaper, prune, broken toy, Jell-O in a sealed bag, ice cube in a sealed bag, and so on
- **Optional:** blindfold

Play musical grab bag where the bag is passed around a circle until the music stops. Whoever has the bag must reach in, grab something, and identify it without looking at it.

Put in a bunch of items just for one player who "grabs and guesses" until making a mistake. Each player keeps all the stuff correctly named. Reload the bag between players.

Practical Tips: Make sure nothing in the bag is wet or has sharp edges.

Make sure players don't pull items out of the bag accidentally, which ruins the fun.

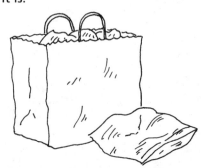

Silly Simon Says

You don't always have to do what Simon says. Kids of all ages will enjoy this variation of the Simon Says game that gives them a chance to add their own creativity to the fun.

Time: 30 minutes

Complexity: Easy–Moderate

What to Do:

1. Have the players stand in a circle.

2. Choose one player to be "Simon" or "It." Simon is to call out true or false statements and act them out in an attempt to get the other players to copy the actions.

3. Here's how to play: Simon says "Jump like a kangaroo," and since this is true, all players should jump around like a kangaroo, just like Simon does. After a few seconds, Simon might say, "Tweet like a bird," "Slither like a snake," or "Fly like a jet." Simon acts out appropriately as the other players follow. Suddenly Simon says something that doesn't make sense, such as "Fly

Materials:
- Enough space for the players to form a circle

like a rabbit." Simon can either pretend to fly or hop like a rabbit in an effort to get the other players to do the same. Players who do follow Simon are out. Players who don't follow Simon stay in the game.

4. Continue playing until only one player is left. That player is the winner.

Variations: Have cards made up ahead of time so players don't have to think up anything. Simon can simply read a card and do what it says.

Have players take turns being Simon instead of just having one player be Simon. This will add extra chaos to the fun.

Practical Tips: Keep the game moving fast so it stays challenging.

Help the players with ideas if they can't think of any. If the game goes on too long with one player being Simon, have another player be Simon for a while.

PASSOVER
Date Varies

Pesach or Passover begins an eight-day celebration commemorating the delivery of the Jews from slavery in Egypt. It's celebrated on the fourteenth of the lunar month of Nisan (March or April). A central part of the Passover celebration, Seder is the ceremony in which families retell the story of the Exodus from Egypt and explain the symbols of the Passover meal.

To prepare for Passover, people clean their houses, wash dishes, and empty refrigerators of foods, especially leavened (regular) bread. On the first night of Passover, families gather to celebrate with the Seder meal; they eat matzo (unleavened bread), drink wine or grape juice, and eat a sumptuous feast. As part of the ceremony, children ask their elders about the customs of Passover—children are included in all areas of Passover as much as possible, to help pass on the drama of the celebration to the next generation.

Haroseth

Haroseth is a traditional spread made during Passover. The ingredients resemble the mortar used to build the pyramids when the Jews were slaves. Sometimes the mixture can taste bitter depending on the herbs used, but this one is sweet and tasty. It tastes great on matzo.

Time: 20 minutes

Complexity: Easy

Ingredients:
- 1 cup chopped apple
- 1/2 cup chopped walnuts or almonds
- 2 teaspoons cinnamon
- 1 teaspoon honey
- 1 tablespoon grape juice or sweet wine
- Matzo

Materials:
- Spoon
- Serving bowl

What to Do:
1. Mix the apples, nuts, and cinnamon with the honey and juice.
2. Serve on matzo during traditional ceremony.

Practical Tip: Have younger children use a nut chopper to chop up the fruit and nuts.

Matzo

Unleavened bread, like matzo, reminds Jews that their ancestors couldn't wait for dough to rise before they escaped from Egypt—they carried matzo with them while fleeing and ate it flat. This year you can make your own matzo.

Time: 30 minutes

Complexity: Moderate—Adult assistance recommended

Ingredients:
- 3-1/2 cups flour
- 1 cup water

What to Do:

1. Mix and knead the flour and water.
2. Roll out the dough on a floured surface, and then transfer it to the greased cookie sheet.
3. Prick the dough several times with a fork and cut into squares with a knife.
4. Bake for 10 to 15 minutes or until lightly brown.

Materials:
- Rolling pin
- Cookie sheet, greased
- Knife
- Fork
- Oven, preheated to 475°
- Large bowl
- Decorated napkins

5. Serve three on top of each other, covered with a decorated napkin.

Variation: Make place cards for each guest by writing names on the small matzo crackers using a toothpick dipped in food coloring.

Practical Tip: During the meal, kids are encouraged to "steal" parts of the matzo and hide them until the dinner is nearly finished, only to be discovered and the last bits eaten so the meal can formally end.

Paper Flowers

Passover is also a celebration of spring. Make these bright paper flowers to welcome spring and to decorate the Seder table.

Time: 30 minutes

Complexity: Easy

What to Do:

1. Cut ten sheets of your favorite colors of tissue paper into 8-inch or 10-inch squares and lay them on top of each other.

2. Accordion pleat the tissues together and tie them off with the strong string in the center.

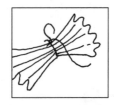

3. Wrap one end of the florist's wire around the center, and keep the rest of the wire straight to use for holding the flower.

Materials:
- 10 sheets of tissue paper (all colors)
- Scissors
- Strong string
- Florist's wire

4. Gently pull out the first tissue from the pleat, then the second, and so on until you've finished five on one side. Turn the flower over and repeat. Turn the flower upside down and repeat for both sides, until you have a colorful fluffy flower.

5. Arrange your flowers in a vase and set them on the table.

Variation: Spray the flowers lightly with your favorite perfume.

Practical Tips: Use thin paper—thick paper will not fold or pull apart easily.

When pulling the tissue out, pull gently and slowly to avoid tearing.

Passover Sponge Cake

Enjoy this traditional Jewish dish usually made in a special pan during Passover. It's tasty anytime of the year.

Serves: 10–12

Time: 30 minutes

Complexity: Challenging—Adult assistance recommended

Ingredients:
- 10 eggs
- 1-1/2 cups sugar
- 1 lemon
- 1/2 cup potato starch
- 1/2 cup pancake meal
- Powdered sugar

Materials:
- Large bowl
- Electric mixer
- Large spoon
- Medium bowl
- Grater
- Rubber spatula
- Ungreased 10" tube pan
- Oven, preheated to 350°
- Knife
- Passover plate

What to Do:

1. Separate the egg yolks from the egg whites.
2. Beat the egg whites in the large bowl until frothy.
3. Slowly add 1/2 cup of the sugar and continue beating until the egg whites become stiff and shiny.
4. Add the remaining cup of sugar to the egg *yolk* in a medium bowl and beat with the electric mixer until smooth and creamy.
5. Grate the rind off of the lemon and add to egg-yolk mixture.
6. Squeeze the juice from the lemon and add to egg mixture (watch for seeds).
7. Using the rubber spatula, fold the potato starch and pancake meal into egg whites, gently but thoroughly.
8. Pour into the tube pan and bake for 1 hour.
9. Remove from the oven and invert pan over the counter. It is important to tradition to cool the cake upside down. When cool, loosen the edges with the knife and turn onto the Passover plate.
10. Dust with powdered sugar.

Practical Tip: Traditional Passover food is served in special Passover dishes. Check to see if those you're serving follow this observance.

EASTER
(Date Varies)

Easter falls on the Sunday following the first full moon after the vernal equinox, between March 22 and April 25. The principal Christian festival, Easter celebrates the resurrection of Jesus Christ from the dead.

Easter is a joyous celebration that usually includes church services, family dinners, and Easter egg hunts. Sneaking into houses, hiding Easter eggs and leaving baskets of goodies, the Easter bunny is also a favorite part of this holiday to children.

By the way, eggs—so prominent at Easter time—are a universal symbol of new life. Be sure to hard boil plenty of eggs for your Easter decorations.

Group Egg Decorating

Here's a way to include the whole family in your egg decorating.

Time: 15 minutes

Complexity: Easy

What to Do:

1. Pass out eggs to everyone at the table.
2. Have everyone draw hair on an egg, then pass it to the right. Have the next person add eyebrows.
3. Continue passing the eggs and have each person draw a part of the face—eyes, cheeks, nose, mouth, ears, moles, eyelashes, chin, and freckles. See what your original egg looks like when all the features have been added.

Materials:
- Hard-boiled eggs (one for each person)
- Permanent felt-tip pens or small markers

Variation: Let everyone draw all the features on an egg—with their eyes closed.

Practical Tip: Have sample cartoon eyes, noses, and mouths on display for ideas.

Candle Eggs

These beautiful candle eggs will add the right touch to your Easter dinner table. Just make sure that no one tries to crack them for breakfast!

Time: 1 hour

Complexity: Challenging—Adult assistance recommended

What to Do:

1. Hollow out several eggs by gently poking a small hole in one end of each egg with the sharp pin or turkey skewer. Scramble the egg inside with the skewer, then let the egg drip out into the small bowl. Rinse clean. Set the eggshells in the egg carton.

2. Melt some old candles or paraffin wax and wax coloring in the double boiler over low heat.

3. Place the funnel over the opening of the egg. Carefully pour the wax into the hollow eggshell in the carton.

4. When the eggshell is full, insert the wired wick into the egg, centering it with a piece of tape for support.

5. Allow the wax to cool and harden, then break off the shell and buff the candle with a soft rag.

6. Heat the bottom end of the candle to soften, then press on flat surface to make it stand up. Or use a candle holder.

Materials:
- Several eggs
- Pin or turkey skewer
- Small bowl
- Egg carton
- Old candles or paraffin wax (available in the baking section of grocery store)
- Wax coloring
- Double boiler
- Small funnel
- Wired wicks
- Tape
- Soft rag

7. Light your candle egg and watch it glow.

Variations: Use several different colors of wax. Layer the colors, letting them cool between additions.

Add glitter and metallic confetti to make your egg sparkle.

Color the wax with old color crayons instead of buying wax coloring.

Practical Tip: Be sure egg shell is dry inside before you fill it.

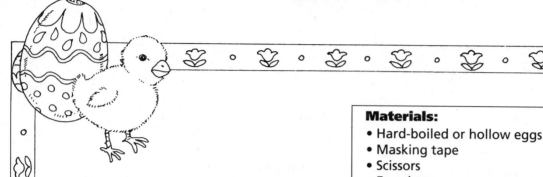

Batik Eggs

Here's a nice change of pace from ordinary purple and pink Easter eggs. Batik is an Indonesian method of hand-printing textiles by brushing wax on the parts not to be dyed. This activity calls for masking tape instead of wax, but the effect is just as interesting.

Time: 30 minutes

Complexity: Easy–Moderate

What to Do:

1. Cut out designs from masking tape.
2. Stick the tape on the eggs and dip the eggs in the dye.

Materials:
- Hard-boiled or hollow eggs
- Masking tape
- Scissors
- Egg dyes
- Cups or bowls

3. Remove the tape when dry.
4. Repeat the sticker process, overlapping some colors before dipping eggs in another color. Work from light to dark colors. Tape over previous color if you wish to retain a particular shade or let them bleed together.

Variation: Instead of tape, use white crayon to resist the dye.

Practical Tip: Use bacon tongs to hold the egg to avoid coloring fingers.

Rainbow Eggs

These colorful eggs will brighten up any Easter basket.

Time: 30 minutes

Complexity: Easy–Moderate

What to Do:

1. Dissolve the egg dye in 2 tablespoons of water in a cup. Add 2 or 3 drops of vinegar.
2. Dampen a piece of cloth with water and wrap it around the egg.
3. Using the eye dropper, drop spots of different colors of dye on the cloth.
4. Twist the cloth tightly around the egg so the colors blend together.

Materials:
- Hard-boiled or hollow eggs
- Egg dyes or food coloring
- Cups of water
- Vinegar
- Eye dropper
- Pieces of cloth

5. Unwrap the egg and let it dry.

Variation: Add glitter to the egg coloring for sparkle.

Practical Tip: Wear rubber gloves to avoid coloring fingers.

Eggshell Mosaic

For once it's okay to smash eggs! But make sure you pick up all the pieces—you'll need them for this activity.

Time: 30 minutes

Complexity: Easy

What to Do:

1. Break the colored eggshells into small pieces.

2. Outline a design on paper or tagboard with the felt-tip pen or marker.

3. Spread glue in one area of the design and fill in with eggshell bits, leaving a slight gap between each piece. Do not cover up your outline. Continue until your design is filled.

4. Allow your mosaic to dry, and then hang it up on a wall.

Materials:
- 6–8 colored eggshells
- 8-1/2" x 11" paper or tagboard
- Felt-tip pen or marker
- Glue
- Varnish

Variation: Decorate Easter eggs as mosaics. Just dye a batch of eggs the traditional way, then remove the shells and glue them onto a blown egg. Cover the eggs with varnish to preserve them.

Practical Tips: Make the eggshell pieces small enough so they're flat but not so small that they become difficult to handle. Spread the pieces onto a plate and press your fingertips in the shells, then transfer to paper.

Use black paper or another dark color for contrast.

Egg Bunny

It's impossible to hatch your hard-boiled Easter eggs into chicks, but you can transform them into darling bunnies. Wanna-be surgeons and designers will love creating these cute critters.

Time: 45 minutes

Complexity: Easy–Moderate

What to Do:

1. Lay a hard-boiled egg on its side and glue on pompoms for feet and a tail. Glue them on slightly under the egg to keep the egg from rolling.

2. Glue on wiggly plastic eyes at the pointy front end.

Materials:
- Hard-boiled eggs
- 5 small pink or white pompoms per egg
- Glue
- 2 wiggly plastic eyes per egg
- Felt-tip markers (red and black)
- Felt (pink and white)
- Scissors

3. Draw on a nose with the red marker and whiskers with the black marker.

4. Cut out ears from the pink felt and small rectangular teeth from the white felt. Then glue the ears on top and the teeth under the nose and whiskers.

Natural Easter Egg Dyes

Do your Easter Eggs look the same year after year? Try some natural dyes for a change. Remember that these colors won't be as bright as the dyes you're used to.

Golden Tan—cook eggs in a small amount of water with brown onion skins.

Pink—soak eggs in a bowl with pickled beets or cranberry juice.

Yellow—dip eggs in a mixture of 1 teaspoon turmeric with 2/3 cup hot water and 1/4 teaspoon vinegar.

Brown—place eggs in 1 tablespoon of instant coffee dissolved in 2/3 cup hot water and 1/2 teaspoon vinegar.

Red—peel off the outside skins of several red onions, put into 2 cups of water, and boil with eggs for 1/2 to 1 hour.

Violet Blue—collect some violet blossoms and set eggs in hot water with the blossoms overnight.

Lavender—add 2 teaspoons of lemon juice to the violet water to get lavender, or soak eggs in grape juice.

Green—add 1/4 teaspoon of baking soda to the violet bowl and the eggs will turn green; or purchase some liquid chlorophyll and soak the shells in that for awhile.

Pink and Blue Pastels—rub cranberries and blueberries over the eggs for a soft, blended coloring.

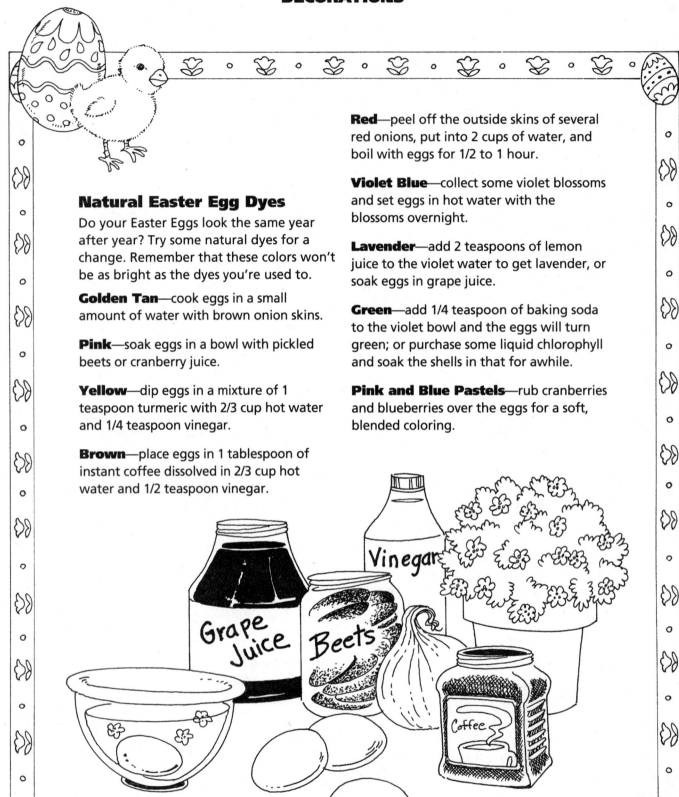

Panorama Egg

What a view! A fun Easter scene is hidden inside this beautiful panorama egg. It does, however, take time and careful work to create this masterpiece.

Time: 3 hours

Complexity: Challenging—Adult assistance recommended

What to Do:

1. Pour the sugar into the large bowl.
2. In the small bowl, stir together several drops of food coloring and one egg white.
3. Add the colored egg white to the sugar and knead until color is blended thoroughly.
4. Spray the egg mold with vegetable-oil spray, and then press sugar into it. Pack it in tightly and allow to harden for exactly 2 hours.
5. Leaving a shell at least 1/2-inch thick, gently scrape sugar out of the egg mold. Carve out small openings at both ends of the egg so you'll have a peephole when the two halves are put together. Dry overnight.
6. Prepare royal icing by combining 3 egg whites, powdered sugar, and cream of tartar. Beat for 7 minutes. Blend in food coloring.

Materials:
- 4 cups sugar
- Large bowl
- Food coloring
- 4 egg whites
- Small mixing bowl
- 4"– 6" plastic or metal egg mold (available at craft stores)
- Vegetable-oil spray (such as Pam)
- 1/2 pound powdered sugar
- 1/2 teaspoon cream of tartar
- Electric mixer
- Decorator icing tube and tip
- Miniature items (candies, flowers, bunnies, chicks, cut-up Easter card figures)
- Easter grass

7. Squirt a small amount of icing in the center of the shell and add the miniature items.

8. Squirt icing around the edge and seal the two halves together. Let dry. Add icing around the sealed edges and on top with a fancy decorator tip, and top with tiny flowers.

9. Peek inside and see the display of miniature items.

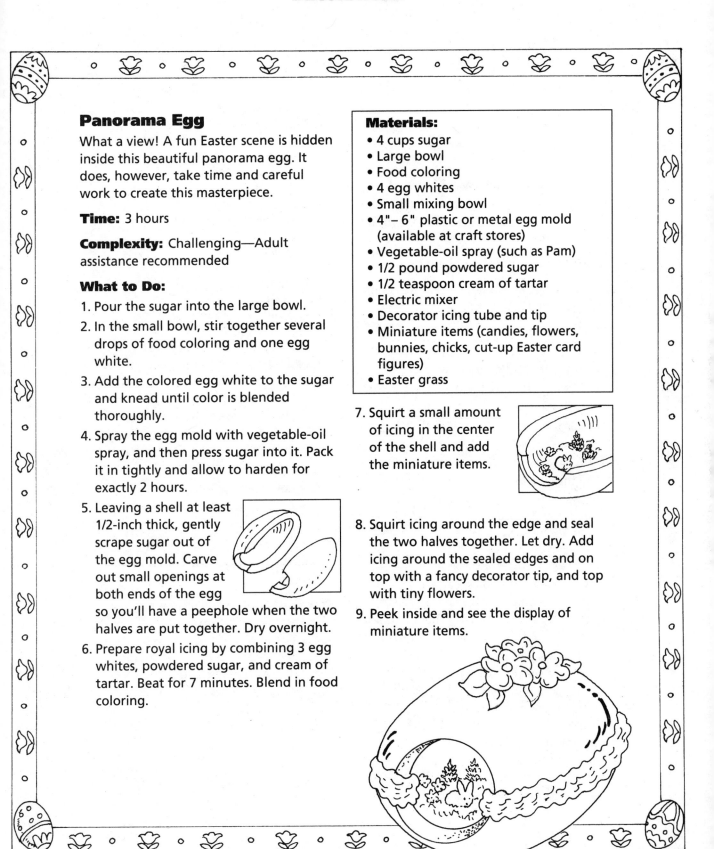

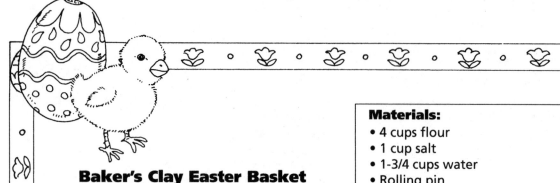

Baker's Clay Easter Basket

A tisket, a tasket, a homemade Easter basket! Here's a fun basket to make and bake for Easter.

Time: 30 minutes (plus baking time)

Complexity: Moderate—Adult assistance recommended

Materials:
- 4 cups flour
- 1 cup salt
- 1-3/4 cups water
- Rolling pin
- Knife
- Small, oven-proof bowl
- Cookie sheet
- Tin foil
- Oven, preheated to 250°
- Varnish (such as Verathane)
- Acrylic paint
- Pipe cleaner, ribbon, or string

What to Do:

1. Mix up a batch of baker's clay by combining the flour, salt, and water.

2. Roll dough flat, to 3/8 inch, and cut into 1-inch-wide strips.

3. Cover the cookie sheet with tin foil, and then place the small oven-proof bowl upside down on it.

4. Lay three strips of dough across the bottom of the bowl, with 1/2-inch space in between each strip. Lay three more strips on top, at right angles, carefully weaving them in and out of the first three strips. Add more strips, weaving them in along the sides, until the bowl is covered.

5. Roll excess dough into two long snakes and twist them together like a peppermint stick. Place the twisted coil around the bottom of the bowl. Make a handle the same way, and lay it

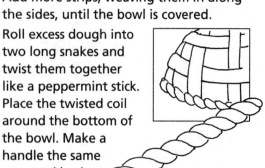

flat on the cookie sheet. The curve of the handle should be the same length as the diameter of the bowl and the two ends should curve up so they can be inserted into the bowl when both have been baked. Poke a hole in each end of the handle and in the top sides of the basket.

6. Bake until firm, 2 to 3 hours. Remove from oven and allow to cool.

7. Remove the dough from the bowl and varnish it for added protection and color.

8. Attach handles with pipe cleaners, ribbons, or string. Use for an Easter basket.

Practical Tip: Include sugarless treats in your Easter basket: furry bunnies, chicks, and ducks; Easter storybooks; seeds to plant in the spring; nuts and trail mix; stickers; plastic eggs filled with party favors; crackers; playdough; or tickets to an Easter movie.

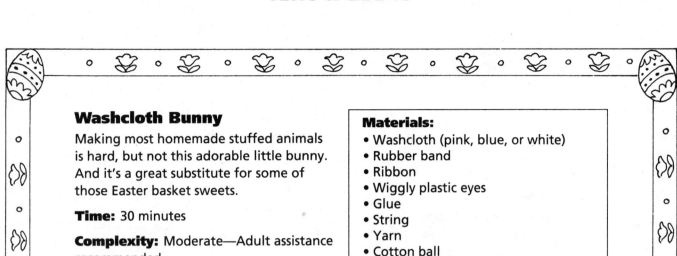

Washcloth Bunny

Making most homemade stuffed animals is hard, but not this adorable little bunny. And it's a great substitute for some of those Easter basket sweets.

Time: 30 minutes

Complexity: Moderate—Adult assistance recommended

What to Do:

1. Place the washcloth flat on the table.

2. Tightly roll one corner to the center of the cloth. Keep the rolled section in place as you turn the cloth around and roll the opposite corner toward the center.

3. Turn over.

4. With the rolled side down, fold the washcloth in half. Then fold back about 2 inches from one end.

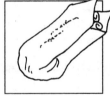
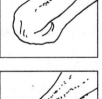

5. Place a rubber band around this section to form the bunny's head.

Materials:
- Washcloth (pink, blue, or white)
- Rubber band
- Ribbon
- Wiggly plastic eyes
- Glue
- String
- Yarn
- Cotton ball

6. Tie a ribbon over the rubber band.

7. Glue on wiggly plastic eyes, a yarn nose, and string whiskers to the head.

8. Glue on the cotton ball for a tail.

Variation: Tie-dye the washcloth to make a multicolored bunny. Or use a little creative twisting and tying and see if you can come up with a chick, duck, or kitten.

Practical Tip: Help younger children with the construction of the bunny since it seems to require more than two hands when your hands are small and not as experienced. For safety, draw on eyes with a permanent marker and sew on nose and whiskers if you're going to give the bunny to a baby.

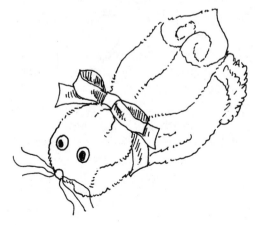

DECORATION

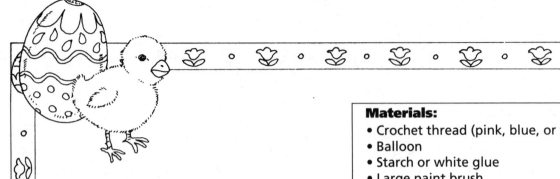

Giant Easter Egg

This giant Easter egg looks like it was laid by a dinosaur! Put it in an Easter basket or hang it up to welcome the Easter Bunny.

Time: 45 minutes

Complexity: Easy—Adult assistance recommended

What to Do:

1. Blow up the balloon and tie a 2-foot piece of thread to the bottom of it.

2. Cover the entire balloon with starch or watered-down glue, using the large paint brush.

3. Wrap the crochet thread around the balloon in one direction, leaving small gaps about 1/2-inch wide so the balloon isn't completely covered. Wrapping doesn't have to be perfect, but it should be somewhat even.

4. Apply another light layer of starch or glue on top of the thread and wrap with another layer of crochet thread in another direction.

5. Repeat one more time until the balloon is covered with crochet thread. (There will be gaps, much like crocheted lace, but the balloon should be fairly well covered with thread.)

Materials:
- Crochet thread (pink, blue, or yellow)
- Balloon
- Starch or white glue
- Large paint brush
- Scissors

6. Hang the balloon from the bottom thread to dry for about 24 hours.

7. When fully dry, pop the balloon and gently pull it out of the thread.

8. Hang the giant egg from the ceiling or place it in a giant Easter basket.

Variations: Use multicolored thread. Although crochet thread works well, you might want to try different yarns and threads for variety.

When the egg is dry, cut a hole in the center and fill it with a stuffed animal or special treat.

You can also flatten the end of the egg by pressing on it gently so it will stand on end.

Practical Tips: Work quickly before the glue or starch dries, or add more when necessary.

Handle the egg with care after it dries as it may cave in if you squish it.

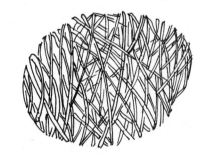

Marshmallow Eggs

Kids of all ages love the ooey, gooey, stuck-to-your-finger mess of marsh-mallows. These marshmallow eggs are sure to be a hit with such a crowd.

Time: 30 minutes (plus time for setting)

Complexity: Easy—Adult assistance recommended

Ingredients:
- Bag of marshmallows
- Margarine or vegetable-oil spray (such as Pam)
- Cornstarch
- 12-ounce bag of chocolate chips
- 1/4 cup margarine
- Decorator frosting tube

What to Do:

1. Grease the plastic egg molds with margarine or vegetable-oil spray, to make removing the marshmallow eggs easier.

2. Melt a bag of marshmallows in the lightly greased, large saucepan over low heat.

3. Pour the melted marshmallows into the plastic egg molds. Allow to set, about 2 hours.

4. When the marshmallow eggs are set, ease them out of the molds and onto the cookie sheet sprinkled with corn-starch. Dust the marshmallows with more cornstarch and let dry, uncovered, for several hours.

Materials:
- Plastic egg molds (available at craft stores)
- Large saucepan, lightly greased
- Stove
- Cookie sheet
- Double boiler or microwave
- Waxed paper

5. Melt the chocolate chips with the 1/4-cup margarine in the double boiler or microwave. Shake excess cornstarch from eggs and set on waxed paper. Spread with chocolate glaze. Chill until firm (about 1 hour). Decorate with frosting tube.

Variations: Color marshmallows with food coloring.

Sprinkle on decorative sprinkles or chocolate for added interest.

Practical Tip: For best results, don't rush the setting and drying times.

EARTH DAY
April 22

Amerca the Beautiful—and let's keep it that way. Earth Day was organized by environmentalists in 1970 and has become more and more popular each year.

Kids have taken action to help the environment in the past few years, forming environmental clubs and organizations.

Earth Day is a day to become more aware of environmental problems. And, it's a day to take action and show you care.

Trash Contest

Take pride in your community! Hold a contest and see who can collect the most trash in half an hour or half a day.

Time: Optional

Complexity: Easy

What to Do:

1. Gather your family and friends together, give everyone a decorated bag in which to collect stuff, set your watches, and take off.

2. Treat the winners (they're all winners) to cookies and milk after the race. Give a special prize to whomever collected the most trash. Stash the trash in a trash can—and don't forget to recycle!

Materials:
- Decorated bags
- Gloves

Practical Tips: Pair younger kids up with older kids or adults.

Be careful picking up broken glass.

Earth's Layers

Anyone who's ever tried to dig a tunnel to China knows that the Earth has many layers. This geological work of art represents the layers of the Earth's formation. It's fun, easy to do, and makes a beautiful gift or decoration.

Time: 45 minutes

Complexity: Easy–Moderate

What to Do:

1. Collect the layering items in the small bags or bowls.

2. Use a folded piece of sturdy paper or large spoon to add a layer to the jar. For example, fill the folded paper with sand and pour it as evenly as possible in the bottom of the jar.

3. Add a second layer of pebbles or whatever you like. It doesn't have to be perfect—the Earth's layers are not perfect. You might have some layers at a slant to make it more realistic.

4. Fill the jar to the top with layers and glue down the lid.

Materials:
- Medium open-mouth jar with lid
- 8–10 items for layering, such as sand, pebbles, shells, seeds, rice, dry beans, popcorn seeds, birdseed, and pasta
- Small bags or bowls
- Sturdy paper or spoon

Variation: Instead of collecting a wide variety of items for the layers, just use white sand or salt and color it with chalk. Pour a small amount of sand or salt on newspaper and gently rub a large piece of colored chalk over it. Set that layer aside and continue the process until the rest of the sand or salt is colored. Layer into the jar. When finished, insert a toothpick into the jar and gently pull it out along the inside of the jar to create an interesting effect. You can also make small birds, trees, and other outlines using this method.

Practical Tip: Don't tilt the jar too far or the layers may mix. Fill it to the very top and seal the lid to prevent it from mixing up if it accidentally tips over.

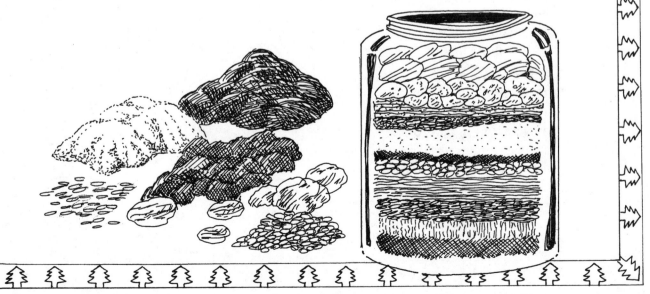

DESIGNS OF NATURE

The Earth is a work of art in itself. Discover the beauty of the Earth on this special holiday with these designs.

Time: 1 hour or more

Complexity: Easy–Moderate

Tree Rubbings
What to Do:

1. Tape paper to the bark of a tree and gently rub a peeled crayon over it until the bark pattern comes through.
2. Label the rubbing with tree type.
3. Make a variety of tree rubbings and compare the different textures.

Nature Rubbings
What to Do:

1. Collect nature items and place one item under a piece of paper.
2. Rub a peeled crayon over it until the image appears.
3. Overlap different items and use other colors to make unique designs.

Track Casting
What to Do:

1. Find animal tracks at the beach, zoo, barnyard, forest, park, or backyard.
2. Follow directions on Plaster of Paris package and mix with water.
3. Stir in a handful of sand.
4. Pour into the track and let harden (it doesn't take very long).

Materials:
- Lightweight paper
- Tape
- Crayons
- Small nature items, such as leaves, twigs, flowers, bushes, herbs, and even small dead insects
- Plaster of Paris
- Sand
- Water
- Pail with pouring lip
- Paint
- Brush
- Sheets of paper
- Rolling pin

5. Carefully pick up the cast and brush off the dirt.
6. Make a cast of your own hand or footprint too.

Leaf Print
What to Do:

1. Collect a variety of dry leaves.
2. Cover one side of each leaf with paint, then place leaves on a sheet of paper until you have a nice design.
3. Place another sheet of paper on top of the leaves and roll with the rolling pin.
4. Peel up the paper and leaves to see the design.

Practical Tip: Collect and set out all the items you're going to use ahead of time.

May

MAY DAY
May 1

Since ancient times people have celebrated May Day with dances, maypoles, and parades. Romans feasted and worshipped the goddess of flowers, Flora. Swedes held ceremonial battles on horseback between Summer and Winter. The English honored the legendary outlaw Robin Hood.

Many May Day celebrations feature a tall decorated tree called a maypole. In history, bringing the maypole in from the woods was a ritual in itself. People also went into the woods before dawn to pick flowers and branches to decorate the tree with. Children wrapped streamers around the maypole.

In the United States this holiday is primarily for children. They make paper May baskets filled with flowers and candy to hang on their friends' doors. They still dance around maypoles, which are more often basketball poles than trees. However you celebrate May Day, it's the perfect time to get outside and enjoy the weather.

Pine-Cone Bird Treat

By May Day birds have returned to most of North America. Your neighborhood birds will love dining on this tasty peanut-butter-and-seeds treat.

Time: 30 minutes

Complexity: Easy

What to Do:

1. Tie the yarn to the top of the pine cone.
2. Spread peanut butter into the crevices of the pine cone.
3. Roll the pine cone in the birdseed or wheat germ.
4. Tie the yarn to a tree branch and watch birds flock to dinner.

Materials:
- Large pine cone
- Colorful piece of yarn (2–3 feet long)
- Peanut butter
- Birdseed or wheat germ
- Spatula or spoon

Variation: Mix oatmeal and water together to create a paste. Spread it on the pine cone and roll in birdseed.

Ice-Cream Cone May Baskets

It's a May Day tradition to make May baskets and hang them on friends' doors. Here's a quick and easy basket that's also edible!

Time: 20 minutes

Complexity: Easy

What to Do:

1. Fill an ice-cream cone with candies, flowers, or small toys.

2. Cut a large circle out of the plastic wrap or cellophane and lay it over the top of the cone.

3. Cut the ribbon into two 2-foot lengths.

4. Wrap the two ribbons around the rim of the cone and tie at opposite sides.

5. Bring the four ends up and tie together in a bow to form a handle.

6. Repeat steps 1 to 5 for each basket you want to make.

Materials:

- Ice-cream cones, one per basket
- Basket fillings (candies, flowers, or small toys)
- Scissors
- Plastic wrap or cellophane
- Narrow ribbon, 4 feet per cone

Variation: Use a paper cup instead of an ice-cream cone for each basket.

Practical Tip: Handle cones carefully so they won't break. Have extras handy.

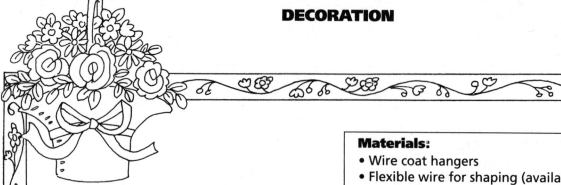

Topiary Garden— Plants in Animal Shapes

Get a little goofy in the garden! It's fun to create and tame these garden pets—you can make a dog, a cat, or even a brontosaurus!

Time: 1 hour

Complexity: Challenging—Adult assistance recommended

What to Do:

1. Bend the hangers and wire into an animal-shaped frame. (Remember, it doesn't have to be perfect!)

2. Soak the sheet moss and sphagnum peat moss in the tub of water until they are good and wet (about 5 minutes).

3. Squeeze out most of the water from the sheet moss and push it into the frame as a lining. This forms the animal's shape.

4. Push the sphagnum moss inside the frame as stuffing. This is the animal's innards.

5. Fill in the outline with pieces of moss and make sure the innards are fully packed.

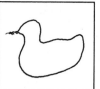

Materials:
- Wire coat hangers
- Flexible wire for shaping (available at hardware stores)
- Sheet moss
- Sphagnum peat moss
- Tub of water
- Plants that are about 4 inches long (creeping fig, ficus vine, or small leaf, needlepoint, jubilee, glacier, or itsy-bitsy ivy)
- Screwdriver
- Hairpins

6. Wash the soil off the roots of the other plants.

7. With the screwdriver, make holes about an inch apart in the moss. Insert the plants' roots into the holes.

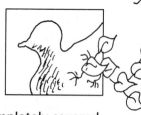

8. Lay the remaining plants along the outside of the frame, pinning them into place with the hairpins. Use many plants if you want it completely covered and you can't wait until it grows in.

9. Water every 2 to 3 days, or when it seems to be drying out.

Practical Tip: Keep your animal in shape by trimming it occasionally and pinning down its new growth. And remember to talk to your new pet often.

Growing Porcupine— Potato Plant Holder

Everyone will love watching this plant take shape. It looks like a porcupine as it grows.

Time: 30 minutes

Complexity: Easy—Adult assistance recommended

What to Do:

1. Cut off the top of the potato.
2. Use the potato peeler or melon baller to hollow out the potato, leaving about a 1/2-inch shell.
3. Put a moist cotton ball inside the potato. Sprinkle some seeds on top of the cotton ball.
4. Glue the buttons on the outside of the potato for eyes, and stick the Popsicle sticks or toothpicks in the bottom of the potato for feet.
5. Set the potato creature near the light and water every day until it grows "prickly" like a porcupine. Then water twice a week as the porcupine takes shape.

Materials:
- Potato
- Knife
- Potato peeler or melon baller
- Cotton ball
- Mustard seed, birdseed, or grass seed
- 2 buttons
- Glue
- 4 Popsicle sticks or toothpicks

Variation: Instead of a porcupine, make a Mr. or Mrs. Potato Head. Use felt-tip pens to draw a face. The seeds grow into hair.

Coloring Flowers

Calling all future scientists! Here's one experiment that's guaranteed to produce colorful results.

Time: 15 minutes

Complexity: Easy—Adult assistance recommended

What to Do:

1. Cut about 2 inches off the bottom of the flower stems.
2. Fill the vase with water.
3. Put several drops of food coloring into the water.
4. Stand the flowers in the water for several hours. Eventually the petals will begin to turn the color of the water in the vase as the flowers "suck up" the colored water through their stems.

Materials:
- Freshly cut inexpensive flowers (carnations, daisies, or daffodils)
- Scissors or knife
- Vase
- Water
- Food coloring

Variation: Try making a flower more than one color by splitting the stem in half and standing each half in a different color of water.

Practical Tip: Add a stalk of celery to see better what is happening.

Sprouting Seeds

Get ready for the gardening season by germinating these seeds indoors. It's a great way to learn about nature and to produce some tasty beans.

Time: 20 minutes

Complexity: Easy

What to Do:

1. Soak the beans in the dish of water overnight.
2. Rinse the beans.
3. Tape the beans to the inside of the sandwich baggy, as shown.

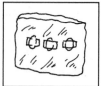

4. Cover the beans with the moist paper towel.
5. Cut a "house" shape out of the green construction paper to fit around the bag and make it look like a "green house."

6. Tape the house to the baggy, and then tape the baggy to a window that receives a lot of light.

Materials:
- 3 beans (pinto beans work well)
- Dish of water
- Sandwich baggy
- Tape
- Moist paper towel
- Green construction paper
- Scissors
- Round orange-juice containers or small pots
- Potting soil

7. In a few days the beans will begin to germinate. When they outgrow the baggy, transplant them to the round orange-juice containers or small pots filled with potting soil.

8. After a few weeks transplant the seeds into the ground, and soon you'll have your own home-grown beans.

Variation: Experiment with a variety of seeds.

Practical Tip: This works best in a sunny, warm window.

Dirt Dessert

This dessert looks like a flowerpot filled with dirt and flowers, but it's really a yummy treat. There are two ways to make Dirt Dessert—the original way or the quick way.

Original Recipe— Pudding and Cookie Pie

Serves: 6–8

Time: 20 minutes

Complexity: Moderate—Adult assistance recommended

Ingredients:
- 1 cup powdered sugar
- 1 8-ounce package cream cheese
- 1/2 cup margarine, softened
- 2 3-1/2-ounce packages instant vanilla pudding
- Milk (for instant pudding)
- 1 12-ounce container Cool Whip
- 1-1/2 packages (20 ounces) Oreo cookies
- Gummy worms

Materials:
- Clean, unused 8" pot (plastic or clay)
- Tin foil
- Plastic flowers
- Blender

What to Do:

1. Combine the powdered sugar, cream cheese, and margarine in the blender.

2. Mix the instant vanilla pudding according to package directions and fold in the Cool Whip. Combine the pudding and cream-cheese mixtures.

3. Line the pot with the tin foil.

4. Crush the Oreo cookies.

5. Put half of the cookie crumbs into the pot. Add the cream mixture and then the other half of the cookie crumbs.

6. Decorate the top of the dessert with plastic flowers and gummy worms. Refrigerate until serving time.

Easy Recipe— Ice Cream and Cookie Pie

Serves: 6–8

Time: 20 minutes

Complexity: Easy

Ingredients:
- Ice cream
- 1 16-ounce box chocolate wafer cookies
- Gummy worms

Materials:
- Clean, unused 8" pot (plastic or clay)
- Tin foil
- Plastic flowers

What to Do:

1. Line the pot with the tin foil.

2. Fill the pot with the ice cream.

3. Crush the cookies.

4. Cover the ice cream with the cookie crumbs.

5. Decorate the top of the dessert with the plastic flowers and gummy worms.

6. Keep in freezer until serving time. Allow to thaw for a few minutes before digging in!

CINCO DE MAYO
May 5

Here's a holiday for everyone who roots for the underdog! Cinco de Mayo is the Mexican national holiday recognizing the anniversary of the Battle of Puebla on May 5, 1862. That day, Mexican troops, outnumbered three to one, pulled together to defeat the French forces of Napoleon.

Mexicans everywhere celebrate this anniversary with parades, dances, and speeches. Children break open piñatas and feast on the treats that pour out. The celebration continues into the night with spectacular food and fireworks. This Mexican holiday is especially popular in the southwestern part of the United States.

Musical Instruments

Everybody loves a Cinco de Mayo parade! Make your parade extra special with homemade musical instruments. Then dress up in bright clothes and hats and make music!

Jingly Bracelet

Sew bells onto elastic, fit the elastic around your hand, and sew to fit. Then slip over your wrist and shake.

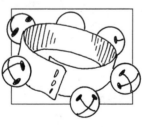

Tambourine

Fill tin-foil pie pans with seeds or beans and staple or glue-gun the pans together. Shake. Use heavy-duty paper plates instead of pie pans for a softer sound.

Rhythm Sticks

Tap wooden dowels or hollow bamboo sticks together to make a rhythm sound.

Rhythm Blocks

Staple sandpaper to two small wooden blocks and rub them together to make a swishy sound.

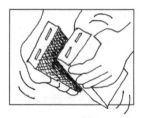

Variation: Offer a concert for your relatives in the backyard during a picnic celebration.

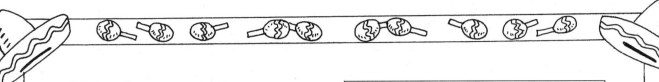

Maracas

Kids love to experiment with many different kinds of musical instruments, especially rhythm instruments. Maracas—often heard in Mexican music—are fun to make and add a happy beat to any music.

Time: 45 minutes

Complexity: Moderate—Adult assistance recommended

What to Do:

1. Combine the flour and water in the large bowl until you get a thick paste.

2. Place a handful of popcorn kernels into the balloon, and then carefully blow it up and tie it.

3. Tape the toilet-paper tube or half a paper-towel tube to the balloon so it forms a handle.

4. Cut the newspaper into 1-inch strips and tear the tissue paper into medium-sized pieces.

5. Dip the strips of newspaper into the flour-and-water paste, and then wrap them around the balloon and tube, being sure to cover them completely several times. Stuff some paper up into the tube before covering it.

6. Cover the balloon and tube with two layers of the torn tissue paper.

Materials:
- 1/4 cup flour
- 2–3 tablespoons water
- Large bowl
- Spoon
- Toilet-paper or paper-towel tube
- Tape
- Balloon
- Popcorn kernels
- Newspaper
- Scissors
- Colorful tissue paper
- Pin
- Felt-tip pens or stickers
- **Optional:** oven, preheated to 450°

7. Let dry for 24 hours or bake in oven for 5 to 10 minutes.

8. When the shell is hard, pop the balloon with a pin inserted directly through the shell.

9. Decorate with the felt-tip pens or stickers. Shake.

Variation: Fill the maracas with different seeds, beans, or sand.

Practical Tip: This can be messy, so cover your work area with newspaper.

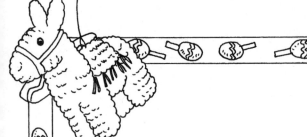

Piñata Party

Why not host a Piñata Party on Cinco de Mayo? Decorate the room in bright colors, serve some tasty Mexican treats, and end the fun with this piñata filled with surprises.

Time: 30 minutes

Complexity: Easy

What to Do:

1. Fill the large paper bag with the toys, candies, stickers, or other treats.

2. Gather the bag at the top and tie it closed with the cord or rope.

3. Decorate the bag with the wrapping paper, crepe paper, or paint.

4. Tape the crepe paper streamers to the bottom of the bag so they will hang down.

5. Hang the piñata from the ceiling with the remaining rope or cord.

6. Have the guests gather around the piñata, not too close though.

7. Blindfold one player with instructions to take three swings at the piñata with the broom handle. If it breaks open, the other players grab what falls out.

Materials:
- Large paper bag
- Small toys, candies, stickers, or other treats
- Long cord or rope
- Bright wrapping paper, crepe paper, or paint and paint brushes
- Crepe paper streamers
- Tape
- Blindfold
- Broom handle

8. If the first player doesn't break the bag open, have another player try. Continue until the bag breaks open.

Variations: Use a lightweight box instead of a bag.

Have the guests make individual piñatas.

Practical Tips: Make sure all the guests are well away from the swinging broom handle so nobody gets hurt.

When the bag breaks open, immediately tell the blindfolded player to stop swinging.

Have some extra goodies on hand in case some of the players don't get any from the piñata.

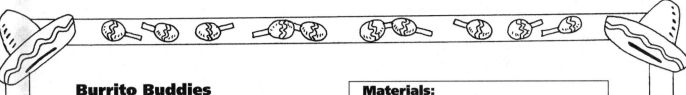

Burrito Buddies

Serve a whole meal in one hand with this burrito. Both kids and adults will enjoy this popular Mexican food.

Serves: 4

Time: 20 minutes

Complexity: Easy—Adult assistance recommended

Ingredients:
- 4 flour tortillas
- 1 9-ounce can refried beans
- 1/2 cup Cheddar and/or Monterey Jack cheese, grated
- Margarine
- 1 cup sour cream
- 2 avocados
- Mild taco sauce

What to Do:
1. Fill the tortillas evenly with refried beans.
2. Spread the grated cheese evenly among the tortillas.
3. Fold the tortillas in half or roll them up.
4. Melt a little margarine in the frying pan on medium-low heat.
5. Place a filled tortilla in the pan, turn the heat up to medium, and cook for 3 to 4 minutes, until the underside of the tortilla begins to turn brown.

Materials:
- Spoon
- Grater
- Frying pan
- Stove
- Spatula
- 4 plates

6. Turn with the spatula and cook for a few more minutes.
7. Serve on plates with sour cream, avocado, and taco sauce.

Variation: Add other Mexican foods to your burrito. Fill with leftover dinner meats, cooked ground beef, other cheeses, onions, chili peppers, or whatever you like. Offer bowls of condiments and let the family choose what they want to add to their basic burrito.

Practical Tips: It's easier to fill the tortilla with beans and cheese before you place it in the pan, but many cooks prefer to set the tortilla in the pan and then fill it.

Be sure to watch the burrito brown—it cooks quickly.

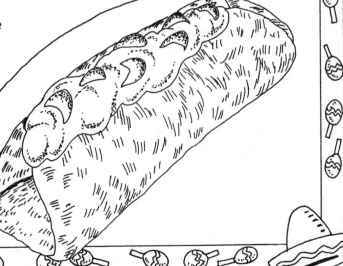

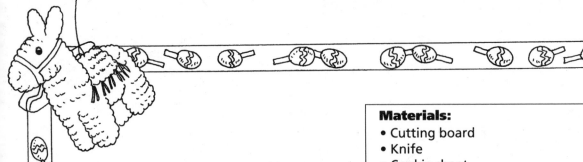

Tortilla Crispies

Replace greasy potato chips with this healthy, Mexican-style treat. Serve them at your Piñata Party.

Serves: 4–6

Time: 20 minutes

Complexity: Easy—Adult assistance recommended

> **Ingredients:**
> • 12 6-inch corn tortillas
> • Vegetable-oil spray (such as Pam)
> • 1/2 teaspoon salt
> • **Optional:** salsa

What to Do:

1. Place the tortillas on a cutting board.
2. Spray the tortillas with the vegetable-oil spray until lightly covered.
3. Sprinkle half of the salt over the tortillas. Turn tortillas over and repeat.
4. Place tortillas on top of each other and cut into quarters.

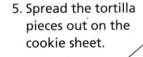

5. Spread the tortilla pieces out on the cookie sheet.

> **Materials:**
> • Cutting board
> • Knife
> • Cookie sheet
> • Oven, preheated to 400°

6. Bake for 8 to 10 minutes, until crisp and lightly browned.
7. Allow to cool. Serve with salsa or plain.

Variations: Omit the salt if you prefer.

Sprinkle on Mexican seasoning, seasoned salt, or Parmesan cheese.

Practical Tips: Make sure the chips are cool before eating them.

Let the leftovers cool completely, and then store them in an airtight container.

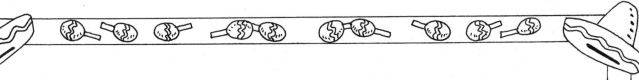

Cinco de Salsa Dip

Here's a great dip to go with your Tortilla Crispies. It tastes even better when it's made with fresh ingredients.

Serves: 4–6

Time: 20 minutes

Complexity: Easy—Adult assistance recommended

Ingredients:
- Vegetable-oil spray (such as Pam)
- 1 9-ounce can refried beans
- 1/2 cup Cheddar cheese, grated
- 1/2 cup Monterey Jack cheese, grated
- 1/2 cup sour cream
- 1 package taco seasoning mix
- 1 tomato, chopped
- 1 3-ounce can chopped olives

What to Do:

1. Spray the cookie sheet or oven-proof platter with the vegetable-oil spray.

2. Spread the refried beans on the cookie sheet or platter.

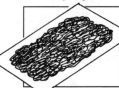

3. Sprinkle on both cheeses.

4. Bake for 8 to 10 minutes, until hot and bubbly. Remove from oven.

Materials:
- Cookie sheet or oven-proof platter
- Spoon
- Oven, preheated to 400°
- Small bowl

5. Combine the sour cream and taco mix in the small bowl. Spread over the beans and cheese.

6. Sprinkle on the chopped tomato and chopped olives.

7. Serve with Tortilla Crispies or other chips or vegetables.

Variations: Use canned bean dip instead of refried beans.

Use mozzarella or American cheese instead of Cheddar and Monterey Jack.

Spread guacamole over the sour-cream layer. Add chopped green onions, chopped mild chili peppers, or other Mexican seasonings.

Use a microwave plate and heat in the microwave instead of the oven.

Practical Tip: Allow the bean-and-cheese layer to cool a few minutes before adding the sour cream so it won't melt.

MOTHER'S DAY
Second Sunday in May

Mother's Day was first observed in 1907 at the request of Anna M. Jarvis of Grafton, West Virginia, who asked her church to honor all mothers on the second anniversary of her mother's death. In 1914 Congress passed a resolution establishing a national Mother's Day. It's a day to express publicly our love and respect for mothers.

Some say that a Mother's Day of sorts, called "Mothering Sunday," existed in the Middle Ages. During this time children often left home at a fairly young age to become apprentices. They were allowed to visit their home on one Sunday each year, Mothering Sunday. Bringing small gifts or cakes home for their mothers, they visited and worked around the house for the day.

Today, many children buy carnations or corsages for their mother to wear on this holiday. Many also make mom breakfast in bed, take her out to brunch or dinner, or send her a card to say thanks.

Potpourri Ball

Mmm—something smells good! This potpourri ball adds a pleasant scent to drawers or closets.

Time: 15 minutes

Complexity: Easy

What to Do:

1. Cover the tennis ball with glue and roll it in the potpourri until it's completely covered.

2. Let dry for 1 hour.

Materials:
- Tennis ball
- Glue
- Potpourri (available at craft stores)
- Ribbon

3. Tie the ribbon around the ball.

4. Hang in a closet or place in a drawer.

Variation: Roll the ball in seeds instead of potpourri to make an attractive decoration.

Practical Tip: Put a thick coat of glue on the ball.

PRESERVING FLOWERS

Kids will be proud to present mom with these decorative flowers on Mother's Day.

Dried Flower Bouquet— Hanging Method

Time: 1–2 weeks

Complexity: Easy

What to Do:

1. Tie the flower stems together loosely.
2. Hang the flowers upside down in a dark room or closet, leaving the door open to provide some circulation.
3. Check them in a week or two, when they should be dry.
4. Wrap them in the tissue paper and give to mom.

Materials:
- Fresh flowers
- String
- Tissue paper

Variation: Press the flowers instead of drying them. Then make a collage to hang on the wall.

Practical Tip: Start this *early* since it takes awhile to dry the flowers.

Dried Flower Bouquet— "Buried Alive" Method

Time: 2 weeks

Complexity: Easy

What to Do:

1. Cover the bottom of the box with cornstarch.
2. Arrange the flowers in the box so they are not touching each other.
3. Slowly add more cornstarch until the flowers are completely covered.
4. Uncover the flowers in about two weeks and wrap them in the cellophane.

Materials
- Fresh flowers
- Large box
- Cornstarch
- Cellophane

Variation: Use borax instead of cornstarch.

Practical Tip: Be patient!

Picture Frame

Here's a simple, inexpensive way to frame favorite photos for mom to display.

Time: 15 minutes

Complexity: Easy

Materials:
- Plastic top from a margarine container
- Scissors
- Paper punch
- Glue
- Felt or paper doily
- Photo
- Yarn or ribbon

What to Do:

1. Cut a triangle in the back of the margarine top, as shown, and fold back to make a stand.

2. Punch a hole in the top of the lid.

3. Glue a circle of felt or a doily on the lid.

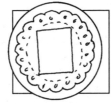

4. Glue the photo onto the felt or doily.

5. String the yarn through the hole and hang the frame up, or tie a decorative ribbon through the hole and stand it up.

Variation: Attach magnet tape to the back of the frame to make a refrigerator magnet.

Practical Tip: Have an adult help younger kids cut the lid.

Homemade Bubble Bath

Every mom needs to get away from it all every once in a while. Here's a gift to make for Mother's Day that will give mom an opportunity to take some time out for herself.

Time: 15 minutes

Complexity: Easy

What to Do:

1 Place the Epsom salts in the glass jar.

2. In the small bowl combine the glycerin with two drops of the food coloring and a few drops of the perfume.

3. Add the mixture to the Epsom salts and stir thoroughly.

4. Use a piece of paper to make a label for the jar. Write "Mom's Bubbles" or whatever you like on the label, and then tape it to the jar.

5. Tie the ribbon around the jar.

Materials:

- 3 cups Epsom salts (available at drug stores)
- Glass jar with lid
- Small bowl
- Spoon
- 1 tablespoon glycerin
- Food coloring
- Perfume
- Paper
- Felt-tip pens or crayons
- Scissors
- Tape
- Ribbon

Variation: Carve a perfumed soap into a heart shape or the first letter of mom's name. Tie it with a ribbon or a pretty washcloth.

Practical Tip: Give mom a few hours off so she can enjoy her gift.

Gumdrop Corsage

After mom is done wearing this colorful corsage, maybe she'll want to eat it! (But don't let her.)

Time: 30–45 minutes

Complexity: Moderate

Materials:
- Small sheet of posterboard, 8-1/2" x 11"
- 5" round paper doily
- Scissors
- Glue
- 6–8 green pipe cleaners
- 6–8 gumdrops (all colors)
- Tissue paper (all colors)
- Skewer
- Ribbon, 1-foot long

What to Do:

1. Out of the posterboard cut a circle the same size as the doily. Glue the doily to the circle.

2. Poke a pipe cleaner into the flat side of each gumdrop to form flower centers on stems.

3. Cut small scalloped circles out of the tissue paper.

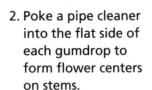

4. Push three or four of the tissue circles onto the end of each pipe cleaner. Then push the circles up to the gumdrops to form the petals around the flower centers.

5. With the skewer, poke holes in the doily-covered posterboard (one hole for each flower).

6. Insert the pipe cleaners into the doily and back out again so the ends of the pipe cleaners are in the front of the doily.

7. Twist the pipe cleaner stems together and tie with the ribbon. Make a bow with the remaining ribbon.

Variation: Make paper flowers out of construction paper and glue them to strips of green construction paper for stems. Write promises to mom on the stems, such as "I will clean my room" or "I will wash the dog." Then do them!

Baked French Toast

Surprise mom on her special day with this easy-to-make breakfast-in-bed presentation.

Serves: 3–6

Time: 45 minutes

Complexity: Easy—Adult assistance recommended

Ingredients:
- 1/4 cup margarine
- 1/2 cup brown sugar, firmly packed
- 1/2 teaspoon cinnamon
- 2 eggs
- 1/4 cup milk
- 6 slices French bread
- 1–2 tablespoons powdered sugar
- 12 ripe strawberries, sliced
- **Optional:** syrup

What to Do:

1. Melt the margarine in the small saucepan on the stove. Or melt it in the microwave-safe bowl in the microwave. Pour into the oven-proof pan.

2. In one small bowl, combine the brown sugar and cinnamon. Sprinkle over the melted margarine.

3. In the other small bowl, combine the eggs and milk. Stir until well blended.

4. Dip a slice of the bread in the egg-and-milk mixture, coating both sides. Place in the oven-proof pan. Repeat for the other slices of bread.

Materials:
- Small saucepan or microwave-safe bowl
- Stove or microwave
- Oven-proof pan
- 2 small bowls
- Spoon
- Tin foil
- Oven, preheated to 375°

5. Pour the remaining egg-and-milk mixture over the bread, cover with tin foil, and bake for 25 minutes. Take the foil off and bake for 10 more minutes.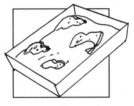

6. Sprinkle the powdered sugar on top of the French toast and top with the sliced strawberries. Serve with syrup, if desired.

Variations: Use regular bread instead of French bread.

Substitute other fruit for the strawberries.

Practical Tips: Present the Mother's Day breakfast to mom in bed on a tray covered with a fancy napkin. Add the newspaper, a card, a flower, and juice or coffee.

Make sure an adult can help out with the cooking. Or substitute foods that don't have to be cooked, such as cereal, a croissant, or a fruit cup.

MEMORIAL DAY
May 30 or Last Monday in May

Memorial Day began around 1868 as a day to honor those who died in the Civil War. Celebrations in most cities and towns included colorful parades led by Civil War veterans and programs with speeches and patriotic songs. People decorated veterans' graves with flowers, ribbons, and flags. Memorial Day became a federal holiday in 1971.

Today, soldiers from all wars are honored on Memorial Day. Flags are flown at half-mast in honor of the dead, and graves are decorated with flowers, wreaths, and miniature flags. Some communities still hold parades and programs, but others observe a quiet holiday. For many, this holiday has become a day to remember all family members and friends who have died.

Crepe-Paper Poppies

Red flowers called poppies are traditionally worn on Memorial Day in memory of the soldiers who died on European battlefields where poppies grew. On Memorial Day, veterans organizations sell real and artificial poppies and donate the proceeds to help disabled veterans. Buy some poppies and try making your own, too.

Time: 20 minutes

Complexity: Easy

What to Do:

1. Cut two 4-inch circles out of crepe paper for each poppy.
2. Place one circle on top of the other.

Materials:
- Red crepe paper
- Scissors
- Green pipe cleaners
- Safety pins

3. Poke two small holes in the center of both pieces of crepe paper.

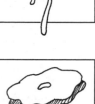

4. Put the end of one pipe cleaner up through one hole, bend it, and bring it back down through the other hole.

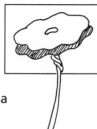

5. Twist that end of the pipe cleaner around the longer end of the pipe cleaner to form a stem.
6. Attach to clothing with a safety pin.

Memorial Day Wreath

Family gatherings have become popular on Memorial Day since it became a three-day weekend. Hang this wreath on your door to remind everyone what the holiday is really about.

Time: 30–45 minutes

Complexity: Moderate

What to Do:

1. Cut stars out of the posterboard in a variety of sizes, using the cookie cutters or stencils as a guide.

2. Spray glue on the stars and sprinkle glitter on them.

3. Tape a piece of the curling ribbon to the back of each star. Curl the ribbon with the scissors.

4. Glue the stars, ribbon-side down, to the wreath. Allow to dry.

Materials:
- Star-shaped cookie cutters or stencils
- Posterboard (red, white, and blue)
- Spray adhesive glue
- Glitter
- Curling ribbon (red, white, and blue)
- Tape
- Glue
- Scissors
- Styrofoam wreath (available at hobby stores)

5. Hang on the front door to greet visitors.

Variations: Use a wreath cut out of posterboard or cardboard.

Instead of stars, decorate the wreath with red, white, and blue wrapped candies.

Practical Tip: Use pins to reinforce the stars if they fall off. Just stick a pin through them into the Styrofoam to secure them.

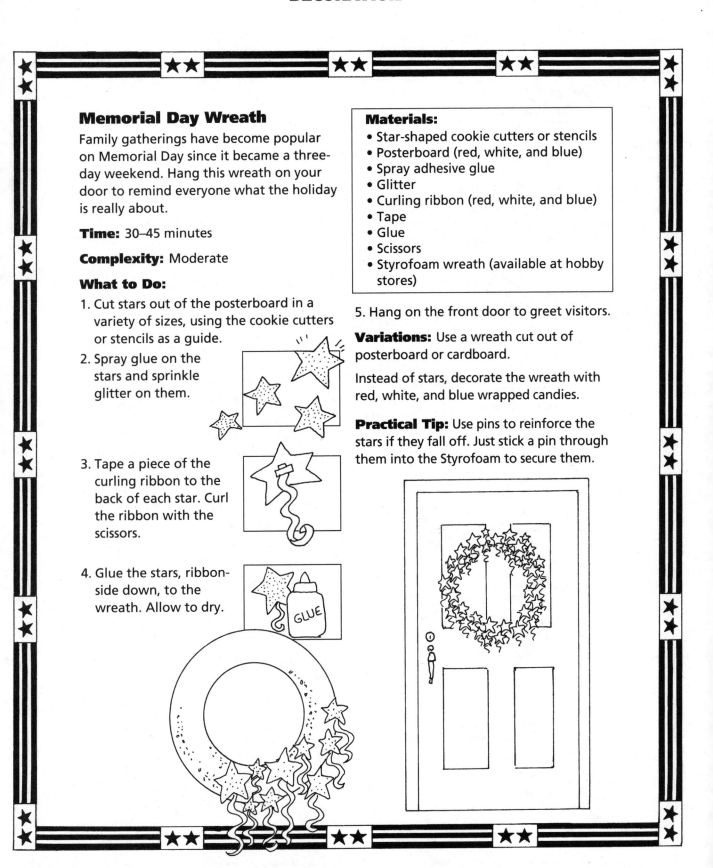

Patriotic Windsock

Instead of flying a flag on Memorial Day, make this red, white, and blue windsock. It's also great to hang up on the 4th of July.

Time: 45–60 minutes

Complexity: Challenging—Adult assistance recommended

Materials:
- 12" x 18" red piece of nylon parachute fabric (available at fabric stores)
- 12" x 18" blue piece of nylon parachute fabric
- 3 squares of white felt
- 5" embroidery hoop (available at fabric and craft stores)
- Glue gun
- Scissors
- 3 feet of twine or string
- **Optional:** sewing machine or needle and thread

What to Do:

1. Sew or glue the red and blue pieces of fabric together along the 18-inch sides, allowing a 1-inch overlap.

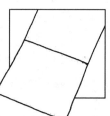

2. Cut the red fabric into 1-inch strips, starting at the unglued end and cutting to where the blue and red fabric meet.

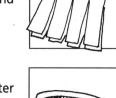

3. Glue the top of the blue fabric to the outer rim of the embroidery hoop. The fabric should be long enough to go all the way around the hoop with an inch overlapping itself to make a seam.

4. Glue the overlapping blue fabric together. Do not glue the red fabric together.

5. Cut eight to ten 2-inch stars out of the felt and glue them to the blue portion of the windsock.

6. Cut the twine or string into three even pieces. Cut three small, evenly spaced holes in the blue portion of the windsock near the rim.

Poke one piece of string through each hole and tie them onto the hoop. Tie the three pieces of the string together about halfway up and again at the end of the strings. Hang up.

Variation: Make a windsock from paper instead of fabric. Decorate the paper first with felt-tip pens or paint. Wrap the paper around an oatmeal box, attach crepe-paper streamers to the bottom, and tie the top with three pieces of twine.

Practical Tip: Use caution around the glue gun—it's very hot. Have two people work on the project together.

June

FATHER'S DAY
Third Sunday in June

The earliest known observance of Father's Day was back in 1908, a year after the first Mother's Day. In 1936 the National Father's Day Committee formed to promote this day honoring dads. The committee also has the difficult task of selecting a Father of the Year. Father's Day became a permanent U.S. holiday in 1972.

On this day children, young and old, take time to tell their fathers how much they mean to them. Some give cards and gifts to their fathers, while others show their appreciation with gifts of action, such as doing household chores, washing the car, or mowing the lawn.

Writing a Poem for Dad

Let dad know how much he's loved on this day by writing a special poem about him. Include the poem on a card or have it framed for a gift.

Time: 15 minutes

Complexity: Easy

What to Do:

1. Think about dad—what he likes to do, what makes him special, funny things he says—and write it all down. Remember, poems don't have to rhyme; they just have to express feelings.

2. Read the poem during dinner, slip it into his coat pocket before he goes to work, or recite it on his answering machine at work.

Materials:
• Paper
• Pen or pencil

Variations: Give dad a poetry book instead of writing a poem.

Read the poem on a tape recorder and give dad the tape for a lasting memory.

Practical Tip: Look through family albums for inspiration.

Father's Day Stencil Card

Parents love to display their children's artwork on their refrigerators. Dad will proudly "show off" this easy-to-make stencil card on his special day.

Time: 15 minutes

Complexity: Easy–Moderate

What to Do:

1. With the pencil draw an outline of dad in the middle of one of the sheets of construction paper.

2. Cut out the outline of dad, creating a hole in middle of the paper that's shaped like dad.

3. Glue the sheet with the hole in it on top of the other sheet of construction paper so dad's shape is the color of the second sheet of paper.

4. Fold the ends of the paper to the middle so the front of the card looks like double doors to the inside of the card.

5. Write something on the outside of the card like "My Two Favorite Words Are . . ." Then write something on the inside like "Dad's Home!"

Materials:
- 2 sheets of construction paper (different colors)
- Pencil
- Scissors
- Spray adhesive or glue
- Felt-tip pens or markers
- **Optional:** envelope

6. Use the felt-tip pens to add details like hair, a face, and clothing to the picture of dad.

Variation: Ask dad to sit near a wall, shine a bright light on the side of his face, and create a silhouette on the wall to trace on a sheet of paper. Glue the silhouette to a large 8-1/2" x 11" card.

Practical Tip: To draw the shape of dad more easily, find a full body photograph and trace the outline.

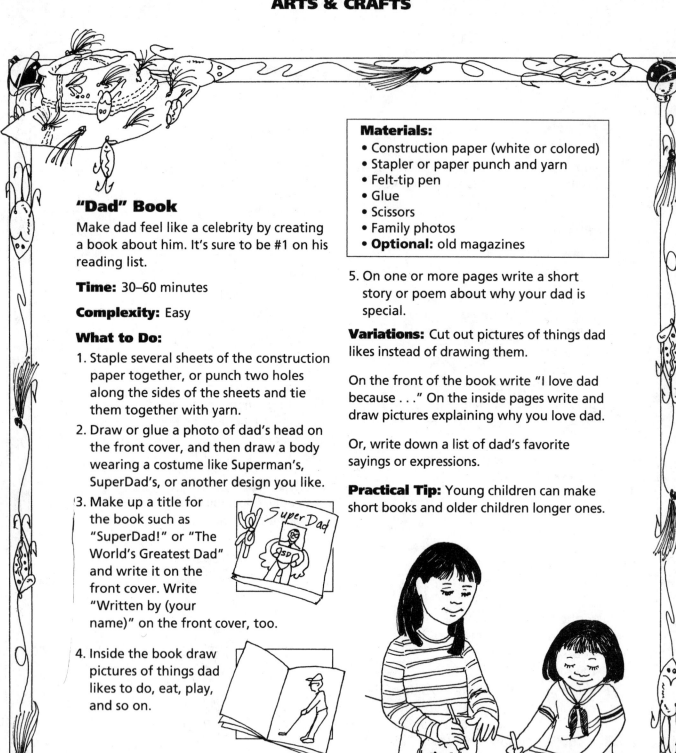

"Dad" Book

Make dad feel like a celebrity by creating a book about him. It's sure to be #1 on his reading list.

Time: 30–60 minutes

Complexity: Easy

What to Do:

1. Staple several sheets of the construction paper together, or punch two holes along the sides of the sheets and tie them together with yarn.

2. Draw or glue a photo of dad's head on the front cover, and then draw a body wearing a costume like Superman's, SuperDad's, or another design you like.

3. Make up a title for the book such as "SuperDad!" or "The World's Greatest Dad" and write it on the front cover. Write "Written by (your name)" on the front cover, too.

4. Inside the book draw pictures of things dad likes to do, eat, play, and so on.

Materials:
- Construction paper (white or colored)
- Stapler or paper punch and yarn
- Felt-tip pen
- Glue
- Scissors
- Family photos
- **Optional:** old magazines

5. On one or more pages write a short story or poem about why your dad is special.

Variations: Cut out pictures of things dad likes instead of drawing them.

On the front of the book write "I love dad because . . ." On the inside pages write and draw pictures explaining why you love dad.

Or, write down a list of dad's favorite sayings or expressions.

Practical Tip: Young children can make short books and older children longer ones.

Miniature Backyard Golf

Putt, putt! Here's an activity the whole family will enjoy on Father's Day. Play individually or in teams.

Time: 30 minutes

Complexity: Easy

What to Do:

1. Make holes for the course by setting cans on their sides.

2. Make obstacles by turning chairs upside down, cutting holes in boxes to send balls through, and thinking up your own creative ideas with items around your house and yard.

3. Get the family together and play. Give

Materials:
- Metal cans, various sizes
- Chairs
- Boxes
- Scissors
- Baseball bats, broomsticks, or golf clubs
- Golf or ping-pong balls

everyone three tries to hit a ball through or around each obstacle. If they miss, they lose their turn. If they make it, they get to keep going.

4. Change the course after each game.

Variation: Keep score. Whoever completes the course in the fewest number of strokes, wins.

Personalized Baseball Hat

Dads love hats. Maybe they wear them because they're in fashion. Maybe it's to keep their heads warm or protect them from the sun. Or maybe it's because they're losing some of that hair. No matter why dad wears a hat, he's sure to love this one.

Time: 30 minutes

Complexity: Moderate—Adult assistance recommended

What to Do:

1. With the felt-tip pens draw a design on the front of the white baseball hat. You might draw golf clubs, a fish dad would love to catch, a favorite team logo, or dad's nickname.

Materials:
- White baseball-style hat
- Permanent felt-tip pens
- 2 pieces of fabric, 4" x 6" long
- Needle
- Thread

2. Sew the pieces of fabric onto the back of the hat to provide extra protection from the sun.

Variation: Pin or glue items onto the hat that are associated with dad's interests, such as golf tees, baseball pins, ski badges, fishing lures, or old concert tickets.

Practical Tip: Omit the flaps if you want the hat to come together quickly and easily without sewing.

Necktie Cake

Dads often get neckties for Father's Day gifts. This year make dad a tie he can eat— a cake shaped and decorated like a tie.

Time: 30 minutes

Complexity: Easy—Adult assistance recommended

Ingredients:
- Cake mix (any flavor)
- 1 can frosting mix
- M & M candies

What to Do:

1. Mix up the cake mix according to package directions. Fill the paper cupcake holder with batter, and then pour the rest of it into the rectangular cake pan.

2. Bake according to package directions. Allow to cool.

3. Cut the cake in half lengthwise. Lay the pieces of the cake end to end on the cardboard covered with tin foil.

4. Place the cupcake at one end of the cake.

Materials:
- 1 paper cupcake holder
- Cupcake tin
- Rectangular cake pan
- Oven
- Knife
- Cardboard covered with tin foil
- Frosting knife

5. Cut the other end of the cake into a V-shape.

6. Frost the cake and decorate it with M & Ms to create a polka-dot tie.

Variations: Decorate the cake with other candies or use frosting in a tube with different tips to create a design.

Copy the design of one of dad's real ties.

Practical Tips: It's easier to frost a cut cake if you freeze it for a while first.

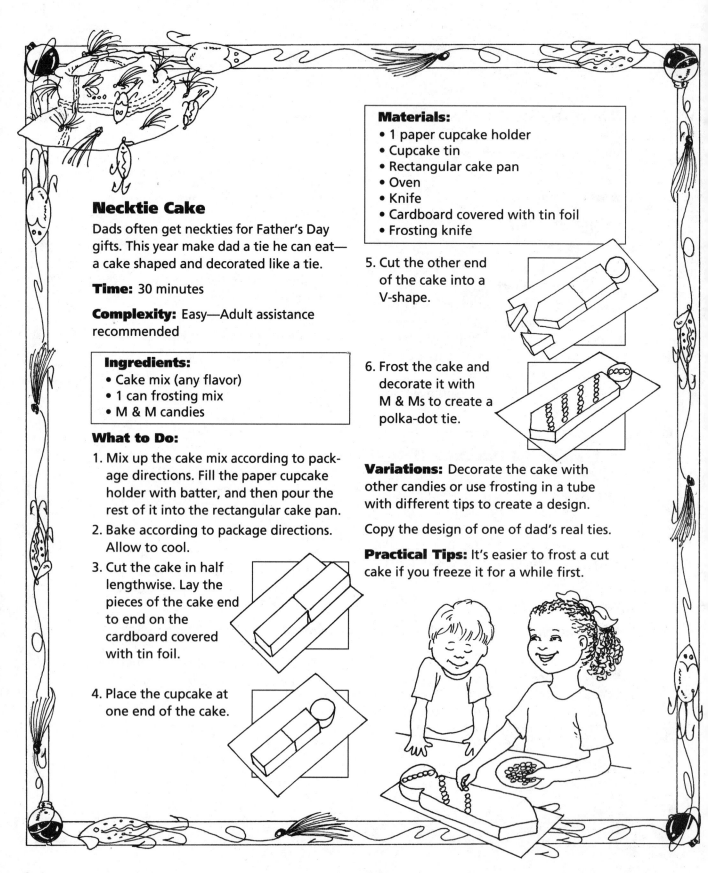

Blueberry Muffins

Greet dad on Father's Day morning with these homemade blueberry muffins. He'll love the special treatment.

Yields: 12 muffins

Time: 30–40 minutes

Complexity: Moderate—Adult assistance recommended

Ingredients:
- 1-1/2 cups flour (white, wheat, or a combination of both)
- 2 teaspoons baking powder
- 1 teaspoon baking soda
- 1/2 teaspoon salt
- 1/2 teaspoon nutmeg
- 1 egg
- 1/4 cup vegetable oil
- 1/2 cup sugar
- 3/4 cup milk
- 2 cups blueberries (fresh or frozen)

What to Do:
1. Place the paper muffin cups in the muffin tin.
2. In the large bowl, combine the flour, baking powder, baking soda, salt, and nutmeg until well blended.
3. In the medium bowl, combine the egg, vegetable oil, sugar, and milk until well blended.
4. Pour the egg mixture into the flour mixture and stir until combined. Do not overmix.

Materials:
- Oven, preheated to 375°
- Muffin tin
- Paper muffin cups
- Large bowl
- 2 large spoons
- Medium bowl
- Spatula

5. Fold the blueberries into the mixture. Batter will be lumpy.
6. Fill each paper muffin cup 1/2 to 3/4 full.
7. Bake for 20 minutes, or until muffins are lightly browned.
8. Remove muffins from muffin tin and allow to cool.

Practical Tip: Serve to dad warm with milk or coffee.

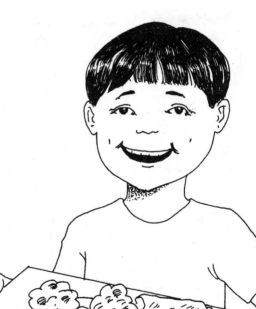

HAPPY "JUNETEENTH"

JUNETEENTH
June 19

Celebrated by African Americans throughout the country, but especially in Texas and the South, this special holiday recalls the day in 1865 when Union General Granger proclaimed the slaves of Texas free. Although President Lincoln issued his Emancipation Proclamation on January 1, 1863, slavery did not really end until the Union victory in April, 1865. According to legend, the slaves in Texas were not freed until June because the news was either withheld so that one last crop could be harvested or delayed because of slow mule travel or the murder of the messenger.

Juneteenth was originally celebrated in Texas and Louisiana. The celebration soon spread to Arkansas, Oklahoma, California, Alabama, and Florida as African Americans moved to these states. Today, it's celebrated throughout the country with picnics, games, and lots of food. Join in one of the many activities and celebrations in your community or host your own Juneteenth celebration.

West African Ginger Ale

Ginger ale, a favorite drink in West Africa, has a spicy taste that tickles the tongue. It will liven up any Juneteenth meal.

Serves: 8–10

Time: 30 minutes

Complexity: Easy—Adult assistance recommended

Ingredients:
- 2 quarts water
- 1/2 pound fresh ginger, peeled and thinly sliced
- 1/2 cup fresh lemon juice
- 1 cup honey
- Ice cubes

Materials:
- Medium saucepan
- Stove
- Large spoon
- Strainer
- Large pitcher

What to Do:

1. In the medium saucepan, combine 2 cups of water and the ginger. Simmer over medium heat for 20 minutes.
2. Stir in the lemon juice and honey. Let cool completely.
3. Strain the ginger mixture into the large pitcher.
4. Add the rest of the water and ice cubes. Let stand until chilled, and then serve.

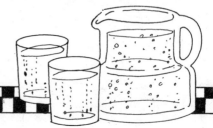

Iron-On Crayon T-shirts

Here's an opportunity to wear your own art. Create African designs, pictures of famous black historical figures, or black-history art for this special celebration.

Time: 30–45 minutes

Complexity: Moderate—Adult assistance recommended

What to Do:

1. Pressing firmly, draw a design on a sheet of the paper with the textile crayons. The design will turn out backwards on the shirt, so draw the pictures or letters accordingly.

2. Place a towel or layers of newspaper on the ironing pad. Then place a sheet of the unprinted white paper on the very top. This will prevent color from bleeding onto the ironing pad.

3. Place the T-shirt on the ironing pad with a sheet of blank paper between the front and the back of the shirt to prevent the colors from transferring to the opposite side of the shirt. Lay the designed paper face-down on the fabric with a piece of the blank paper on top of it to prevent the colors from smearing onto the iron.

Materials:
- White T-shirt, mostly polyester with some cotton in it
- Textile dye crayons (available at craft stores)
- 4 sheets of blank white paper
- Towel or newspaper
- Ironing board
- Iron
- Scissors
- Colorful beads

4. Set the iron to the cotton setting with no steam. Iron until the image becomes slightly visible through the paper.

5. Carefully remove the designed paper. The design will come out in brilliant colors and will remain on the fabric permanently.

6. Cut a fringe design along the bottom of the sleeves and the bottom of the T-shirt. Attach large, colorful beads to each of the fringe strands and tie them on securely.

Variation: Fringe a pair of knit pants, such as bicycle pants, and add beads to those strands too.

Blackberry Surprise

Food is an important part of Juneteenth celebrations. This blackberry dessert is like a cobbler but is cooked on the stove instead of in the oven. It's delicious served with ice cream on the side.

Serves: 6

Time: 30 minutes

Complexity: Moderate—Adult assistance recommended

Ingredients:
- 5 cups blackberries
- 2/3 cup sugar
- 2/3 cup water
- 1 teaspoon vanilla extract
- 1-3/4 cups flour
- 2 tablespoons sugar
- 2-1/2 teaspoons baking powder
- 3/4 teaspoon salt
- 1/3 cup margarine, cut into pieces
- 1/2 cup + 3 tablespoons milk
- Ice cream

What to Do:

1. In the frying pan, combine the blackberries, 2/3 cup sugar, and water. Bring to a boil over medium heat, stirring occasionally.
2. Reduce to low heat and simmer for approximately 5 minutes, until thickened.

Materials:
- 10" frying pan with lid
- Stove
- Spoon
- Medium bowl
- Tablespoon
- Serving bowls

3. Stir in the vanilla.
4. While the blackberries are simmering, combine the flour, 2 tablespoons of sugar, baking powder, and salt in the medium bowl.
5. Cut the margarine into the flour mixture until it's crumbly.
6. Stir in the milk to make a soft dough.
7. Drop 12 heaping tablespoons of dough into the simmering blackberries.
8. Cook uncovered for 10 minutes. Then cover and cook for another 10 minutes.
9. Divide into serving bowls. Serve with ice cream.

Variation: Instead of blackberries, use another favorite berry, peaches, or plums.

Practical Tip: Keep margarine chilled until ready to use to make it easy to cut into crumbs.

Sweet Potato– Peanut Butter Tarts

Sweet potatoes and peanut butter sounds like an unusual combination. But this dessert blends them together to make a sweet and tasty treat.

Yields: 18 tarts

Time: 1 hour

Complexity: Challenging—Adult assistance recommended

Crust Ingredients:
- 2-1/2 cups flour
- 1 teaspoon baking powder
- 1/4 teaspoon salt
- 8 tablespoons (1 stick) margarine, cut into pieces
- 1/2 cup smooth peanut butter
- 1/3 cup ice water

Filling Ingredients:
- 2 medium sweet potatoes (1 pound)
- 8 tablespoons (1 stick) margarine, softened
- 1-1/2 cups sugar
- 1 teaspoon vanilla
- 1 teaspoon cinnamon
- 1/4 teaspoon salt
- 1 cup evaporated milk
- 2 large eggs, beaten
- Vegetable-oil spray (such as Pam)
- 1/4 cup heavy cream, chilled
- 2 tablespoons powdered sugar

What to Do:
1. First make the crust. In the large bowl, combine the flour, baking powder, and salt. Cut in the margarine and peanut butter until crumbly.
2. Sprinkle in water until the dough is moist enough to hold together.
3. Roll the dough into a ball, wrap it in waxed paper, and chill for 1 hour.

Materials:
- Large bowl
- Large spoon
- Waxed paper
- Medium saucepan
- Stove
- Potato peeler
- Mixer
- Rolling pin
- Cookie cutter or cup
- Muffin tin
- Fork
- Oven, preheated to 350°
- Knife

4. Next make the filling. In the medium saucepan, cook the sweet potatoes in boiling water until tender (about 25 minutes). Drain and cool slightly, then peel and mash.
5. Combine the potatoes and softened margarine. Stir until the margarine melts.
6. Stir in the sugar, vanilla, cinnamon, and salt. Then beat in the milk and eggs. Chill until ready to use.
7. Roll half of the dough out until it's about 1/8-inch thick. Use a cookie cutter or cup to cut the dough into circles. Repeat until all the dough is used.
8. Spray the muffin tin with vegetable-oil spray. Place the dough circles into the muffin cups, press into sides, and prick the bottom and sides of the dough with a fork.
9. Fill each muffin cup with 1/4 cup of the filling.
10. Bake for 10 minutes, then run a knife around the inside of each cup, lift out, and cool.
11. Whip the cream and powdered sugar until soft peaks form. Top each tart with whipped cream and serve immediately.

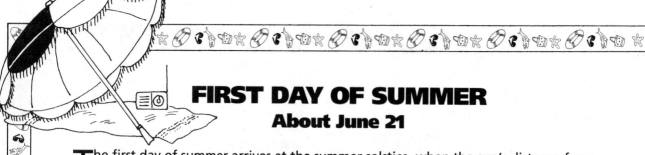

FIRST DAY OF SUMMER
About June 21

The first day of summer arrives at the summer solstice, when the sun's distance from the celestial equator is greatest. This is also the longest day of the year in the northern hemisphere—the Arctic Circle experiences daylight for twenty-four hours.

The arrival of summer also officially welcomes summer vacation. School is out, there's no more homework, and hot weather is finally here! Start planning the special outings, daily activities, chores, and goals for summer now before those endless summer days magically slip away.

Pinwheel

The warm summer winds have arrived. Carry this homemade pinwheel outside and watch it spin and spin.

Time: 20 minutes

Complexity: Moderate

What to Do:

1. Cut a sheet of the construction paper into a 9-inch square.
2. Decorate both sides with the felt-tip pens and glitter.
3. With the ruler, draw diagonal lines from the corners so they cross in the middle.
4. Cut along the lines *almost* to the middle.

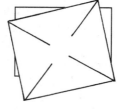

Materials:
- Construction paper
- Scissors
- Felt-tip pens
- Glitter
- Glue
- Ruler
- Thumbtack
- Pencil or wooden dowel
- Tape

5. Bend every other corner to the middle and poke the thumbtack through the tips and the center of the pinwheel.

6. Push the thumbtack into the pencil or dowel, near one end, leaving space between it and the pinwheel. Blow the pinwheel or swing it through the air.

Summer Activity Calendar

Summer brings vacations to far-away and not-so-far-away lands, lazy days at the beach, and countless ball games and activities. Whatever this summer brings to your family, a calendar of your plans will keep the whole family on track.

Time: 15–30 minutes

Complexity: Easy

What to Do:

1. With the ruler and pen or marker make a grid with five spaces down and seven spaces across on each sheet of paper or tagboard. Write June, July, and August on the top of the grids. Fill in the appropriate dates on these months.

2. Fill in the days you already have plans for (birthdays, vacations, when to start packing for vacation, the day summer school starts, Father's day, Juneteenth, the 4th of July).

3. Brainstorm with your family about what they want to do on the rest of the summer days. Fill in the calendar with your plans.

Materials:
- 3 sheets of construction paper or tagboard
- Ruler
- Felt-tip pen or marker
- Thumbtack

Suggestions: Make a pizza. Go to the zoo. Start a collection. Make paper dolls. Learn a code. Read a murder mystery. Camp in the backyard. Have a sleepover party. Go skating. Make a crossword puzzle. Learn to braid hair. Collect bugs and classify them. Visit your grandparents. Go to a movie. Walk to town. Read comics all day. Go fishing. Collect cans for money. Have a lemonade stand. Try some temporary tattoos. Have a carnival. Start a dog-washing service. Climb a tree. Practice skateboarding. Learn the latest dances. Try out for a drama production. Write a short story. Create a cartoon character. Go to the beach. Learn the harmonica. Have a jacks marathon. Design clothes. Make a race car. Change your hairstyle. Create a computer game. Make it to the 9th level in Super Mario 3.

4. Hang the calendar up in the kitchen or somewhere everyone will see it every day.

Variation: Use a pre-existing calendar to write your summer plans on.

Practical Tip: Use another calendar for reference when you're filling in the correct days and dates of your summer calendar.

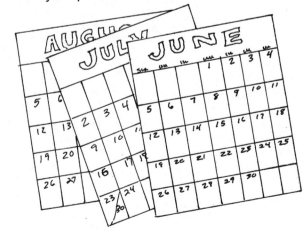

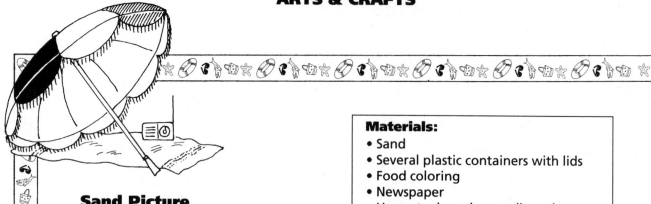

Sand Picture

Ahhh, the smooth feel of sand slipping between your toes. You don't have to be at the beach to make these beautiful sand pictures. Wherever you make them, they'll remind you of sunny days at the beach.

Time: 30 minutes (plus drying time)

Complexity: Moderate

What to Do:

1. Put sand in the plastic containers and add a few drops of food coloring—a different color for each container.

2. Cover and shake the containers or stir until the sand is completely colored.

3. Spread the colored sand out on newspaper for a few minutes and let it dry while you color more.

4. Using the pencil, draw a design on the tagboard or cardboard.

5. Spread glue on the outline of the design.

6. Cover the outline with one color of sand. Shake the excess sand back into its container.

7. Spread glue onto another area of the design, and then fill it in with another color of sand. Repeat until your entire design is complete.

8. Allow to dry (about an hour). Hang up on a wall.

Materials:
- Sand
- Several plastic containers with lids
- Food coloring
- Newspaper
- Heavy tagboard or cardboard
- Pencil
- Glue

Variation: If you're at the beach, clear a smooth area of sand. Then draw a simple design in the sand with a stick. Fill in the areas with a fine layer of colored sand, creating a tropical scene, multicolored parrot, or colorful flower.

Practical Tip: Do this activity outside or in a garage or basement where you won't mind the sand that gets left behind.

Homemade Hurricane

Hold onto your hat, it's hurricane season! Here's a fun way to learn more about this awesome windstorm.

Time: 20 minutes

Complexity: Easy

What to Do:

1. Attach the Tornado Tube to a bottle according to package directions.

2. Fill one bottle with water, food coloring, and glitter.

3. Close the bottles using the tube, then turn the bottles over so the water is on top.

4. Swirl the top bottle to create a whirlpool, and watch the hurricane appear as the water moves to the bottom bottle.

5. Add a little boat to the bottle if you want some more excitement.

Materials:

- 2 plastic soda or water bottles (2-liter size)
- Tornado Tube (available at toy or school supply stores)
- Water
- Food coloring
- Glitter
- **Optional:** miniature toy boat

Variation: Make oceans in a bottle by filling the bottle with 2/3 water and 1/3 oil, adding glitter, sequins, or sparkles, and sealing with the cap.

Practical Tip: Try to figure out what's happening and why.

Frisbee Golf Tournament

In Beaver, Oklahoma, they hold a cow-chip-throwing contest this month. If you don't have any cow chips lying around, well, you're lucky. You can have just as much fun with Frisbees as with the authentic chips.

Time: 20 minutes

Complexity: Easy

What to Do:

1. With the acrylic paints, paint designs or your names on the Frisbees. Let them dry.

2. Set up your Frisbee golf course in the yard. Use objects such as sticks, boxes, or

Materials:
- Frisbees (one for each player)
- Acrylic paints
- Paint brushes
- Large yard
- Felt-tip pens or small cards with numbers on them

tables that the Frisbees must land in or hit. Number each goal with felt-tip pens or small cards.

3. Have the players toss their Frisbees to each goal, one at a time. Keep score by counting how many "strokes" it takes to land on or around each goal.

Variations: Give each player a different-colored Frisbee instead of painting them.

Use plastic lids from ice-cream pails instead of real Frisbees.

Practical Tip: Let the players practice awhile before you start the game.

Homemade Badminton

Here's a great game for the beach or the backyard that you create yourself.

Time: 15 minutes

Complexity: Moderate

What to Do:

1. Bend the wire hanger into an oval shape, so it looks like a racquet.

2. Twist the ends of the hangar together to make a handle.

Materials:
- Wire hanger
- Nylon stocking
- Yarn or string
- Nerf ball, sponge, or ping-pong ball
- Volleyball net or long string

3. Pull the nylon stocking over the top and wrap it tightly around the handle.

4. Wrap yarn or string around the handle to make it secure and easy to hold.

5. Hit the Nerf ball, sponge, or ping-pong ball back and forth across the volleyball net or long string stretched between two trees.

Cooling Fan

Sometimes the hot summer weather can be too much. Make this fancy fan to keep your cool.

Time: 20 minutes

Complexity: Easy

What to Do:

1. Glue ribbon, lace, or string across the top side of the construction paper. Cut to fit.

2. With the felt-tip pens, crayons, or colored pencils make a colorful design on the rest of the paper.

3. Add the glitter, sequins, or puffy paints to the design.

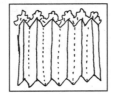

4. Fold the paper into 1/2-inch creases back and forth accordion-style.

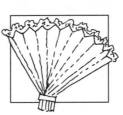

5. Tape the bottom end closed. Fan yourself when you get hot.

Materials:
- Construction paper or cardstock, 11" x 14"
- Ribbon, lace, or string
- Glue
- Scissors
- Felt-tip pens, crayons, or colored pencils
- Glitter, sequins, or puffy paints
- Tape

Variations: Use two pieces of colored paper, each a different color, to make a two-tone fan.

Make a giant fan with an extra-large piece of paper.

Fold the fan first, and then decorate every other strip one way and the alternate strips another way. Then you'll have two designs depending on how you hold the fan.

Practical Tip: The cardstock paper makes a more powerful and sturdier fan, so use it if you're really hot.

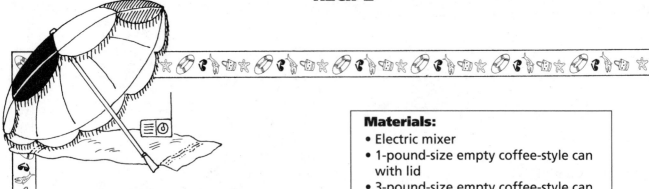

Homemade Strawberry Ice Cream

You'll need the whole family to make this frosty treat. But the results are simply delicious!

Yields: 2-1/2 cups

Time: 30–45 minutes

Complexity: Moderate

Ingredients:
- 1 cup heavy cream
- 1 cup milk
- 1 egg, beaten
- 1/2 cup sugar
- 1 teaspoon vanilla
- 1/3 cup strawberries, diced
- 20 cups crushed ice
- 1-1/2 cups rock salt

Materials:
- Electric mixer
- 1-pound-size empty coffee-style can with lid
- 3-pound-size empty coffee-style can with lid
- Table knife
- Large spoon
- Bowls
- Spoons

What to Do:
1. With the electric mixer, mix the cream, milk, egg, sugar, vanilla, and strawberries together in the small can.
2. Cover the small can and set it inside the larger can.
3. Layer about 10 cups of the crushed ice alternately with about 3/4 cups of the rock salt in the space between the cans.
4. Cover the large can and roll it back and forth between two family members for about 10 minutes.
5. Open the outer can and empty the remaining ice and water.
6. Lift out the small can, wipe the lid dry, and remove the lid.
7. Using the knife, scrape the ice cream from the sides of the can and stir well.
8. Cover the can and place it inside the large can again.
9. Repack the large can with another 10 cups of crushed ice and 3/4 cup salt.
10. Cover and roll for 5 more minutes.
11. Serve in bowls.

Variation: Substitute other fruits for the strawberries.

Practical Tip: Mix the ingredients in a bowl first if desired, and then pour into the small can.

July

CANADA DAY
July 1

While people in the United States celebrate Independence Day on the 4th of July, Canadians celebrate on July 1 in remembrance of the 1867 confederation of their country. Although loyal to Great Britain, regions of Canada wanted to unite to form their own government. On July 1, 1867, the British government approved their plan and the Dominion of Canada became an independent country.

Canada Day is celebrated much like the 4th of July in the U.S., with parades, picnics, and fireworks. Since the Independence Days of Canada and the U.S. are so close together, a week-long International Freedom Festival is held each year in bordering Windsor, Ontario, and Detroit, Michigan. The Detroit River separates the two cities and the river is central to the festivities, which include fireworks, water parades, sky diving, concerts, and art exhibits.

Crayon Melt

Here's a creative way to use all those worn-down crayons in the bottom of the crayon bucket. Melt the crayons into a Maple Leaf design in honor of Canada Day.

Time: 2-1/2 hours (including melting time)

Complexity: Easy

What to Do:

1. Lay the newspaper over the work area and place a sheet of construction paper in the center.

2. Sharpen the crayons, collecting the shavings in bowls by color.

3. Arrange the shavings on the construction paper in a Canadian leaf design, flag, or other shape.

Materials:
- Newspaper
- Construction paper
- Pencil or crayon sharpener
- Crayons
- Bowls

4. Carefully carry the picture outdoors on a hot, still day and leave it to melt for a few hours in the sun.

Variation: Melt under a low-heat iron using paper towels on top to absorb the wax and protect the iron.

Practical Tip: Don't make the design too detailed because the colors may run into each other as they melt.

Paper Firecrackers

Fireworks displays are central to both Canada Day and 4th of July celebrations. Real firecrackers are dangerous to play with—these paper firecrackers are a fun alternative. They can really make a bang!

Time: 5 minutes

Complexity: Easy

What to Do:

1. Cut a piece of paper into a square of about 7 or 8 inches.

2. Fold the square in half so the bottom edge of the sheet comes within 1/2 inch of the top edge.

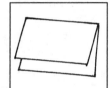

Materials:
- Paper
- Scissors

3. Fold the square in half again from side to side so the flap is on the inside. Crease the fold well.

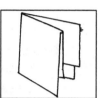

4. Hold the paper firecracker tightly between your thumb and index finger at the open corner where the paper is only two thicknesses thick.

5. Quickly flick your arm and wrist downward. The inside flap of the paper will pop out and make a loud snap.

Fishing Hole

Canada is famous for its great fishing. If you can't trek to the north woods, try fishing at home with this activity.

Time: 30 minutes

Complexity: Easy

What to Do:

1. Make a fishing pond by rounding the corners of one sheet of the posterboard.

2. Cut out fish, alligators, turtles, and frogs from the construction paper. Use the felt-tip pens to add details. Attach a paper clip to the mouth area of each animal. This will be your "hook."

Materials:
- Several sheets of posterboard (blue or green)
- Construction paper
- Scissors
- Felt-tip pens
- Paper clips
- Dowels or rulers
- Yarn or string
- Magnet tape

3. Tie a piece of yarn or string about 2 feet long to the dowel or ruler. Attach a small piece of magnet tape to the end of the string and start fishing.

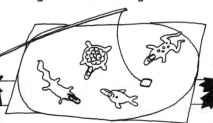

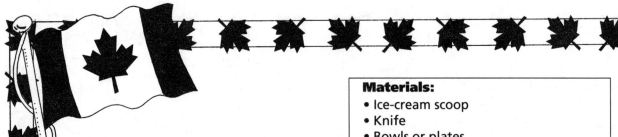

Ice-Cream Pie with Leaf Design

I scream, you scream, we all scream for ice cream. Keep cool on Canada Day with this yummy ice-cream pie. Make it with Maple Nut and Rocky Road ice cream or your two favorite flavors.

Serves: 8–10

Time: 30 minutes

Complexity: Easy

Ingredients:
- 2 flavors of ice cream (1 quart of each)
- Chocolate cookie pie crust
- Chocolate sauce
- Whipped cream

What to Do:

1. Soften one carton of ice cream on the counter or in a microwave.
2. Spread a thin layer of the chocolate sauce on the crust.
3. Spread the softened ice cream on the crust, filling the pan a little over half full. Smooth the ice cream with the knife and place the pie in the freezer for about an hour.
4. Soften the other carton of ice cream.
5. Spread a layer of the chocolate sauce over the first layer of ice cream.

Materials:
- Ice-cream scoop
- Knife
- Bowls or plates
- Spoons
- **Optional:** tiny Canadian flag, microwave

6. Add a second layer of ice cream to the pie, creating a mound. Freeze for another hour.

7. Drizzle more chocolate sauce over the pie. Return to the freezer until ready to serve.

8. When ready to serve, create a leaf design with the whipped cream on the top of the pie.

9. If desired, stick in a small Canadian flag.
10. Cut the pie into slices and serve in bowls or on plates.

Variation: Make your own pie crust: mix crushed chocolate wafers or cookies with a little melted butter and press into a pie pan.

Practical Tip: Be sure to refreeze between ice-cream fillings for easier handling.

Maple Nut Bars

These yummy maple nut bars are a tasty way to celebrate the independence of the Maple Leaf nation.

Yields: 12–16 bars

Time: 1-1/2 hours

Complexity: Moderate—Adult assistance recommended

Bar Ingredients:
- 2 cups flour
- 1/2 teaspoon baking soda
- 1/2 cup brown sugar, packed
- 1/2 cup margarine, softened
- 1 cup pure maple syrup
- 1 egg
- 2 teaspoons vanilla
- 1 cup walnuts
- Vegetable-oil spray (such as Pam)

Frosting Ingredients:
- 1/2 cup margarine, softened
- 2 ounces cream cheese, softened
- 1 tablespoon brown sugar, packed
- 3 tablespoons pure maple syrup
- 1/4 cup + 2 tablespoons powdered sugar

What to Do:

1. First make the bars. In a medium bowl, combine the flour and baking soda. Mix well and set aside.

2. In the large bowl, use the electric mixer to combine the brown sugar and the margarine. Add the maple syrup, egg, and vanilla. Beat until smooth.

Materials:
- 2 medium bowls
- Large spoon
- Large bowl
- Electric mixer
- Oven, preheated to 325°
- Baking pan, 8" x 8"
- Toothpick
- Cooling rack
- Frosting knife

3. Combine the flour mixture and the walnuts with the sugar mixture. Do not overmix.

4. Spray the baking pan with vegetable-oil spray, and then pour in batter.

5. Bake for 40 to 45 minutes or until a toothpick inserted in the center comes out clean. Allow to cool for 15 minutes, and then turn it upside down on the cooling rack and allow to cool completely.

6. Make the maple frosting. In a medium bowl, combine the margarine and cream cheese, using the electric mixer. Add the brown sugar and maple syrup and beat until smooth.

7. Slowly add the powdered sugar and mix until smooth. Add more powdered sugar if the frosting seems thin.

8. Spread frosting on the bars.

Variation: Sprinkle nuts on top on the frosted bars, too.

FOURTH OF JULY
July 4

Oooh, aah! The 4th of July means brilliant fireworks and jubilant parades in America today. But we also try to remember what we're celebrating—the anniversary of the signing of the Declaration of Independence in 1776, when the Continental Congress declared the United States of America independent from Great Britain.

In the preamble to the Declaration of Independence, Thomas Jefferson wrote that "all men are created equal" and that they have a right to "life, liberty, and the pursuit of happiness." The declaration also contains a section listing twenty-eight grievances against King George III of Great Britain, and a section that terminated the allegiance of the colonies to the British Crown.

Berry Sparkler Sundaes

This blueberry-and-strawberry sundae is always delicious, especially on hot July days. It's also very fitting for the 4th of July because it's red, white, and blue.

Time: 15 minutes

Complexity: Easy—Adult assistance recommended

> **Ingredients:**
> • Vanilla frozen yogurt or ice cream
> • Blueberries
> • Strawberries
> • Lemon extract
> • Colored sugar cubes

What to Do:

1. Scoop the frozen yogurt or ice cream into bowls and top with the blueberries and strawberries.

> **Materials:**
> • Ice-cream scoop
> • Bowls
> • Spoons
> • Match or lighter

2. Soak the colored sugar cubes in the lemon extract. Place a cube on top of each sundae, and light it.

3. Serve immediately.

Variation: Top your sundaes with sparkly pipe cleaners for artificial flames.

Practical Tip: Watch young children around flames.

Homemade Map

The 4th of July presents the perfect time to learn more about our country. You can explore different areas of the country without leaving home by making a homemade map of the whole country, a state, or individual communities.

Time: 1 hour or more

Complexity: Moderate

What to Do:

1. If you're using the plywood option, paint the wood with green paint.

2. Design a map on paper using an existing map as a reference. Using your design as a model, transfer the map to the plywood or tagboard.

3. Include geographical features such as rivers, lakes, and mountains; favorite points of interest such as amusement or national parks; and homes of friends and relatives.

4. Paint a street that goes across the map and past favorite points of interest along the way. Fill in the details with paint or make structures out of construction paper and glue them on.

5. Paint the board with shellac to protect it.

Materials:

- Large piece of plywood or green tagboard
- Paint
- Paint brushes
- Map
- Paper
- Pencil
- Construction paper
- Scissors
- Glue
- Shellac

Variation: Make a map from fabric. Make the "country" out of green fabric, appliqué on the points of interest, and add details with permanent felt-tip pens.

Practical Tip: If you want to make a really large map, buy plywood in small sections for easy storage, and then assemble them at home.

PATRIOTIC COSTUMES

Planning on attending a local 4th of July parade? Join in the fun instead of watching from the sidelines. Here are two costumes to wear as you march down the street and celebrate the Red, White, and Blue.

Giant Firecracker

Materials:
- 2 sheets of heavy red tagboard
- Stapler
- Scissors
- Sparkly pipe cleaner
- Headband
- Red shorts

What to Do:

1. Staple the ends of the red tagboard together to form a tube.

2. Cut out two eyeholes.

3. Bend the sparkly pipe cleaner around the top of the headband to look like a fuse. Put the headband on.

4. Put on red shorts.

5. Slip on the tube. Keep your hands down at your sides and hold the tube up with your fingers. March down the street.

Paul Revere

Materials:
- Piece of cloth
- Marker
- Red, white, and blue clothing
- Paul Revere style hat (from costume or thrift store)
- Hobby horse or homemade one out of brown construction paper

What to Do:

1. With the marker make a sign on the cloth that reads "The British Are Coming," or make it funny and write "The British Aren't Coming Anymore!" or "The Parade Is Coming!"

2. Dress in red, white, and blue clothes.

3. Hop on the hobby horse and ride through town warning the villagers.

Variation: Come as another famous character from history, such as George Washington with an ax and a handful of cherries or Thomas Jefferson writing the Declaration of Independence.

Homemade Water Slide

The 4th of July usually means hot weather. Cool off on a homemade water slide.

Time: 15 minutes (to set up)

Complexity: Easy

What to Do:

1. Lay the plastic piece out on a clear area of the lawn. Don't put it too close to trees, shrubs, birdbaths, or anything else that you might run into accidentally.
2. Secure the corners of the plastic in the ground with tent hooks or heavy (but not sharp) objects.
3. Turn the hose nozzle on the "spray" setting and set it at the edge of the plastic, with the water running down lengthwise.
4. Run, slip, and slide, making up contests as to who can go the fastest or farthest, who can do the most spins, and so on.

Materials:
- Plastic sheet, tablecloth, shower curtain, or large garbage bag
- Tent hooks or heavy (but not sharp) objects
- Hose with spray nozzle

Variations: Gather all the neighborhood kids together and stage a water war. Use squirt guns, water balloons, or lunch baggies filled with water and tied off (add a few drops of food coloring for a special effect). Or fill a bucket with sponges and water and toss them at each other. Or hurl plastic buckets full of water at each other and use umbrellas or cookie sheets as shields.

Practical Tip: Move the water slide to a new place after half an hour to avoid damaging the lawn.

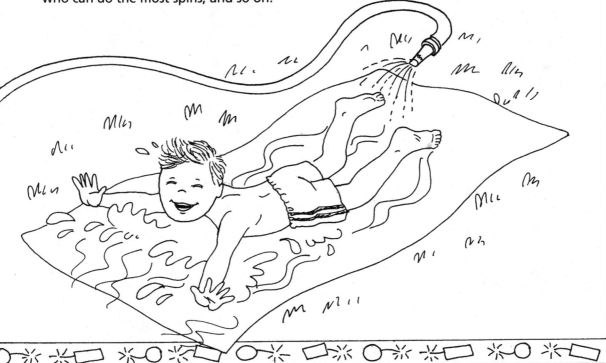

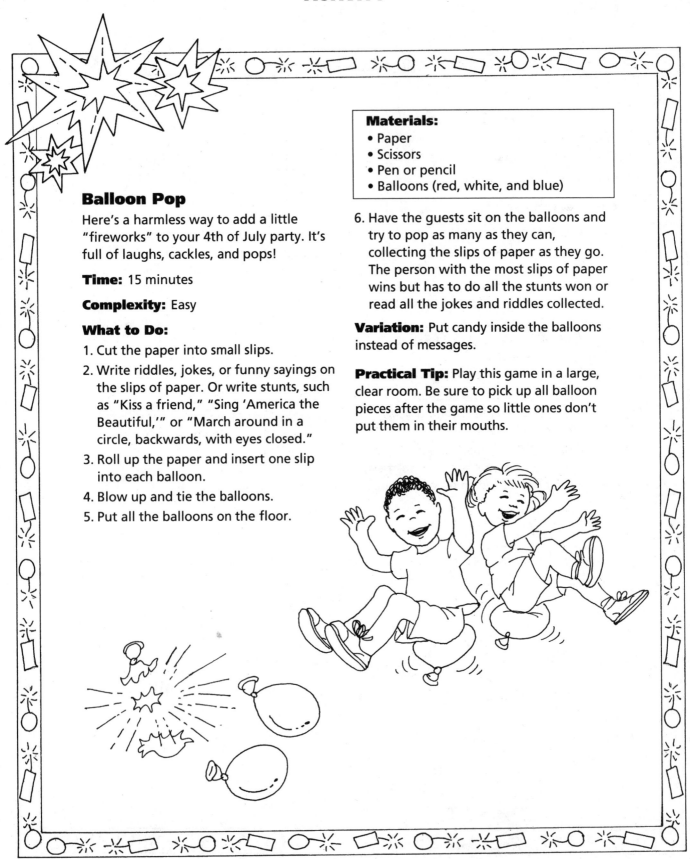

Balloon Pop

Here's a harmless way to add a little "fireworks" to your 4th of July party. It's full of laughs, cackles, and pops!

Time: 15 minutes

Complexity: Easy

What to Do:

1. Cut the paper into small slips.
2. Write riddles, jokes, or funny sayings on the slips of paper. Or write stunts, such as "Kiss a friend," "Sing 'America the Beautiful,'" or "March around in a circle, backwards, with eyes closed."
3. Roll up the paper and insert one slip into each balloon.
4. Blow up and tie the balloons.
5. Put all the balloons on the floor.

Materials:
• Paper
• Scissors
• Pen or pencil
• Balloons (red, white, and blue)

6. Have the guests sit on the balloons and try to pop as many as they can, collecting the slips of paper as they go. The person with the most slips of paper wins but has to do all the stunts won or read all the jokes and riddles collected.

Variation: Put candy inside the balloons instead of messages.

Practical Tip: Play this game in a large, clear room. Be sure to pick up all balloon pieces after the game so little ones don't put them in their mouths.

Angel-Food Flag Cake

It's time to show the flag! This angel-food cake makes an impressive centerpiece and serves a lot of hungry people!

Serves: 8–12

Time: 30 minutes

Complexity: Easy—Adult assistance recommended

Ingredients:
- Rectangular angel-food cake
- Whipped cream or Cool Whip
- Strawberries
- Blueberries

What to Do:

1. Bake the angel-food cake according to package directions or buy a cake from a bakery.
2. Slice the cake and place the pieces into the rectangular glass pan. 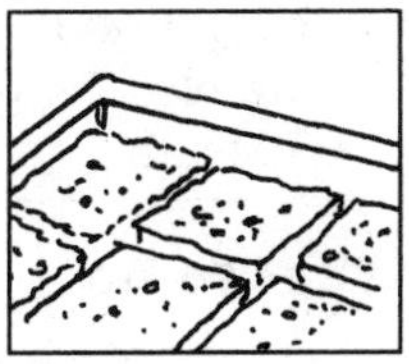
3. Cover the cake with whipped cream or Cool Whip. 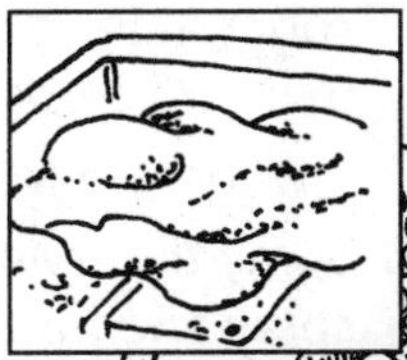
4. Slice the strawberries.

Materials:
- Knife
- Rectangular glass pan
- Spoon
- Small plates
- Forks

5. Decorate the cake with the strawberries and blueberries in a flag design.

6. Refrigerate until serving time.

Variation: Use a regular cake instead of angel food. Add other fruits to the top of the cake.

Practical Tip: Don't refrigerate the cake longer than an hour or the whipped cream will get hard.

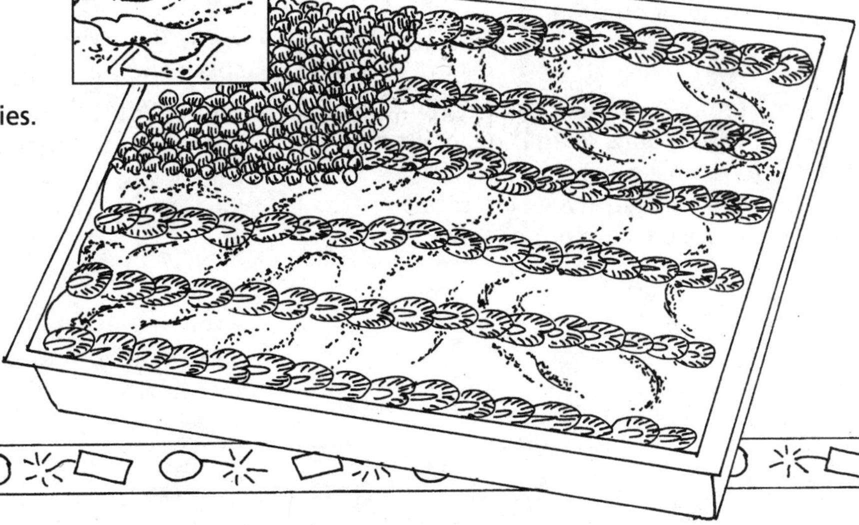

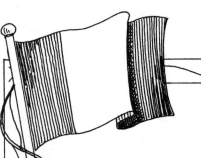

BASTILLE DAY
July 14

On this day in 1789, citizens of Paris captured and nearly destroyed the Bastille, a state prison. Although it actually held few prisoners, the Bastille was a symbol of the cruel French monarchy. Under the king, the rich paid no taxes on their land and lived luxuriously while the poor endured heavy taxes and starvation. Anyone who spoke out against the injustice was thrown into prison. The fall of the Bastille prison thus marked the beginning of the French Revolution that overthrew the monarchy and sought a democratic government.

People worldwide celebrate Bastille Day to remember democratic ideals. Grand parades, block parties, dances, and music are part of this joyous celebration. As in the U.S., fireworks are enjoyed at dusk.

French Crepes

Celebrate Bastille Day with French crepes. These thin pancakes are filled with fruit and topped with whipped cream or syrup.

Serves: 4

Time: 1 hour

Complexity: Moderate—Adult assistance recommended

Ingredients:
- 1-1/2 cups flour
- 1 tablespoon sugar
- 2 cups milk
- 2 eggs
- 1 teaspoon vanilla
- 2 tablespoons margarine, melted
- Vegetable-oil spray
- 1 cup fresh strawberries, sliced
- Whipped cream or berry syrup

Materials:
- Large bowl
- Electric mixer
- Large spoon
- Frying pan
- Stove
- Spatula

What to Do:
1. In the large bowl, combine the flour, sugar, milk, eggs, vanilla, and margarine. Beat until smooth.
2. Refrigerate for 30 minutes.
3. Spray the frying pan with vegetable-oil spray and heat over medium.
4. Pour in enough batter to cover the bottom of the pan. Batter should be thin. Cook until lightly browned, turn, and cook until other side is lightly browned.
5. Remove to a plate. Fill with sliced strawberries and fold over both sides. Serve with whipped cream or berry syrup.

Homemade Candles

The French use a lot of candles in their festivities. These candles symbolize the burning of the Bastille.

Time: 30–45 minutes

Complexity: Moderate—Adult assistance recommended

What to Do:

1. In the double boiler, slowly and carefully melt the candles or paraffin with dye or coloring.
2. Fill the milk carton 1/2 full with small ice cubes.
3. Set a long wick in the center.
4. Pour the wax over the ice.
5. Add more ice cubes to fill the carton, and then add the rest of the wax.
6. When the wax has cooled (about 15 minutes), pour off the water.
7. When the wax is completely firm, tear off the carton and you'll find what's left of the Bastille! It's a candle!

Materials:
- Candles or paraffin
- Candle dye or food coloring
- Double boiler
- Stove
- Milk carton
- Small ice cubes
- Long wicks

Variation: Use old broken crayons to add color.

Practical Tip: Use extreme caution around hot wax.

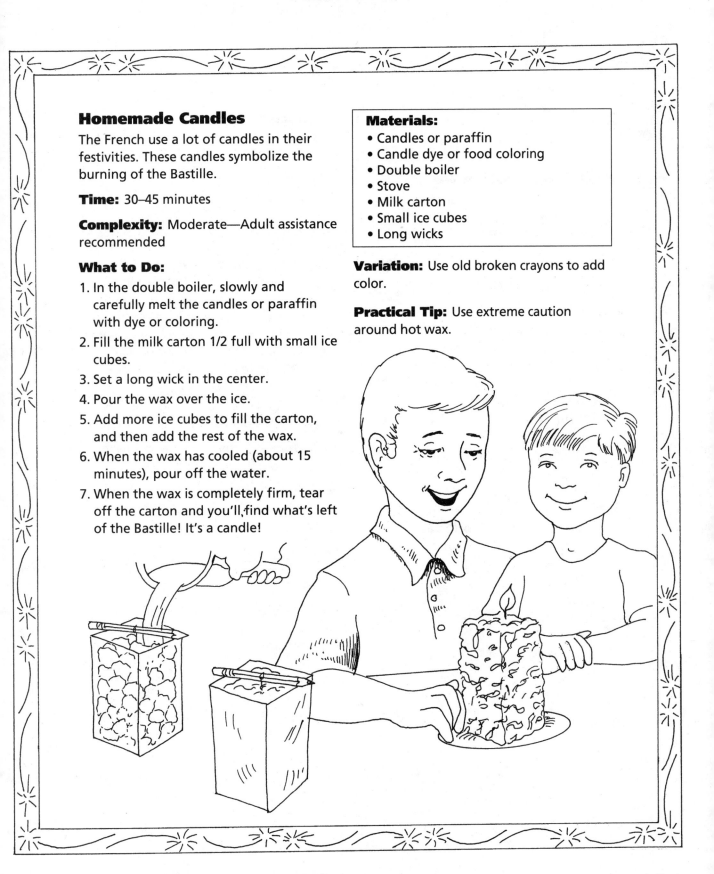

French Revolution Game

Here's a game for the whole family. It's a lot like the game Battleship, but you're looking for French flags.

Time: 30 minutes

Complexity: Moderate

What to Do:

1. Using a permanent felt-tip pen, make a grid eleven spaces across and eleven down on the top of the four box pieces. Use the ruler to make the lines straight.

2. Number from one to ten across the top, allowing an empty space in the upper left-hand corner.

3. Skipping the first square again, write the letters R-E-V-O-L-U-T-I-O-N down the left-hand column.

4. Cover the grids with clear Contact paper, then set the box top and bottom at right angles so your opponent can't see inside.

5. Decide who wants to be the revolutionist and who wants to be the monarch. Then, mark five French flags on your upper grid with a water-based felt-tip pen (not permanent) without your opponent seeing.

Materials:
- 2 dress-size boxes, about 11 inches or more in length and width
- Permanent felt-tip pens
- Ruler
- Clear Contact paper
- Water-based felt-tip pens
- Damp cloth

6. Take turns trying to guess where the other player's flags are hidden by calling off points on the gird such as R–8, I–5, and so forth. If your guess is correct, your opponent must tell you. If you're wrong, your turn is over. Whoever first guesses where all five of their opponent's flags are wins the game.

7. When the game is over, wipe the grid clean with a damp cloth and start again.

Variation: Hide only one flag to make the game extra challenging.

Practical Tip: Be sure to mark down what numbers you have called at the bottom grid so you won't repeat yourself.

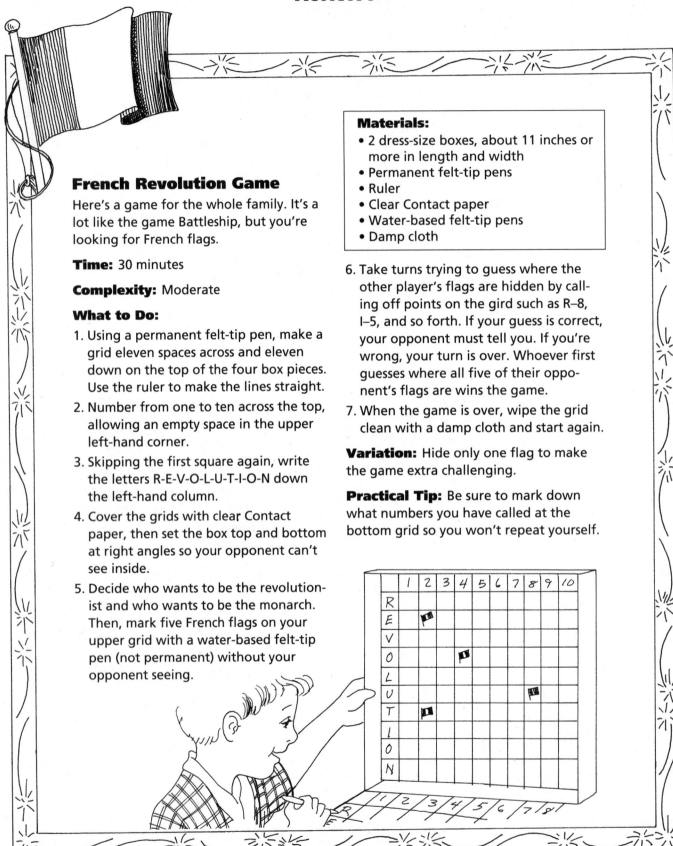

August

SUMMER VACATION DAYS

Technically August doesn't have any holidays in it, but when you think about it, the whole month is like one long holiday! August is vacation month, that special time of year when parents cram their kids into the back seat of their compacts and head for Vacation City, using the narrowest, windiest scenic routes they can find. After an hour's chorus of "Are We There Yet?" to the tune of "99 Bottles of Beer on the Wall," everyone's a little batty.

August is also a month of togetherness for many families, when everyone breaks away from hectic schedules to play with each other. It's a great time to explore new lands or just to hang out together in your own community.

_____

Learning Sign Language

Learn a new language while you're traveling—sign language. Practice the American Sign Language alphabet until you know it by heart. Then spell your name, your friends' names, street signs, and short sentences. If you learn it with somebody else, you'll be able to talk to each other without making a sound—and nobody can eavesdrop.

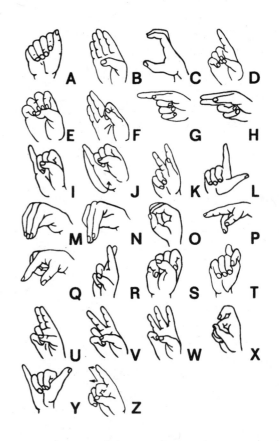

Travel Box

Don't forget to pack a travel box as you load up the car for vacation. Fill it with things to keep busy with during those long car, plane, or train trips.

Time: 30 minutes

Complexity: Easy

What to Do:

1. Glue old postcards or travel pictures to the tin container or box.
2. Cover the box with clear Contact paper.
3. Tape the cereal box inside the decorated box to hold books, pads of paper, and postcards.
4. Tape the orange-juice can upright in one corner of the decorated box to hold pens, pencils, and crayons.
5. Tape the envelope inside the decorated box to hold stickers, paper dolls, and other small items.
6. Fill the box with travel items mentioned under materials.

Variations: Instead of a box, fill a backpack or carry-bag with lots of travel items.

Prepare a travel box as a gift for a friend or relative going on a trip. Wrap each item up in gift wrap and include a note to open one new item every day or hour of the trip.

Practical Tip: Don't forget to include old favorites, such as a blanket, teddy bear, or pillow.

Materials:

- Tin container, cigar box, old lunch box, cardboard box, or other carrying case
- Postcards and/or pictures from travel magazines
- Glue
- Scissors
- Clear Contact paper
- Cereal box
- Orange-juice can
- Legal-size envelope
- Wide packing tape
- Stuff to put inside, such as sticker books, coloring books, dot-to-dot books, activity books, comic books, paperback books, song books, crayons, markers, white glue, small scissors, pads of paper, hand-held video games, small radio or cassette player with headset, blank and recorded tapes of songs or stories, small toys or dolls, action figures, puppets, small travel games, slinky, playdough, silly putty, Etch-a-Sketch, magic slates, View Master, the beginning of a postcard collection, address books, stationery, grooming items, nonperishable snacks, juice boxes, flashlight, or Band-Aids

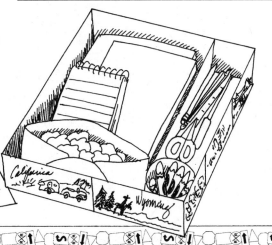

Traveling Checkerboard

"Are we almost there?" This checkerboard with magnetic pieces is a great way to keep riders occupied on car and plane trips.

Time: 30 minutes

Complexity: Easy

What to Do:

1. Using the black marker and the ruler, draw a grid on the cookie sheet with sixty-four squares, eight across and eight down.

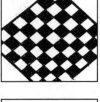

2. Color the squares alternately with the red and black markers so your cookie sheet looks like a checkerboard.

3. Cut the magnet tape into small pieces and stick them to the bottom of the checker pieces.

4. Have a checker tournament on your new board in the car—the pieces won't slip off when you go over a bump.

Materials:
- Cookie sheet
- Permanent markers (red and black)
- Ruler
- Magnet tape
- Scissors
- 24 checker pieces

Variations: Make your own checker pieces out of baker's clay. (See recipe on page 21.)

Play chess instead of checkers on your new travel board by sticking magnet tape to the bottom of chess pieces.

Practical Tip: Keep the pieces in a large baggy when you're not playing so you won't lose any.

Alphabet Highway

A, B, C, D . . . Finding letters in alphabetical order on signs and license plates is a favorite car game that can be played on any road with signs.

Number of Players: 2 or more

Time: Open

Complexity: Easy

What to Do:

1. Watch for signs or license plates along the road and pick out words that contain letters you need. Start with "A" and continue picking out words with the other letters in order. Two players cannot pick the same letter from the same sign.

Materials:
• A road with plenty of signs

2. Play until someone gets through the entire alphabet or you reach your destination.

Variations: Call out words that begin with the letter of the alphabet you are on. Or instead of words, locate objects that begin with the letters of the alphabet, in order. For example, if you see a car, call out "A—automobile, C—Car, or F—Ford."

Limit players on the left side of the car to signs on the left side of the road; players on the right side of the car to signs on the right side of the road.

Practical Tip: Give younger players a few seconds head start or assistance from adults.

Name That Tune

Who's up on the Top 40? Find out by playing this guessing game with a radio.

Number of Players: 3 or more

Time: Open

Complexity: Moderate

What to Do:

1. Turn the radio dial slowly across your portable radio and stop each time you get to a tune.

2. Whoever correctly names the tune first gets a point. Another point is awarded if the player can also name the artist.

Materials:
• Portable radio
• Pen or pencil
• Paper

3. Keep score on paper. Play until someone gets ten points or you reach your destination.

Variation: Sing or hum a song and have the others guess the title.

Practical Tip: If a song goes on too long and no one can name it, move on.

Materials:
• Pen or pencil
• Paper

The DJ Game

Try guessing song titles based on one-word clues. You'll be surprised at how many song titles you remember.

Number of Players: 2 or more

Time: Open

Complexity: Easy

What to Do:

1. Have one player think of a popular song and say only one word from the song, such as "Happy" from "Happy Birthday to You."

2. The next player tries to guess the song. If the player guesses a song that contains the right word, but is not the song the first player was thinking of, the player who guessed gets one point. The player who guessed then takes a turn at choosing a song.

3. The player gets two points for a correct guess. Then the player who chose the first song has to choose another one

(this gives the guesser more chances to get more points).

4. If the player who is guessing cannot name a song using the key word, the player who thought of the song gets two points and must announce what the song was. The turn goes to the guesser.

5. Keep score on paper. Play until someone gets ten points or you reach your destination.

Variation: Describe a song instead of giving a word clue, such as "a song about water." Play the same as above.

Practical Tip: Designate someone to keep score.

Name Chain

Good spellers are needed for this fast-moving game. See how long you can keep the chain going.

Number of Players: 2 or more

Time: Open

Complexity: Moderate

What to Do:

1. One player says a first name.
2. The next player says another first name, but it must begin with the last letter of the previous name. For example, the first player says JohN, the

Materials:
• A quick mind

second player says NicK, the third player says KathY, the fourth player says YvonnE, and so forth.

3. If you stump your opponent, your opponent gets an "N." The first one to spell "Names" is out of the game.

Variation: Use cities, foods, animals, and lots of other categories.

Practical Tip: Don't say names that end in the letters x, q, or z.

Nick, Kate, Ellen, Neil,

What's His Name?

Here's a variation on the old "20 Questions" game.

Number of Players: 3 or more

Time: Open

Complexity: Easy

What to Do:

1. One player thinks of a person, real or fictional, but famous or at least known to the group. (Include cartoon characters.)
2. The other players take turns asking "yes" or "no" questions.
3. Limit the guesses to twenty or keep going until someone guesses or all give up. If someone guesses correctly, move on to the next player.

Materials:
• **Optional:** pens or pencils
• **Optional:** paper

Practical Tips: Here are some good questions to begin with: "Is it a male/female? Is it a child/adult? Is it real/fictional? Is it famous/friend? Is it animal/human? Is it cartoon/story character? Is it in show business/politics?"

Some good characters to try are Bugs Bunny, Santa Claus, Grumpy, Cookie Monster, Yourself.

Write down the answers to the questions so you won't repeat questions and to help figure out who it is.

Materials:
- Flashlights (2 per team)
- Paper
- Pens or pencils
- Cards or paper with Morse code on it (one per player)

Flashlight Messages

Everyone gets a thrill out of sending and receiving secret messages. When night falls, use flashlights and the Morse code to play this secret-message game.

Time: 30 minutes

Complexity: Challenging

What to Do:

1. Split the players up into partners or teams of four or six players each.

2. Split the partners or teams across the yard, making as large a space between them as possible. Half of each team will be sending the message while the other half receives it.

3. Give half of each team a simple message to send to their partners. Use messages like "Time for dessert," "Go into the house," "Sing a song."

4. Teams send the message by using long and short flashes of light for the dashes and dots of the Morse code. Use a waving light to signal "Ready for message" and "Please start over." Also, be sure to have senders pause between each letter and pause longer between words.

5. Give a prize to the first team to send and receive the message correctly.

6. Play again but have different players send and receive another message.

Variation: Instead of giving light signals, give sound signals by using a whistle or harmonica. You'll need a different sound maker for each team.

Practical Tips: Keep the messages simple.

Teams need to pay attention to their own partner and decode the message quietly so they don't help other teams figure it out.

Teams can invent their own way to signal word breaks.

International Morse Code

A	•—	**N**	—•
B	—•••	**O**	———
C	—•—•	**P**	•——•
D	—••	**Q**	——•—
E	•	**R**	•—•
F	••—•	**S**	•••
G	——•	**T**	—
H	••••	**U**	••—
I	••	**V**	•••—
J	•———	**W**	•——
K	—•—	**X**	—••—
L	•—••	**Y**	—•——
M	——	**Z**	——••

Gorp

This high-energy food is a must for any camper. Give everyone a baggy full and head out for a long hike.

Time: 5 minutes

Complexity: Easy

Ingredients:
- Nuts, such as peanuts, cashews, almonds, walnuts, hazelnuts, sunflower seeds, and dried coconut
- Dried fruit, such as raisins, apricots, dates, apples, candied pineapple, and banana chips
- M & Ms and/or Reeses Pieces
- Yogurt-covered raisins and/or peanuts

Materials:
- Large bowl or bag
- Large spoon
- Zip-lock baggies

What to Do:
1. In a large bowl or bag mix equal amounts of the nuts, fruit, and candy.
2. Fill a baggy full of the mixture for each camper.

Variation: Make an all-fruit or all-nut mix.

Practical Tip: Gorp makes you thirsty, so bring a thermos of water along on your hike.

S'mores

Gather around the campfire and make S'mores. Sandwiches never tasted so good as these made with graham crackers, chocolate, and gooey marshmallows.

Serves: 6

Time: 15 minutes

Complexity: Easy—Adult assistance recommended

Ingredients:
- 12 marshmallows
- 3 chocolate bars
- 6 large graham crackers

What to Do:
1. Break the graham crackers and chocolate bars in half.
2. Place the chocolate halves on six graham cracker halves.

Materials:
- Long barbecue fork or roasting stick
- Napkins

3. Roast the marshmallows over the fire, and then stick two marshmallows on each chocolate-covered graham cracker. Use the plain graham cracker halves to top the sandwiches.
4. Press closed, let the heat of the marshmallow melt the chocolate bar, and eat.

Variation: Use mint-flavored or dark-chocolate bars.

Practical Tip: Don't burn the marshmallows. Golden-brown marshmallows make the best-tasting S'mores.

OVERNIGHT CAMPOUT

August is the perfect time to have a campout—the weather's warm, the stars are out, and all you need are some campers and a few pieces of camping equipment to make it happen. Kids will love this outing even if it's only in your backyard.

Invitations

Write the party details with a permanent felt-tip pen on tiny flashlights or packages of dried camp food. Or cut out tiny construction-paper tents that open up and write the party details inside the tents. Send or hand deliver the campy invitations to guests.

Decorations

Use tents, sleeping bags, or whatever you plan to use in your campout as decorations. Place the camping gear on a nearby picnic table. Set out flashlights, comics, snacks, and so on. If your campout is at home, make the area look like a mountain camp by drawing a mural of a mountain to tack on the fence.

Activity

Have a nighttime scavenger hunt in the backyard. Split the guests up into two teams and give each team a list of items to find. Set a time limit to collect everything. Tell them not to take anything that is not on their list, because it might be on the other team's list. Include such things as "a bug, a leaf, some litter, a toy, a piece of garden hose, a gardening tool, and some camping equipment." Whoever collects the most things on their list wins.

After the traditional ghost stories, tell funny stories and jokes before going to sleep.

Food

Serve traditional campout food, such as hot dogs, baked beans, and S'mores for dessert.

Favors

Send your guests home with small flashlights, comic books, freeze-dried camp food, compasses, or other camping equipment.

Variation: Have a family campout in your backyard. Look at the stars and share camping memories.

Practical Tip: If it rains, move the party indoors and hang up a paper moon and stars.

September

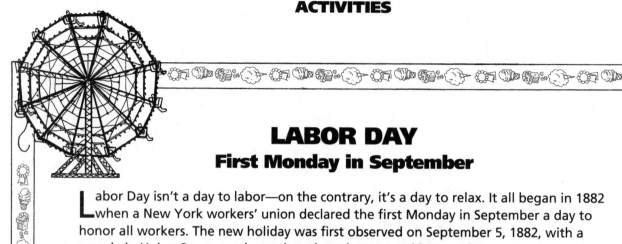

LABOR DAY
First Monday in September

Labor Day isn't a day to labor—on the contrary, it's a day to relax. It all began in 1882 when a New York workers' union declared the first Monday in September a day to honor all workers. The new holiday was first observed on September 5, 1882, with a parade in Union Square and speeches about better working conditions, shorter work days, and higher wages. A few years later, in 1894, Labor Day became a national holiday. (Many other countries honor workers on May 1, the traditional May Day.)

Today this holiday marks the end of summer vacations, the reopening of schools, and the beginning of fall activities. State fairs, picnics, and visits to friends are common outings for many families on this day of relaxation.

Family Excursions

Labor Day weekend is your last chance to check off the remaining items on your summer activity list. So pack up the family and take an overnight vacation or a one-day trip to a local fun spot. Here's a list of suggestions.

- Visit the zoo and imitate the animals.
- Go to the park and have a scavenger hunt.
- Pack your lunch in backpacks and take a bike trip.
- Go to an ice-skating rink and cool off.
- Take in a matinee movie and bring your own favorite candy.
- Visit a farm and learn what it's like to be a farmer.
- Go to a planetarium and watch the stars in broad daylight.
- Have a bring-something-to-share picnic with other families and sample new foods.
- Visit a rest home and bring along a fun activity or game to play with the residents.
- Go out to lunch at a foreign restaurant and taste new foods.
- Go to a sports event, wear the team colors, eat vendor's food, and root for the home team.
- Go to a local park and get a game of Frisbee going.
- Get up early, watch the sunrise, and have a breakfast picnic.
- Go to a lake and float boats, fish, or swim.
- Learn a new sport such as horseback riding, golf, or badminton.
- Take a short train ride to a nearby town—and back again.

Lemonade Stand

Fresh, squeezed lemonade is a real thirst-quencher. Setting up and running a lemonade stand is a great way to make a little spending money during hot weather.

Time: 20 minutes

Complexity: Easy–Moderate

Ingredients:
- 6 lemons
- 6 cups cold water
- 6–12 teaspoons sugar
- Ice cubes

What to Do:

1. Cut the lemons in half.
2. Squeeze the lemons over the juicer or by hand into the pitcher.
3. Add water and sugar according to taste and stir until well blended.
4. Add ice to keep it cold.
5. Set up a table, make colorful signs, and serve lemonade over ice cubes in cups to thirsty customers. Charge ten cents a glass and five cents for refills.

Variations: Make pink lemonade by adding three to four strawberries to the lemon juice and whirling it in a blender until smooth.

Materials:
- Knife
- Large pitcher
- Large spoon
- Plastic or paper cups
- Table
- Large sheet of paper or tagboard
- Markers
- **Optional:** juicer

Set up other weekend businesses, such as selling arts & crafts made during the summer; tutoring a younger child in needed back-to-school subjects; performing chores for neighbors, such as mowing lawns, weeding gardens, or washing windows; collecting recyclable items that can be turned in for cash; or washing cars or bikes.

Practical Tips: If it's a really hot day, freeze the lemonade before opening for business and serve icy slushes to overheated customers.

Make the lemonade with clean hands and utensils and keep it cool in a cooler with plenty of ice.

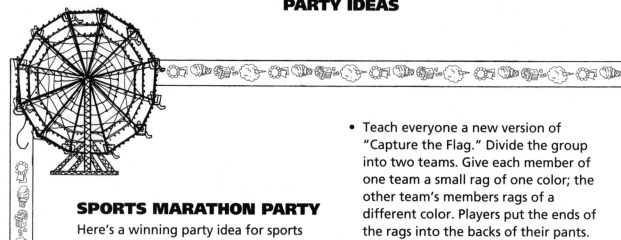

SPORTS MARATHON PARTY

Here's a winning party idea for sports enthusiasts. They'll love the exercise and variety of activities.

Decorations

- Decorate the party room or backyard with sports equipment, such as baseball bats, footballs, and mitts.
- Put up posters of favorite athletes, set out sports cards, and hang pennants.
- Make the tablecloth look like a giant scorecard, game board, or large sports pennant.
- Use the sports pages for place mats, and set up a table centerpiece of Ace bandages, Ben-Gay, baseballs, sports cards, and anything related to sports.

Games

- Set up lots of different games for people to play, such as croquet, badminton, softball, lawn bowling or lawn darts (safety ones), basketball, and miniature golf.
- Have tournaments or marathon games, make up new rules for old games, or have rotations where everyone plays a game until time is called. Then have everyone rotate to the next game.

- Teach everyone a new version of "Capture the Flag." Divide the group into two teams. Give each member of one team a small rag of one color; the other team's members rags of a different color. Players put the ends of the rags into the backs of their pants. When play begins, set everyone free to run and grab as many of the opposite rags as they can. The team that first gets all the other team's rags, wins.

Food

- Ask everyone to bring lunch in a decorated bag. Encourage interesting, intriguing, and attractive artwork on the bags. Set all the bags on the table. At lunch time, have the youngest party guest choose one of the decorated lunch bags. Work up to the oldest. This way everyone gets a new lunch, perhaps something unfamiliar. Share the surprise of finding what's inside.
- Have plenty of sports drinks, such as Gatorade, available.

Burger Dogs

Hamburgers don't have to be round. These hotdog-shaped burgers will please everyone at your holiday picnic.

Serves: 4

Time: 15 minutes

Complexity: Moderate—Adult assistance recommended

Ingredients:
- 1 pound lean ground beef
- 4 slices of American cheese
- 4 hotdog buns
- Condiments (mustard, catsup, relish, onion, tomato)

Materials:
- Grill
- Spatula
- Plates
- Napkins

What to Do:

1. Shape the ground beef into four logs about 6 to 7 inches long.
2. Grill until browned and cooked, about ten minutes, turning once.
3. Top with cheese slices.
4. Serve in hotdog buns with condiments.

Space Invader Salad

This salad may look a little "alien" at first, but closer examination reveals that it's made with common ingredients that are nutritious and tasty. It's a good way to include some other food groups at your picnic or barbecue.

Serves: 4

Time: 10 minutes

Complexity: Easy

Ingredients:
- 1 cup cottage cheese
- 1/4 cup shredded carrots
- 2 tablespoons raisins
- 4 slices of pineapple
- A variety of additives, such as cherry halves, dried fruit, chow-mein noodles, chopped nuts, coconut, carrot circles, celery sticks, and so on

Materials:
- Large spoon
- Medium bowl
- 4 plates

What to Do:

1. In the medium bowl, mix the cottage cheese with the shredded carrots and raisins, reserving a few raisins to use for eyes or other decorations.
2. Scoop the mixture onto four plates.
3. Top each scoop with a pineapple slice to begin the space invader's face.
4. Decorate the face with the additives to make creatures from Mars.

BACK-TO-SCHOOL

As summer draws to a close, it's time to get ready for school again! It's a time to assemble school supplies and gym clothes, organize study areas in the home, and adjust to new schedules. It's an exciting and sometimes scary time for kids. They'll have new teachers, classes, friends, and responsibilities. The beginning of the new school year can also be emotional for parents—whether children are entering kindergarten or ninth grade, they've reached another milestone in their lives.

Preparing for the school year may be an elaborate or simple task for your family. Each family is different. However you prepare for the school year, just make sure you're ready when that first bell rings.

Educational Place Mats

Learn fun new facts while eating breakfast with educational place mats. They're easy to make, so change them as each "subject" is mastered.

Time: 30–45 minutes

Complexity: Easy—Adult assistance recommended

What to Do:

1. Decorate a sheet of white construction paper using felt-tip pens, crayons, and glitter, or glue on magazine pictures of a favorite hobby or interest. For example, draw or glue down pictures of dinosaurs from a coloring book.

2. Outline the drawings or pictures in black felt-tip pen and label them. (Name the dinosaurs, for example.)

3. Cover both sides of the paper with the clear Contact paper, allowing the Contact paper to extend 1/8 inch beyond the construction paper as a border.

Materials:
- White construction paper
- Felt-tip pens, crayons, and/or glitter
- Glue
- Scissors
- Clear Contact paper
- **Optional:** old magazines or coloring books

Variations: Try a star chart of the constellations, different types of insects, baseball stars, different kinds of fish, varieties of flowers, colors, maps, foreign words and phrases, pictures of famous buildings and sites worldwide, pictures of famous people, or breeds of dogs, cats, or horses.

Practical Tip: The Contact paper is tricky to use so adults should assist with this.

Pasta Pencil Holder

Everyone loves to eat pasta in spaghetti, soups, and salads, so why not use pasta to create interesting crafts—like this pencil holder made out of alphabet pasta?

Time: 45 minutes

Complexity: Easy—Adult assistance recommended

What to Do:

1. Spread the alphabet pasta out on the newspaper.
2. Use the paint brush to brush a thick coat of the glue on the jar, and then roll the jar in the pasta, picking up the pieces as you go. Fill in any bare areas with leftover letters.
3. Allow the glue to dry.
4. Go outside and spray the letters on the jar with a favorite color of enamel paint and allow to dry.
5. Fill with pencils or other school supplies.

Materials:
- Alphabet pasta
- Newspaper
- Empty jar or can
- White glue
- Paint brush
- Enamel spray paint

Variations: Color the alphabet noodles before gluing them to the jar by soaking them in a mixture of food coloring and vinegar or alcohol for a few minutes. Allow them to dry on a paper towel. Roll the glue-covered jar in the noodles, and then spray with clear Verathane or another varnish.

Color the noodles with a felt-tip pen.

Use a variety of pasta noodles, beans, seeds, or other items to cover the jar.

Practical Tips: For safety, use a plastic jar instead of a glass one.

Decorate the lid if you plan to close the jar.

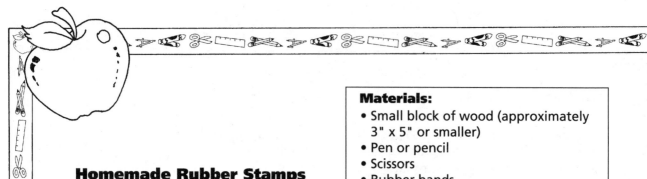

Homemade Rubber Stamps

Kids can't wait to make their own special marks on paper, letters, and reports with these homemade rubber stamps.

Time: 45–60 minutes

Complexity: Moderate

What to Do:

1. Draw a design such as your name, hearts, stars, or "I Love You" messages on the wood with the pen or pencil.

2. Cut rubber bands into pieces that will fit the design.

3. Brush the rubber cement on the design and carefully place the pieces of the rubber bands on top of the design. Let dry for 5 to 10 minutes.

4. Press the rubber stamp on the ink pad and then on paper.

Variation: Cut designs out of thick posterboard and glue them onto wood blocks for a different kind of stamp.

Materials:
- Small block of wood (approximately 3" x 5" or smaller)
- Pen or pencil
- Scissors
- Rubber bands
- Rubber cement
- Ink pad
- Paper

Practical Tip: Keep the designs simple so it will be easier to make an exact fit with the rubber bands.

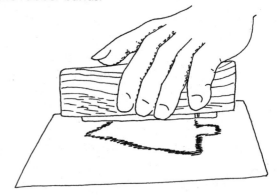

Creating Study Space

It's hard to do homework at the kitchen table. Here are some ideas to help you create a fun but functional study space for the upcoming school year.

- Set up a special table or desk for study. Make sure it's the right size.
- Set up a bookshelf. Stock it with a good dictionary and other reference books.
- Hang up a calendar to keep track of project deadlines and upcoming events.
- Get a good supply of pencils, pens, erasers, rulers, paper, and art supplies.

- Invest in a computer for the whole family to use.
- Cover an entire wall with clear Contact paper, and then write on the walls with water-based magic markers. Put learning posters underneath the Contact paper for studying the parts of the body, world geography, or multiplication tables. Add some game boards.
- Buy a section of corkboard at a lumber store and nail it to all or part of one wall. Frame it with wood to make it more attractive. You can leave the cork showing or cover it with a favorite fabric and change the fabric as you like. Use thumbtacks to display artwork, notes, and pictures.

- Make a map mural. Find a map of your local area, the U.S., the world, or other geographical areas, and pin it to corkboard. Stick pins in favorite or familiar places and attach colored yarn to show distances. Circle places you've been to.

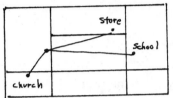

- Buy a plastic paper-towel holder and screw the holder into the bedroom wall at arm's level. Fill it with a roll of butcher paper (available at art stores). Make sure that the paper unrolls against the wall. Create pictures right against the wall, or cut off a piece and work at an easel or desk.
- Nail or glue strips of Velcro horizontally or vertically on the wall. Also sew small bits of Velcro onto stuffed animals, light jackets, and any kind of cloth toy or item. Stick them on the Velcro strips. This is a handy way to show off a stuffed animal collection or keep track of jackets.
- Create some new storage areas to help keep rooms neat and clean. Collect ice-cream tubs and cover them with fabric, wallpaper, or paint. Stack them on their sides or set them on shelves. Old lunch boxes make good storage containers for small things—plastic figurines, jewelry, or crayons.

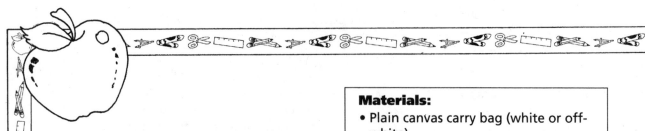

Personalized School Bag

This personalized school bag is a great help to students carrying all those books, papers, and pencils to school. Each bag will be unique.

Time: 30–60 minutes

Complexity: Moderate—Adult assistance recommended

Materials:
- Plain canvas carry bag (white or off-white)
- Pencil
- Fabric crayons
- Paper towels
- Iron and ironing board
- **Optional:** newspaper, vegetable peeler, scissors

What to Do:

1. With the pencil draw a picture or design, such as a favorite cartoon character, superhero, or your name, on the canvas bag.

2. Draw over the pencil lines with the fabric crayons, pressing hard.

3. Lay the canvas between a few layers of damp paper towels.

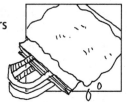

4. With the iron on a low setting, press the paper towels until they're dry.

5. Peel off the paper towels and repeat until the crayon wax is gone from the bag and only the color is left.

Variations: To add extra color, peel the paper off of the fabric crayons. Grate the crayons into separate color piles on the newspaper. Sprinkle colors inside the design outlines and press with the iron as described above.

After the bag has been colored with the crayons and pressed, dye the bag in a favorite color. The crayon color will resist the dye color, leaving the design on a colorful background.

Practical Tips: For safety make sure adults do the ironing part of this activity.

Paper towels don't need to be damp if you don't have any water handy.

Don't pile the shaved crayon peelings too thickly inside the design or it will be difficult to iron off the wax.

Fruit Leather

Like the fruit rolls sold in grocery stores, this fruit leather is a hit with kids and parents because it's sweet and nutritious.

Time: 15 minutes (plus cooking time)

Complexity: Moderate—Adult assistance recommended

Ingredients:
- 2-1/2 cups fruit puree, such as plums, apricots, peaches, or nectarines
- Vegetable-oil spray (such as Pam)

What to Do:
1. Spray the nonstick pan or cookie sheet with the vegetable-oil spray and set aside.
2. In the medium saucepan, bring the fruit puree to a boil and stir until it thickens.

Materials:
- Nonstick pan or cookie sheet
- Stove
- Medium saucepan
- Large spoon
- Oven, preheated to 250°
- Plastic wrap

3. Pour the mixture onto the pan or cookie sheet and spread to 1/4-inch thickness.
4. Bake for 2 to 3 hours, until dry and no longer tacky.
5. Carefully tear the fruit up into smaller pieces and roll the pieces up in the plastic wrap. Store in refrigerator.

Variation: Cover a cookie sheet with heavy-duty plastic wrap, pour thickened fruit mixture on, and place in the sunlight for 2 to 3 days.

Apple Boats

What more could a person ask for in a snack? This refreshing, high-protein after-school snack covers three food groups. But the best part is that kids will love eating it.

Time: 10 minutes

Complexity: Easy—Adult assistance recommended

Ingredients:
- 2 green apples
- 1/4 cup peanut butter, chunky style preferred
- 3 tablespoons peanuts, chopped
- 1/4 cup Rice Krispies
- 3 tablespoons raisins
- 2 slices Cheddar cheese

Materials:
- Knife
- Small bowl
- Spoon

What to Do:
1. Cut the apples in half and remove their cores, leaving hollows for the peanut-butter mixture.
2. In the small bowl, combine the peanut butter, peanuts, Rice Krispies, and raisins.
3. Spoon the mixture into the prepared apple halves.
4. Make sails with triangular pieces of cheese set on top and stuck in the peanut-butter mixture.

GRANDPARENT'S DAY
First Sunday following Labor Day

Grandparent's Day, celebrated on the first Sunday in September following Labor Day, began in 1978 to honor those special people we call Grandma and Grandpa.

It's a day for grandchildren to send their grandparents cards and gifts but also just to spend time with them to show their love! It's also a day for family stories. Kids will be amazed at what their grandparents remember about their parent's childhood as well as other tales from their family's history.

"I Love You" T-shirt

Grandparents delight in showing off arts and crafts made by their grandchildren. This personalized T-shirt is sure to become a favorite item in their wardrobe.

Time: 30–45 minutes

Complexity: Easy–Moderate

What to Do:

1. Use the puffy paints to write "I Love You" or another message on the front of the T-shirt. Also, outline your hand with the puffy paints and carefully write "Grandma" or "Grandpa" inside the hand.
2. Color the inside of each letter with a permanent felt-tip pen in a light shade.
3. Wrap up and give to your grandparent.

Materials:
- Large white T-shirt
- Puffy paints
- Permanent felt-tip pens

Variations: Have your picture made into a decal, cut it out in the shape of the "I Love You" sign, and have it pressed onto the shirt. Outline in puffy paints and give to a grandparent.

Make your own design or special message on the shirt.

Practical Tips: Allow to dry thoroughly before wrapping.

Wash the T-shirt in cold water.

Puzzle Picture

Grandparents never tire of looking at pictures of their grandchildren. Here's a picture they'll have to put together—it's a puzzle made out of a favorite photo.

Time: 45 minutes

Complexity: Moderate

What to Do:

1. Enlarge a funny or cute photo of the grandchildren at a photo or copy store.

2. Using the spray adhesive or photo mount spray, glue the photo onto the piece of tagboard. Be sure to glue the entire photo to the tagboard.

3. When the glue is dry, draw puzzle-piece shapes on the back of the tagboard with the felt-tip pen.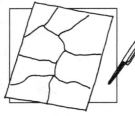

4. Cut along the lines to form the puzzle pieces. Don't make them too small or too large.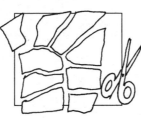

5. Put all the pieces in the box or large envelope (which you can also decorate) and your surprise picture is ready.

Materials:
- Photo of grandchildren
- Tagboard
- Spray adhesive or photo-mount spray
- Felt-tip pen
- Scissors
- Box or large envelope

Variation: If you have any pictures of grandchildren and grandparents together, even better.

Practical Tip: When put back together, the puzzle photo can be mounted on tagboard and framed. Hobby stores also have special glue for bonding together completed jigsaw puzzles.

Materials:
- Pen or pencil
- Paper
- Quiet and comfortable place
- **Optional:** tape or video recorder

Grandparent Interview

This activity gives kids a chance to pretend they're reporters. It's also a fun way for them to discover new things about their grandparents and their family history.

Time: 1 hour

Complexity: Easy

What to Do:

1. Make a list of questions to ask during the interview. Some good ones are: What was life like for you when you were my age? What were your parents and siblings like? What was school like? What did you want to do when you got older? What was my parent like as a child?

2. Pretend to be a reporter and interview the grandparent. Record the interview on an audio- or videotape for a lasting memory.

Variations: Take turns asking questions to each other.

Take notes during the interview and write a story about the grandparent afterwards. Give a copy of the story to the grandparent.

Practical Tip: Be a good listener.

Family Tree

Grandparent's Day is the perfect time to gather information together and create a family tree. Kids will enjoy chatting with their grandparents and discovering where they came from and who they are related to.

Time: 45–60 minutes

Complexity: Easy

What to Do:

1. Ask your grandparents from both sides of the family to tell you the names of all your relatives, as far back as they can remember. Write the names down on a piece of paper, grouped in families.

2. Draw a tree trunk on the brown construction paper, cut it out, and glue it onto the posterboard.

3. With the black felt-tip pen, write your name in the center of the trunk.

4. Cut two branches out of the brown construction paper, one for your mother's family and one for your father's family. Label each branch with the appropriate family's last name.

5. Add more branches for extending family groups and glue them onto the posterboard.

6. Cut leaves out of the green construction paper and write the names of your relatives on the leaves.

7. Assemble the leaves together in family groups and glue them onto the branches. Repeat for all family members until you have a full family tree with lots of branches.

Materials:
- Sheet of paper
- Pen or pencil
- Large sheet of white posterboard
- Fine-tipped black felt-tip pen
- Construction paper (brown and green)
- Scissors
- Glue

Variations: Use photos or draw pictures of your family members instead of or in addition to writing their names on the tree.

Add details to the tree, such as birthdates, places of birth, and so on.

Give the tree some fruit by having the kids be apples and the adults be oranges. Or have the girls be apples and the boys be oranges.

Instead of a tree, make a circus, pyramid, fan, rainbow, staircase, or other grid for building your genealogy chart.

Practical Tips: Make a rough draft of the chart and then transfer it to the posterboard.

Talk to other relatives and go through old photo albums if grandparents are not available to talk to.

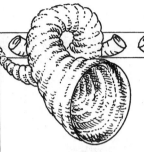

ROSH HASHANAH
(Date Varies)

Rosh Hashanah means "head" or beginning of the New Year. It occurs on the first day of the Jewish month of Tishri and marks the beginning of an observance covering ten days, culminating with Yom Kippur, the solemn Day of Atonement.

Originally a harvest festival, Rosh Hashanah is celebrated at the new moon. The shofar, a ram's-horn trumpet, is sounded at sundown and the festivities begin with a special holiday meal. In the days that follow, Jews reflect on the year past and their hopes for the year ahead. Many attend services at temples or synagogues.

The Jewish High Holy Days end with Yom Kippur, the Day of Atonement, which is considered the holiest Jewish holiday. It's a day for fasting, repentance, and seeking forgiveness.

Apple and Honey Treat

Serve a traditional sweet treat on Rosh Hashanah to assure the family that the coming year will be "a sweet year."

Time: 20 minutes

Complexity: Easy—Adult assistance recommended

Ingredients:
- Apples
- Jar of honey
- Hallah (white bread usually twisted into a braid but served smooth and round during this holiday)

What to Do:
1. Cut the apples into slices and remove the cores.
2. Place the apple slices on the serving plate with pieces of hallah.

Materials:
- Knife
- Serving plate

3. Dip into honey and eat.

Variations: Core an apple and fill it with honey. Dip apple wedges into the apple well.

Slice the apples crosswise to make circles, remove the cores, and place on plate. Fill the holes with honey. Serve with dates and almonds.

Warning: Honey should not be served to children under two.

Pop-Up Greeting Card

A pop-up greeting card is a fun way to carry Rosh Hashanah wishes to family and friends. It's also a great way to begin a new year.

Time: 30 minutes

Complexity: Moderate

What to Do:

1. Cut a rectangle out of the blue construction paper and a smaller one out of the white paper.

2. Fold the white rectangle in half.

3. Make two small cuts at the fold on an angle.

4. Put glue around the edges of the white paper.

5. Glue the white rectangle inside of the blue one. Let the glue dry.

6. Fold the card in half.

7. Open the card, fold the center piece outward while the outer edges remain folded inward.

8. Press the card shut to crease it again.

9. On the outside write something about a special friend, like a memory of something fun you've done together. You might write "I have a special friend

Materials:
- Blue construction paper
- White paper
- Glue
- Scissors
- Felt-tip pens

who loves to play baseball." Then open the card and write around the pop-up part something like, "Happy New Year to my friend." On the pop-up part write the friend's name so it jumps out in 3-D: "Benjamin Samrick!"

Variation: Make up your own design for the card.

Practical Tip: Adults might need to help younger kids with the folding part of this card.

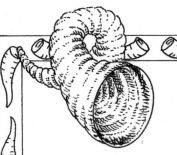

Holiday Fruit Pizza

Honey cakes and pieces of apples dipped in honey symbolize a sweet year to come and are popular at Rosh Hashanah. It's also customary to eat "funny fruit" or fruit you haven't eaten before or for a long time during Rosh Hashanah.

Serves: 8–10

Time: 20 minutes

Complexity: Moderate—Adult assistance recommended

Ingredients:
- Refrigerator sugar-cookie dough
- 2 8-ounce packages of cream cheese
- 1-1/4 cups sugar
- 1/2 teaspoon vanilla
- Sliced fruits (kiwi, guava, papaya, or other favorites)
- 2-1/2 tablespoons cornstarch
- 1/2 cup cold water
- 1 cup orange juice
- 1/4 cup lemon juice

What to Do:

1. Slice the cookie dough into thin circles, then press the circles together and smooth them into a round pizza pan so there are no holes between the slices.

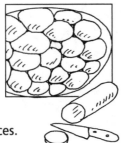

Materials:
- Knife
- Round pizza pan
- Oven
- Electric mixer
- Small saucepan

2. Bake according to package directions, until lightly browned.

3. Mix the cream cheese with 1/4 cup of the sugar and the vanilla. Spread on top of the cooled dough. Top with sliced fruits in a circular pattern.

4. Dissolve the cornstarch in cold water. Add orange juice, lemon juice, 1/2 cup cold water, and 1 cup sugar.

5. Pour the mixture into the small saucepan and heat over low heat until thick. Cool, then spoon over fruit.

6. Refrigerate for 1 hour, and then cut into wedges and serve.

Variation: Choose a variety of different fruits to decorate the dough and make a design with the fruit.

Practical Tip: Cut the fruit in thin slices and allow space between the fruit to fill with glaze.

October

COLUMBUS DAY
Second Monday in October

Celebrated on the second Monday in October, Columbus Day honors Christopher Columbus's arrival in the Bahamas on October 12, 1492. Columbus Day has become a controversial holiday in recent years, especially for Native Americans, as it marks the beginning of European domination over their lands. Many historians do not believe that Columbus was the first to discover America or that he was a hero. Nonetheless, the holiday serves as a tribute to the New World rather than one particular man.

The first Columbus Day celebrations in the U.S. took place on October 12, 1792, in both New York and Maryland. President Franklin D. Roosevelt proclaimed Columbus Day a federal holiday on October 12, 1937. In 1968, President Lyndon B. Johnson moved the holiday to the second Monday in October to create a three-day weekend. Today we celebrate this holiday with parades and parties.

Sailor's Delight

Ships ahoy! This healthy snack looks like sailing ships. Pretend they're the Niña, Pinta, and Santa Maria and have them for a treat on Columbus Day.

Time: 10 minutes

Complexity: Easy

Ingredients:
- Cantaloupe
- Cherries
- Grapes
- Raisins
- Cheese slices

What to Do:

1. Cut the cantaloupe into sizable slices, keeping on the rind.

Materials:
- Wooden skewers
- Knife
- Plates

2. Push a cherry, grape, and raisin to the end of each skewer.

3. Poke two holes on opposite ends of each cheese single and poke a skewer through the holes to form sails.

4. Add more fruit on top of the cheese and stick the skewer into the cantaloupe.

Variations: Use paper sails instead of cheese; write the names of the ships or pirate logos on the paper sails.

Use toothpicks instead of skewers.

Columbus Diorama

Re-create Columbus's world in miniature. All you'll need are a few basic craft supplies and your imagination.

Time: 30–60 minutes

Complexity: Moderate

What to Do:

1. Place the shoe box on its side and begin re-creating the scene of Columbus landing in America inside it.

2. Use paint, crayons, or markers to color the inside of the box. Color a sky at the back and top. Add clouds, land, and ocean. Extend the ocean onto the bottom side of the box.

3. Glue sand to the edge of the land to create a shoreline.

4. Make trees out of construction paper and glue them to the land.

5. Glue glitter and fish cut out of construction paper to the ocean.

6. Make ships out of walnuts. Crack the walnuts in half, remove the nuts, and fill them with playdough. Make sails out of paper taped or glued to toothpicks to stick into the playdough. Or make ships out of construction paper. Place the ships on the ocean.

7. Use your imagination to add other details to the scene.

Materials:
- Shoe box
- Paint, crayons, or markers
- Paint brushes
- Construction paper
- Scissors
- Tape
- Glue
- Walnut and nut cracker
- Playdough
- Toothpicks
- Glitter
- Sand

Variations: Cut a hole in the lid of the box and put the lid back on the box. Cut holes in the top of the box so light can come in. Peer through the hole to see your scene.

Use a larger box

Practical Tip: Plan out your scene before you get started.

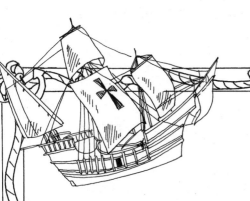

Around the World Game

Christopher Columbus explored the world by sailing to new lands. You can explore the world by playing this game. Keep a map handy to identify the places you're "traveling" to.

Time: 30 minutes

Complexity: Easy–Moderate

What to Do:

1. Before the game, fill the suitcase with items from around the world.

2. Have the players sit in a circle with the map or globe in the middle.

3. Give the suitcase to a player. Tell the player to open the suitcase and pull something out without looking. After closing the suitcase, the player is to look at the item and tell the other players what the item is and where it came from.

4. Tell the player to find the location on the map or globe. If the player cannot find the location, the player seated on the right gets to try. Continue until someone identifies the item and locates it correctly.

Materials:
- Suitcase
- Items from different parts of the world, such as a fan from China, maracas from Mexico, jewelry from Africa, a book from Russia, tea from England, mittens from Alaska, a lei from Hawaii, a clock from Switzerland, and so on
- World map or globe

5. Award a point to the player who gets the correct answer.

6. Continue passing the suitcase around the circle until everyone has had a turn.

Variation: Use food from around the world. Go to an international food or import store and buy candy, cookies, crackers, or other foods from various countries. Put the food items in a picnic basket. Let the players keep the treats they pull from the basket.

Practical Tip: Have clues ready in case the players have trouble identifying where the items came from. Or let the players put their fingers on the map and call out "hot" or "cold" as they trace a path to the right location.

Columbus Spaghetti

This spaghetti recipe uses tuna instead of red meat—just the way sailors might have made it while at sea.

Serves: 4

Time: 45 minutes

Complexity: Easy—Adult assistance recommended

Ingredients:
- 1 small garlic clove, chopped
- 2 tablespoons olive oil
- 3 tablespoons parsley, chopped
- 1-1/2 cups canned Italian tomatoes in juice, chopped
- 1 can (10 ounce) tuna in water, drained
- 1 pound spaghetti noodles, cooked
- **Optional:** 3 tablespoons margarine, Parmesan cheese

What to Do:
1. Sauté the garlic in the olive oil until lightly browned.
2. Add the parsley. Stir and cook for 30 seconds.
3. Add the tomatoes and their juice. Simmer uncovered over low heat for 20 to 25 minutes, stirring occasionally.
4. Break the tuna into small chunks and add to the sauce, mixing well.
5. Remove from the heat and stir in the margarine, if desired.
6. Serve over the cooked spaghetti noodles. Add Parmesan cheese, if desired.

Materials:
- Stove
- Medium saucepan
- Large spoon
- Large serving bowl

Variations: Serve the sauce over other types of pasta instead of spaghetti, such as twisted macaroni or wheel-shaped pasta.

Buy enriched spaghetti made from spinach or other vegetables. Or serve over rice for a Spanish taste.

Practical Tip: Use your favorite can or jar of spaghetti sauce if you want to save time. Just add the tuna as you heat the sauce, and dinner will be ready in a jiffy.

DECORATION

UNITED NATIONS DAY
October 24

This holiday commemorates the founding of the United Nations in 1945. The United Nations is an organization of nations who work together to secure peace throughout the world. Fifty nations signed the initial charter; today over 150 are members.

Perhaps the best known UN agencies are UNICEF (United Nations Children's Fund), which works to improve the health and welfare of children and mothers, and WHO (World Health Organization), which successfully eradicated small pox from the earth. The office of the High Commissioner for Refugees is also, unfortunately, very active.

On this holiday people take time to learn about the traditions, food, and people of other nations.

International Flags

Here's a creative way to appreciate the flag of our country as well as the flags from other countries.

Time: 30 minutes

Complexity: Easy

What to Do:

1. Create new designs for the U.S. flag using red, white, and blue construction paper. Try to have your new design represent something special about this country.

2. Make flags for other countries. Choose colors and designs that represent something about the countries.

Materials:
- Construction paper (all colors)
- Scissors
- Glue
- Pictures of flags of the world

3. Talk about your flags and the designs you chose. Then look at the pictures of the real flags to see how your flag compares.

Variation: When the flags are complete, guess which country they represent before the flag-maker tells you.

AROUND THE WORLD PARTY

Kids are intrigued with the foods, customs, and life-styles of other countries. Have a party on United Nations Day to celebrate the diversity in our world.

Time: 2 hours

Complexity: Moderate

What to Do:

1. Send out invitations on postcards from different parts of the world. Or make your own postcards from cut-up maps. Write the party details in with the black felt-tip pen. Ask the guests to dress in clothes that represent another country and to bring a food dish from that country to share at the party.

2. Decorate the party room with posters, travel brochures, and postcards from different parts of the world. Hang flags from different countries from the ceiling or the walls.

3. Cut out shapes of other countries from construction paper and glue or tape them to full sheets of construction paper and use as place mats.

4. Play a variety of music from other countries during the party.

5. Ask trivia questions from different parts of the world. Or play a game of "Where in the World Is Carmen Sandiego?"

6. Send the guests home with small flags or other souvenirs from different countries.

Materials:
- Maps
- Black felt-tip pen
- Globe
- Food from different countries (brought by your guests)
- Flags, souvenirs, posters, travel brochures, postcards, and music from different countries
- Construction paper (all colors)
- Scissors
- Glue or tape

Variation: Ask each guest to bring a set of stamps from a different country. Provide stamp books, and exchange stamps so everyone goes home with a beginning international stamp collection. For more information on UN stamps, write: United Nations Postal Administration, P.O. Box 5900, Grand Central Station, New York, NY 10017.

Practical Tip: Assign a different country to each guest so a wide variety of countries are represented at the party.

HALLOWEEN
October 31

Halloween is an ancient celebration combining Druid rites and Christian customs. Thousands of years ago European Druids began the new year on what is now November 1. They believed it was the beginning of winter, that winter and summer were at war, and that on the night before the new year, the army of winter, including ghosts, goblins, and witches, would approach. People tried to frighten these evil beings away by building huge bonfires and wearing masks and animal skins. When Christianity arrived, November 1 became All Saints' Day or All Hallows' Day. And the night before this day was known as All Hallows' Eve, or Halloween.

What originated as a frightening holiday has become a fun holiday for kids, who continue the tradition of dressing up in costumes. The best part for many kids is going out into the night "Trick or Treating." Like the ghosts and goblins they imitate, if they aren't given candy treats, they just might pull some trick on you.

Skeleton Person

What's more scary than a skeleton showing through a person? This spooky drawing will thrill trick-or-treaters on Halloween.

Time: 30 minutes

Complexity: Easy

What to Do:

1. In heavy black felt-tip pen or crayon draw a skeleton on one of the large sheets of white paper
2. Place another sheet of paper over the skeleton. Tape them together so they won't slip apart.
3. Draw a second picture on the outer sheet of paper, covering the skeleton with a face, hands, clothes, and shoes.

Materials:
- 2 large sheets of white paper
- Heavy black felt-tip pen or black crayon
- Crayons (all colors)
- Tape

4. Tape the resulting picture to the window with a light behind it or hold it up to a lamp, so that the skeleton shows through the person.

Variation: Personalize your skeleton by adding a photograph of a family member to the outer drawing.

Practical Tip: Make the picture at night and tape it on the window, then watch the surprise when the sun shines through it in the morning.

HORRIFIC HAUNTED HOUSE

Eeeeeeeeekkk! Everyone likes to get a little spooked on Halloween. These tips will help you turn your garage into a spooky maze of surprises.

- Hang spiderwebs made from yarn, or buy stringy stuff at the store and squirt it all over as your guests walk in.
- Make a headless horseman. Stuff old clothes with newspapers and set a pumpkin in its lap for its head. Paint a face on the pumpkin with glow-in-the-dark paint.
- Paint "eyes" all around the room with glow paint or use glow-in-the-dark stickers.
- Play a ghost record or a tape of creaky sounds and eerie screams. Or make your own scary sounds. Blow across the tops of different sized bottles to make weird moaning sounds; breath heavily into a large empty bucket or bin to make an echo sound; and scream into a paper tube.
- Create tunnels from large cardboard boxes or card tables and blankets for the victims to crawl through.
- Set up silly gravestones with your guests' names on them.
- Have the guests put their hands in bowls of Jell-O and Slime and tell you what they feel as you introduce yourself as Dr. Frankenstein. Cold baked beans, spaghetti, and oatmeal also work well.
- Ask friends to be "dead" bodies that suddenly come to life. Wrap them up in sheets.
- Wear costumes to suit your theme, such as the Mad Scientist, Frankenstein's Laboratory, the Witch's Cottage, and so on.

COSTUMES

The most memorable Halloween costumes are often homemade. Here are some fun and spooky costumes that are easy to make.

Pumpkin

Here's the perfect costume to wear while you're waiting for "the great pumpkin" to arrive.

Time: 30–45 minutes

Complexity: Challenging—Adult assistance recommended

What to Do:

1. Cut two large circles out of the orange fabric.

2. Sew the circles together, leaving openings for legs, arms, and head.

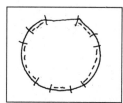

3. Turn the top over 1/2 inch and run a drawstring through it.

Materials:
- Orange fabric
- Scissors
- Needle
- Orange thread
- String
- Green felt
- Old newspapers, tissues, fabric, or pillows
- Green tights and shirt or pajamas

4. Cut out a green hat from felt in the shape of a pumpkin stem.

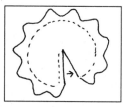

5. Sew two pieces of string onto the hat to tie under your chin.

6. Put on the green clothes, slip on the pumpkin suit, and stuff it with newspapers, tissues, fabric, or pillows.

7. Pull the drawstring closed.

Variation: With a black marker draw a face on your pumpkin after it's sewn together.

Practical Tip:
Make sure the costume is comfortable, especially if it's going to be worn for an extended period of time.

Quick Favorites:

Mummies are spooky favorites. Tie-dye an old white sheet so that it has splotches of red all over it. Allow it to dry. Cut or tear the sheet into strips and wrap it around your body. Add some make-up to your face for the "long dead" look. Or use a plain sheet or a flowered one for a tropical mummy. Be sure to leave mouth, nose, and eyeholes.

Glow-in-the-Dark Skeletons will chill your bones. Put on black clothes, such as tights, a shirt or leotard, gloves, and socks. Attach glow-in-the-dark masking tape where bones are, cutting rounded edges for the ends.

Pinocchio and Gepetto make a great pair traveling together. Pinocchio wears a white shirt, red or black shorts, suspenders made from braid trim, a Peter Pan hat, and a long putty nose. Gepetto wears knickers, a big billowing shirt, a hat, and glasses. Attach yarn to the shoulders, hands, and knees of Pinocchio, draw on "joints" with eyebrow pencil, and attach the yarn ends to a wooden "X." Then have Gepetto "work" the Pinocchio puppet.

Peter Pan or Robin Hood, two old favorites, wear green tights and leotards or green pajamas (you can use the pajamas later for sleeping). Cut jagged edges on a green shirt for both, and add a hat, feathers, and a belt with a homemade cardboard knife attached.

Raggedy Ann wears an old dress, a white apron with a small red heart on it, and white tights with red tape wrapped around the legs. Add a red yarn wig for hair, draw on some freckles with eyeliner, and brush on lots of blush.

Superman, Spiderman, and the Incredible Hulk are quick and easy superhero costumes. The bodies are made from tights and leotards, or pajamas—red and blue for Superman, red for Spiderman, and green for Hulk. Superman wears colored jockey underwear over the tights, a cape, and a big letter "S" on the front of his shirt; Spiderman wears a fishnet cap and a spider on the front of his shirt; and Hulk pads his body with fabric or towels and wears cut-off jeans.

Mickey Mouse is a perennial favorite. Wear black tights, a blue shirt, red shorts with big white felt buttons on the front. Then add a black piece of rope for the tail. Glue black tagboard ears to a headband. Put on black socks over the shoes if you don't have black shoes. Add make-up for whiskers, and color the nose red.

Guess What It Is Game

What's in the bag? Great Green Gobs of Greasy Grimy Gopher Guts? This traditional Halloween game always provides plenty of thrills and chills as the guests feel the foreign objects.

Time: 30 minutes

Complexity: Easy

What to Do:

1. Put the fruits and vegetables, or "innards," in the plastic bags. Cover them with the brown paper bags so the players can't see what's inside.

2. Tell a scary story as you pass around the "innards" and have the guests feel what's inside. Or sing "Great Green Gobs of Greasy Grimy Gopher Guts."

Materials:
- Fruits and vegetables that resemble body parts, such as an old, softening carrot for a finger, Jell-O for a liver, large cooked macaroni noodles for intestines (guts!), cooked spaghetti for brains, 2 large peeled grapes for eyeballs, popcorn kernels for teeth, a canned apricot half for a tongue, and a soft, ripened tomato for a heart
- Plastic bags
- Brown paper bags

3. Have the players guess what they are really feeling. Award a prize to the player who gets the most answers right.

Variation: Use your imagination to come up with other body parts.

Practical Tip: Show the players what the items really are after the game is over.

Apple on a String

Here's an apple-eating game that's just as tricky as bobbing for apples, but you won't get wet playing this game.

Time: 15 minutes

Complexity: Easy

What to Do:

1. Hang the apples from the ceiling on long pieces of string.

2. Say "Go" and have the players eat the apples without using their hands.

3. The first player to finish an apple is the winner.

Materials:
- Apples
- String
- Scissors

Variation: Make the game easier by using marshmallows or doughnuts instead of apples.

Practical Tip: Encourage the players to use a shoulder to help them "capture" the apple and eat it.

Crystal Ball Piñata

Look into the magic crystal ball and see your future. Goodies are in store for you if you have this crystal ball at your party—it's a piñata!

Time: 30 minutes

Complexity: Moderate

What to Do:

1. Blow up a large balloon and cover it with papier-mâché (follow package directions on how to apply), or cover the balloon with liquid starch and crepe paper. Allow it to dry.

2. Paint the ball black and sprinkle on glitter. Allow it to dry again.

3. Cover with glow-in-the-dark star stickers.

4. Cut open a small hole at the top and fill with candies.

Materials:
- Large balloon
- Papier-mâché or crepe paper and liquid starch
- Black paint
- Paint brush
- Glitter
- Glow-in-the-dark star stickers
- Scissors or knife
- Small candies
- String
- Plastic bat

5. Tie with string and hang from the ceiling.

6. Turn off the lights, let the ball glow in the dark, and then take turns swinging the bat.

Variations: Instead of painting the ball black, use black crepe paper.

Paint on stars with glow-in-the-dark paint instead of using stickers.

Fill the piñata with small magic tricks or made-up fortunes instead of candy.

Practical Tip: Use caution when swinging at the piñata. Don't turn all the lights off.

Gauze Ghost

What's Halloween without a ghost? Use this spooky ghost as a table centerpiece—or hang it from the ceiling to greet the witches and monsters who stop by for a Halloween treat.

Time: 10 minutes

Complexity: Moderate—Adult assistance recommended

What to Do:

1. Use the scissors to round the corners of the 6-inch piece of gauze or cheesecloth.

2. Pour the liquid starch into a bowl and dip the gauze or cheesecloth in it completely.

3. Set the bottle on the newspaper.

4. Drape the wet gauze or cheesecloth over the bottle and allow it to dry for 24 hours.

5. After completely dry, use the black felt-tip pen to draw a face on the ghost.

6. Place the ghost on your table for a centerpiece or thread string through the top of the ghost and hang it from the ceiling.

Materials:
- 6" square of surgical gauze or cheesecloth
- Scissors
- Liquid starch
- Bowl
- Newspapers
- Empty soap or drink bottle
- Black felt-tip pen
- **Optional:** string

Variations: Color the liquid starch with food coloring to make a colorful ghost.

Glue on wiggly plastic eyes instead of drawing them on or glue on eyes and a mouth cut out of felt.

Practical Tips: This is messy, so use plenty of newspapers.

Although the ghost will retain its shape once the starch dries, it is still delicate and should be handled with care.

Jack-O'-Lantern Candy Holder

Everybody likes to make jack-o'-lanterns for Halloween. Most are carved out of pumpkins, which are too messy to hold candy. Here's a jack-o'-lantern that doubles as a container for trick-or-treat goodies.

Time: 30–45 minutes (plus drying time)

Complexity: Easy–Moderate

What to Do:

1. Cut the newspaper into 1-to-2-inch strips.

2. Blow up the balloon and tie it.

3. Cover the balloon with newspaper strips dipped in the flour-and-water paste or liquid starch.

4. Cover the whole balloon two or three times, and let it dry completely (2 to 3 hours or overnight).

5. Pop the balloon and paint the ball orange. Add some black eyes, a nose, and a mouth.

6. Cut a zigzag-patterned top off of the pumpkin holder, poke holes in the sides, and attach a piece of the yarn for a handle.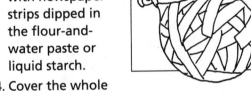

Materials:

- Newspaper
- Scissors
- Balloon
- Flour-and-water paste or liquid starch
- Orange paint
- Black paint
- Paint brush
- Yarn
- Shellac

7. Shellac the holder and allow it to dry.

Variation: Make a witch's head or a big bat instead of a pumpkin.

Practical Tip: This is messy, so work over newspapers and wear a smock.

Popcorn Pumpkins

Pop up a batch of popcorn and make these Halloween treats. They look and taste great

Time: 45–60 minutes

Complexity: Moderate—Adult assistance recommended

Ingredients:
- 2 cups white corn syrup
- 1 tablespoon vinegar
- 1 teaspoon salt
- 2 teaspoons vanilla
- Orange food coloring
- Green food coloring
- 1 medium bowl popped popcorn
- 1 small bowl popped popcorn
- Butter
- Raisins

What to Do:

1. Heat the corn syrup, vinegar, and salt in the saucepan until it reaches 250° on the candy thermometer.

2. Add the vanilla, and then pour 2/3 of the mixture into the large bowl and color it with the orange food coloring.

3. Pour the remaining mixture into the medium bowl and color it with the green food coloring.

4. Pour the hot orange mixture onto the medium bowl of popcorn. Mix well with a spoon. Pour the hot green mixture onto the small bowl of popcorn. Mix well with a spoon.

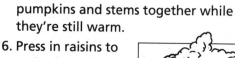

Materials:
- Saucepan
- Stove
- Candy thermometer
- Large bowl
- Medium bowl
- 2 large spoons
- Plastic wrap

5. When the popcorn is warm (not hot), use buttered hands to form the orange into balls and the green into stems. Press the pumpkins and stems together while they're still warm.

6. Press in raisins to make faces. Wrap the popcorn pumpkins in plastic wrap.

Variation: Omit raisins, but cut out facial features from black construction paper and glue onto the plastic wrap.

Practical Tip: Work quickly but keep hands buttered to prevent burnt fingers.

Jack-O'-Lantern Oranges

Kids get a lot of candy on Halloween. Here's a treat that's sweet and delicious naturally. And best of all, it looks like a jack-o'-lantern.

Time: 20 minutes

Complexity: Easy—Adult assistance recommended

Ingredients:
- Oranges
- Can of frozen orange juice

What to Do:

1. Cut the tops off of the oranges in a zigzag pattern.
2. Lift off the tops and scoop out the insides.
3. Draw jack-o'-lantern faces on the outsides of the shells with the black permanent felt-tip pen.
4. Mix up the can of frozen orange juice according to package directions. Squeeze the juice from the orange pulps and mix with the orange juice. Pour the juice into the orange shells and set in the freezer for several hours.

Materials:
- Knife
- Spoon
- Pitcher
- Black permanent felt-tip pen
---

5. To eat, set on counter for a few minutes to partially thaw, or peel back the orange shells.

Variation: Fill the orange shells with orange sherbet or vanilla pudding tinted orange. Decorate the orange shells with chocolate frosting.

Practical Tip: Make these at night and freeze overnight so they're ready to go in the morning.

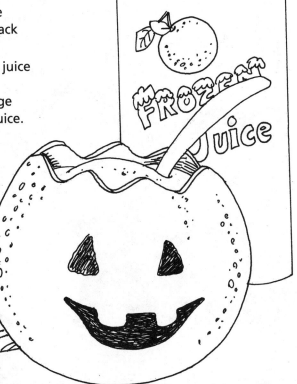

Halloween Punch

Here's a fruity, spicy punch that warms you up. It's a must for a Halloween party.

Time: 30 minutes

Complexity: Easy—Adult assistance recommended

Ingredients:
- 1 pumpkin
- 1 quart apple juice
- 1/2 cup lemon juice
- 5 cloves
- 1 teaspoon nutmeg
- 2 cinnamon sticks

What to Do:
1. Clean out the pumpkin, removing all seeds and strings.

Materials:
- Knife
- Large spoon
- Paper towel
- Felt-tip pens
- Large pan
- Stove

2. Blot the inside with a paper towel.
3. Draw a jack-o'-lantern face on the outside of the pumpkin with the felt-tip pens and refrigerate.
4. Prepare punch by mixing the apple juice, lemon juice, cloves, nutmeg, and cinnamon sticks in a large pan and bringing the mixture to a boil.
5. Simmer for 10 minutes. Serve in the pumpkin shell.

Variation: Fill the pumpkin with favorite soup or stew and serve for lunch or dinner.

Dracula's Blood Yogurt and Ice-Cream Mixture

This creepy drink is sure to bring kids running up for refills. It's made with fruit, yogurt, and ice cream.

Serves: 6

Time: 5 minutes

Complexity: Easy

Ingredients:
- 16 ounces plain yogurt
- 1/2 teaspoon vanilla
- 1 10-ounce package frozen strawberries
- Ice cubes
- Strawberry ice cream

Materials:
- Blender
- 6 tall glasses

What to Do:
1. Mix the plain yogurt, vanilla, and frozen strawberries in the blender until smooth.
2. Pour the mixture into tall glasses with ice cubes or chill.
3. Top with a spoonful of strawberry ice cream.

Variation: Try another flavor of ice cream instead of strawberry.

Floating Hand

Yipes! There's a hand floating in the Halloween punch! Don't worry—it's scary, but safe.

Time: 10 minutes (plus freezing time)

Complexity: Easy

Ingredients:
- Red drink mix
- Water

What to Do:
1. In the pitcher mix up the red drink mix according to package directions.
2. Fill the new rubber glove with the red drink. Tie the end with string.
3. Put the filled glove in the freezer and allow it to freeze.

Materials:
- Pitcher
- Large spoon
- String
- New rubber glove
- Fine scissors

4. When frozen, cut the glove off carefully and float the remaining "frozen hand" in a bowl of punch.

Variation: Serve a red hand made of frozen Jell-O.

Practical Tip: Wash and clean the rubber glove thoroughly to remove any residues before using it.

Baked Pumpkin Seeds

Don't let all those pumpkin seeds you pulled out of your pumpkin go to waste. Bake them up and pop them in your mouth—delicious!

Time: 45 minutes

Complexity: Easy—Adult assistance recommended

Ingredients:
- Pumpkin seeds
- 3–4 tablespoons margarine
- **Optional:** salt or seasoning

What to Do:

1. Spoon pumpkin seeds out of a pumpkin.

2. Clean the pumpkin seeds.

Materials:
- Large saucepan
- Stove
- Cookie sheet
- Large spoon
- Oven, preheated to 350°

3. Melt margarine in a large saucepan and mix in the seeds.

4. Spread the seeds out on the cookie sheet, sprinkle with a little salt or seasoning, if desired, and bake, stirring about 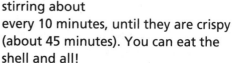 every 10 minutes, until they are crispy (about 45 minutes). You can eat the shell and all!

Variation: Omit the margarine if you prefer.

November

VETERANS DAY
November 11

We celebrate Veterans Day on November 11, the day when World War I ended on the eleventh hour of the eleventh day of the eleventh month of 1918. The holiday, originally called Armistice Day, became Veterans Day in 1954 to honor veterans from all wars.

On this day the president or one of his representatives lays a wreath of flowers at the Tomb of the Unknown Soldier in Arlington National Cemetery in Virginia. The memorial actually comprises three tombs that represent all the unidentified soldiers who lost their lives in WWI, WWII, and the Korean Conflict.

Today the holiday is sometimes celebrated on the Monday closest to November 11. Whenever they observe it, many communities hold parades or programs in honor of this day of remembrance.

Flag T-shirt

Show the red, white, and blue. It's easy to turn a plain, white T-shirt into a patriotic flag to wear on this special day.

Time: 30–45 minutes

Complexity: Moderate—Adult assistance recommended

What to Do:

1. Cut stripes out of the red iron-on fabric.
2. Cut stars out of the blue iron-on fabric.
3. Arrange the stripes and stars on the white T-shirt in any shape or design you like. You can form the American flag (traditional except for the blue stars), or you can create a new look for the stars and stripes.

Materials:
- Red iron-on fabric
- Blue iron-on fabric
- White T-shirt
- Iron
- Scissors

4. Iron on the fabric and wear your shirt proudly for the day.

Variation: Outline the stars and stripes with red and blue puffy paints for a 3–D effect.

Practical Tip: Use a star-shaped cookie cutter or other predrawn star to help you make your stars exact.

Thank-a-Veteran Card

Today would be a nice day to send a veteran a special card, to thank him or her for supporting our country. Send the card to a veteran you know or call your local Veterans Administration office for names.

Time: 30 minutes

Complexity: Moderate

What to Do:

1. Glue the red and blue sheets of construction paper together.

2. Fold the paper in half.

3. Cut several small stars or one big star out of the front of the card so you can see the inside of the card, which will be the other color.

4. Open the card up and set it on the newspaper. With the eye dropper, drop diluted white poster paint on the bottom right-hand side of the inside of the card.

5. With the straw, blow the paint upwards causing a wispy branchlike design. Repeat if necessary to cover the inside card with more "bursts" of white paint, creating a "star-spangled" sky lit up with "fireworks."

Materials:
- 1 sheet of red construction paper
- 1 sheet of blue construction paper
- Glue
- Scissors
- Newspaper
- Eye dropper
- Straw
- White poster paint, slightly diluted with water
- Paint brush

6. With the white paint, write "Oh, say, can you see . . ." on the outside of the card. Then write "Thanks for protecting our country!" on the inside of the card.

Variations: Use white paper and red and blue paint to make "bursts" of "fireworks."

Add glitter before the paint dries.

Practical Tip: Young children may have a hard time understanding how to blow on straws because they're used to sucking on them. Give them a quick lesson by having them blow a scrap of paper off the table. You might also cut a small slit at the top of the straw, which will keep them from inhaling and won't interfere with blowing.

"Oh, say, can you see..."

THANKSGIVING
Fourth Thursday in November

Turkey Day! The first Thanksgiving was held by the Pilgrims in Plymouth, Massachusetts, after their first harvest sometime around 1621. They invited Native Americans to join in the celebration, and all enjoyed a feast of deer, goose, duck, oysters, eel, bread, fruit, and cornmeal pudding.

President George Washington proclaimed November 26, 1789, a national Thanksgiving Day, so people could offer thanksgiving and prayer for prosperity, freedom, and hope. The day was not accepted nationally, however, until 1863, when President Lincoln declared Thanksgiving to be the last Thursday in November. President Franklin D. Roosevelt moved the holiday to the fourth Thursday in November in 1941.

Today Thanksgiving is usually celebrated as a family day rather than a public holiday. Families gather together and eat too much turkey, stuffing, cranberry sauce, sweet potatoes, and pumpkin pie. Then they all take a nap!

Turkey Napkin Rings

Thanksgiving dinner can be very messy—be sure to have plenty of napkins and napkin rings on the table. These turkey napkin rings complement your holiday table.

Time: 30 minutes

Complexity: Easy

What to Do:

1. Cut the cardboard tubes into 1-1/2-inch rings.
2. Glue ribbon around each cardboard ring.

Materials:
- Cardboard tubes, such as paper-towel tubes
- Scissors
- Colorful ribbon
- Glue
- Brown paper or cloth napkins
- Construction paper

3. Cut out a turkey face from construction paper, leaving a flap at the neck to glue onto the ring. Cut the flap in half, fold it in different directions, and glue it upright to the tube, as shown.

4. Stuff a napkin through each ring to make a turkey body and back feathers.

Turkey Place Mats

Kids can contribute to the holiday meal by making these turkey place mats.

Time: 30 minutes

Complexity: Easy—Adult assistance recommended.

What to Do:

1. Cut out scallop shapes from three sides of the brown construction paper, leaving one long side straight. Use as much of the paper as you can to make it large.

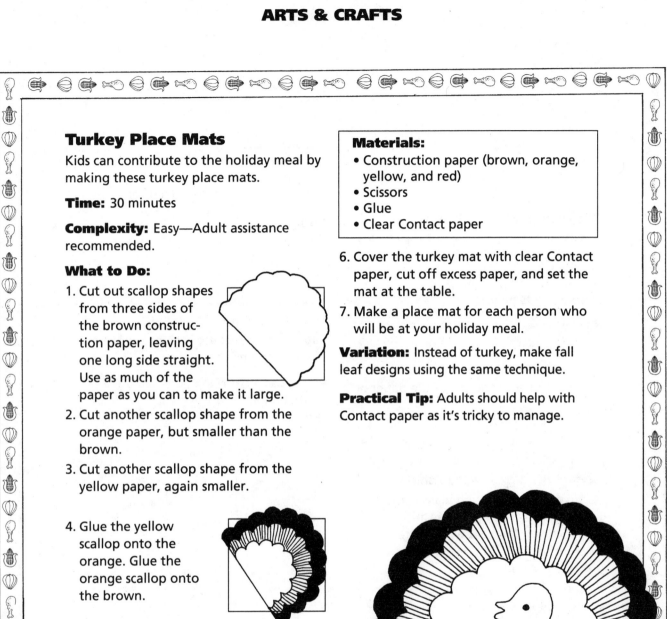

2. Cut another scallop shape from the orange paper, but smaller than the brown.

3. Cut another scallop shape from the yellow paper, again smaller.

4. Glue the yellow scallop onto the orange. Glue the orange scallop onto the brown.

5. Cut a small turkey head from the red construction paper and glue it onto the yellow paper.

Materials:

- Construction paper (brown, orange, yellow, and red)
- Scissors
- Glue
- Clear Contact paper

6. Cover the turkey mat with clear Contact paper, cut off excess paper, and set the mat at the table.

7. Make a place mat for each person who will be at your holiday meal.

Variation: Instead of turkey, make fall leaf designs using the same technique.

Practical Tip: Adults should help with Contact paper as it's tricky to manage.

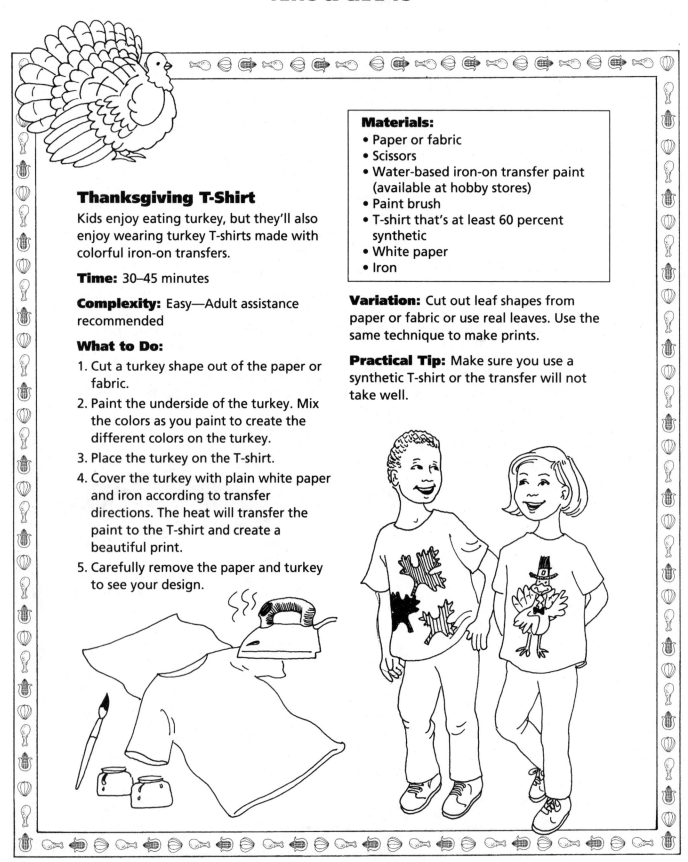

Thanksgiving T-Shirt

Kids enjoy eating turkey, but they'll also enjoy wearing turkey T-shirts made with colorful iron-on transfers.

Time: 30–45 minutes

Complexity: Easy—Adult assistance recommended

What to Do:

1. Cut a turkey shape out of the paper or fabric.
2. Paint the underside of the turkey. Mix the colors as you paint to create the different colors on the turkey.
3. Place the turkey on the T-shirt.
4. Cover the turkey with plain white paper and iron according to transfer directions. The heat will transfer the paint to the T-shirt and create a beautiful print.
5. Carefully remove the paper and turkey to see your design.

Materials:
- Paper or fabric
- Scissors
- Water-based iron-on transfer paint (available at hobby stores)
- Paint brush
- T-shirt that's at least 60 percent synthetic
- White paper
- Iron

Variation: Cut out leaf shapes from paper or fabric or use real leaves. Use the same technique to make prints.

Practical Tip: Make sure you use a synthetic T-shirt or the transfer will not take well.

Hand Turkey Puppet

Gobble, gobble! These turkeys make great leading characters in a Thanksgiving play.

Time: 30 minutes

Complexity: Easy

What to Do:

1. With a pencil trace your hand on a paper plate.
2. Cut out the paper handprint.
3. Cut "feathers" out of the construction paper and glue them onto the fingers of the paper hand.
4. Draw a face on the turkey with the crayons or markers and tape or glue a Popsicle stick to the back of the paper hand.

Materials:
- Paper plate
- Pencil
- Scissors
- Glue
- Construction paper
- Color crayons or markers
- Popsicle stick
- **Optional:** tape

Variations: Use real feathers (available at hobby stores) instead of paper.

Draw on the turkey's face with puffy paints for a 3-D effect.

Instead of gluing the puppet to a Popsicle stick, cut out two paper plates in the shape of your hand and glue all edges of the hand together except the wrist side. Decorate one or both sides of the hand. Slide the puppet onto your hand like a glove and use during your puppet show. Or decorate an old glove as a turkey.

Practical Tip: Be sure to let the puppet dry before using it or it may fall apart.

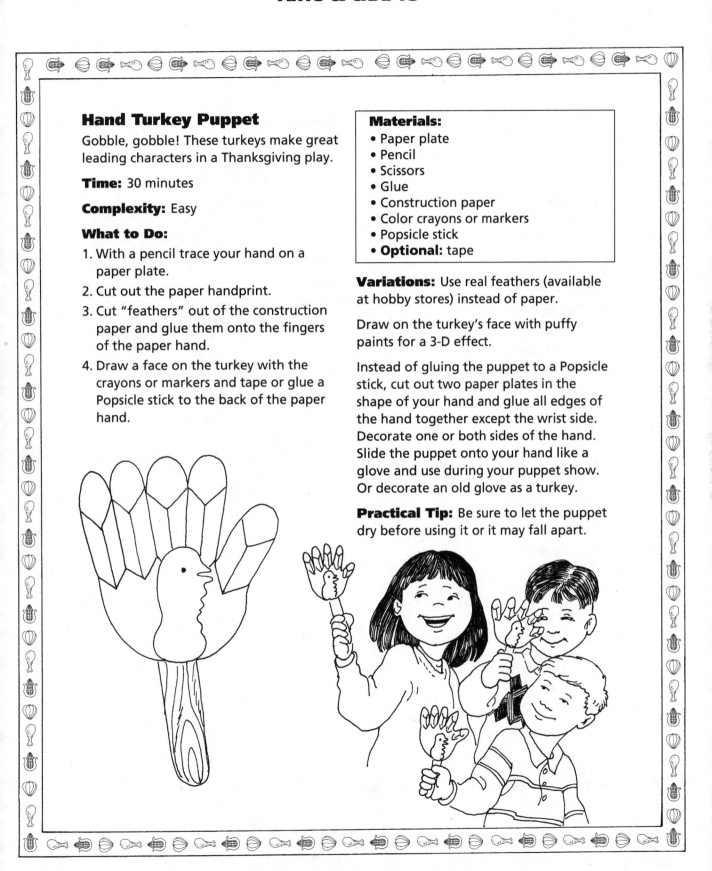

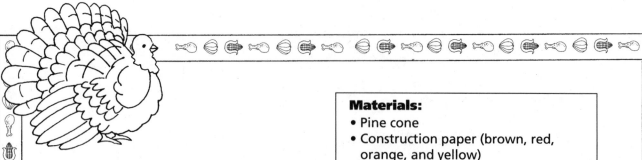

Pine-Cone Turkey

Create these holiday turkeys to decorate the holiday table or to keep as pets.

Time: 20 minutes

Complexity: Easy

What to Do:

1. Cut small, medium, and large scallops out of the construction paper.

2. Glue the scallops to the pine cone for the turkey's feathers.

3. Cut a head out of the construction paper and glue onto the pine cone.

4. Glue the wiggly plastic eyes onto the head.

5. Cut feet out of the brown construction paper and glue onto the bottom of the pine cone.

Materials:
- Pine cone
- Construction paper (brown, red, orange, and yellow)
- Glue
- Wiggly plastic eyes

Variation: Instead of construction paper, use colored or natural feathers from a hobby store.

Practical Tip: Glue is tricky to use on a pine cone, so work slowly and carefully. Don't use too much glue.

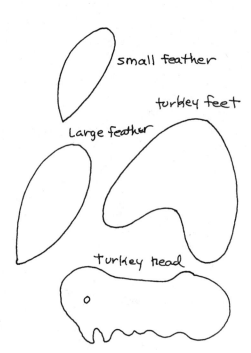

small feather

turkey feet

Large feather

turkey head

Dream Catcher

The legend of the dream catcher comes from the Ojibwa, who believe that the night air is filled with dreams, both good and bad. The dream catcher captures the dreams that float by. The good dreams slip through the center hole and slide down to the person sleeping below, while the bad dreams get tangled in the web. Make your own dream catcher in honor of the Native Americans at the first Thanksgiving.

Time: 1 hour

Complexity: Challenging—Adult assistant recommended

What to Do:

1. Glue or twist a hoop together.

2. Tie one end of the web material you are using to the hoop.

3. Begin stitching a web by looping the web material completely around the hoop. Be sure to catch each loop about itself before going to the next one, as shown. Space the stitches evenly apart, pulling loops tight to the hoop.

4. Start a second row by following the same steps for the first row, but go around the middle of the loops from the first row instead of the hoop. Periodically add beads, trinkets, or charms to the web.

Materials:

- Hoop material, such as willow twig, basket reed, pipe cleaner, embroidery hoop, or grapevine
- Glue
- Web material, such as thread, yarn, string, dental floss, or fishing line
- Fastener, such as a leather strip, leather shoe lace, yarn, or narrow ribbon
- Feathers
- Beads, small trinkets, or charms

5. Continue adding rows until you have a hole in the center the size you desire. Tie a small knot at the end of the web material to hold it in place.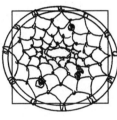

6. Attach feathers to the web by gluing them to the hoop or inserting them into small openings in the hoop.

7. Tie a fastener to the hoop to hang the dream catcher up by.

Variation: For another web style, start as above, but in the second row loop around the same point as the first row.

Practical Tip: Work slowly and carefully for best results.

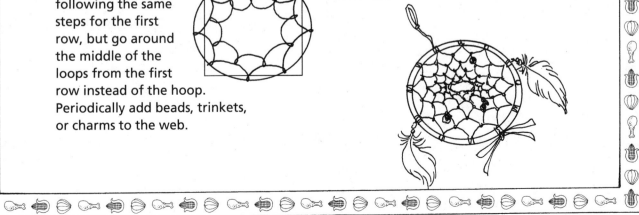

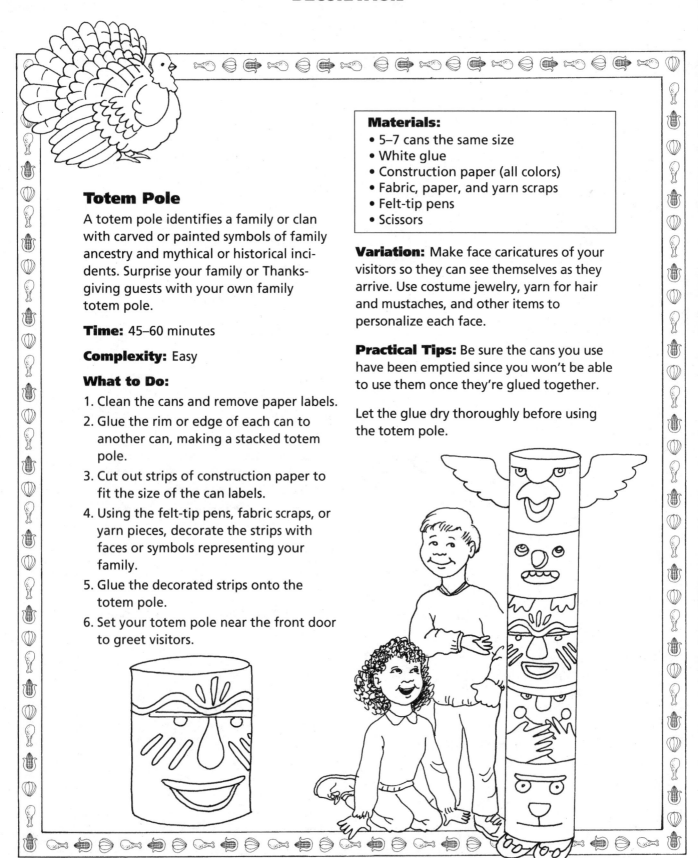

Totem Pole

A totem pole identifies a family or clan with carved or painted symbols of family ancestry and mythical or historical incidents. Surprise your family or Thanksgiving guests with your own family totem pole.

Time: 45–60 minutes

Complexity: Easy

What to Do:

1. Clean the cans and remove paper labels.
2. Glue the rim or edge of each can to another can, making a stacked totem pole.
3. Cut out strips of construction paper to fit the size of the can labels.
4. Using the felt-tip pens, fabric scraps, or yarn pieces, decorate the strips with faces or symbols representing your family.
5. Glue the decorated strips onto the totem pole.
6. Set your totem pole near the front door to greet visitors.

Materials:
- 5–7 cans the same size
- White glue
- Construction paper (all colors)
- Fabric, paper, and yarn scraps
- Felt-tip pens
- Scissors

Variation: Make face caricatures of your visitors so they can see themselves as they arrive. Use costume jewelry, yarn for hair and mustaches, and other items to personalize each face.

Practical Tips: Be sure the cans you use have been emptied since you won't be able to use them once they're glued together.

Let the glue dry thoroughly before using the totem pole.

THANKSGIVING DAY SONG

Traveling on Thanksgiving Day? Pass
the time by singing this traditional Thanksgiving Day song. It'll get everyone
in the mood for homemade pumpkin pie.

Thanksgiving Day

Over the river and through the wood,
   To Grandfather's house we go;
     The horse knows the way
     To carry the sleigh
   Through the white and drifted snow.

Over the river and through the wood—
   Oh, how the wind does blow!
     It stings the toes
     And bites the nose
   As over the ground we go.

Over the river and through the wood,
   To have a first-rate play.
     Hear the bells ring,
     "Ting-a-ling-ding!"
   Hurrah for Thanksgiving Day!

Over the river and through the wood,
   Trot fast, my dapple-gray!
     Spring over the ground
     Like a hunting hound,
   For this is Thanksgiving Day.

Over the river and through the wood,
And straight through the barnyard gate . . .
     We seem to go
     Extremely slow—
   It is so hard to wait!

Over the river and through the wood—
   Now Grandmother's cap I spy!
     Hurrah for the fun!
     Is the pudding done?
   Hurrah for the pumpkin pie!

—Lydia Marie Child

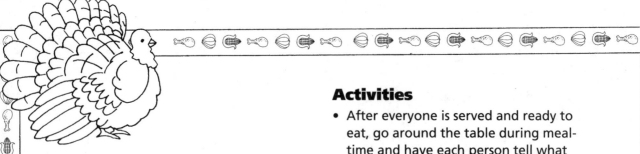

THANKSGIVING DAY CELEBRATION

Here are some ideas to make your Thanksgiving Day celebration extra special.

Decorations

- Hang up autumn mobiles to give the party room an outdoor look and to add some fall colors. Collect a bunch of leaves and pine cones from the yard. Tie colored yarn around each leaf or pine cone. String a long piece of yarn kitty-corner from one corner of the party room to the other, then repeat from other corners. Hang leaves from yarn. Or cut out tree branches from brown construction paper and tape them to a wall or on top of a tablecloth. Then glue the leaves and pine cones to the tree branches.

- Decorate the table with a display of Indian corn, colorful gourds, and leaves in a big wicker or cornucopia basket. To make your own cornucopias, curve brown construction paper into a cone shape and place corn and gourds inside. Lay it on its side and add more corn, gourds, and leaves tumbling out.

- Hollow out a pumpkin and fill it with flowers or fall leaves. Or cut a pineapple in half, hollow it out, attach a construction paper or felt turkey head for one end and use the pineapple leaves for the tail end. Fill it with fruit salad.

Activities

- After everyone is served and ready to eat, go around the table during meal-time and have each person tell what they are thankful for. This is a good time to share stories about what each one appreciates about life, friends, family, and so on. If you get a chance, write these down and save them to read at next year's Thanksgiving gathering.

- Ask a friend from another country or culture to make something traditional from their heritage. Then exchange dishes and enjoy the new foods during the meal.

Game

- Have the guests sit in a circle and begin a rhythm by having them first slap their legs, then clap their hands, then snap their fingers. Each time they snap their fingers one guest must name something to be thankful for, taking turns around the circle. If players miss the beat and can't come up with something, they are out of the game and the rest continue.

Food

- Make individual pumpkin pies for your guests that reflect their personalities. Buy or make graham-cracker shells for each guest in individual aluminum pans. Make pumpkin pie filling according to directions on the can and pour into the shells. Bake for 20 to 25 minutes or until done. Allow to cool. Create eyes, nose, and mouth with candy corn. Create hair with whipped cream.

Turkey-Shaped Cheese Appetizer

Serve an appetizer that looks like a turkey! Your guests will gobble it up.

Serves: 6–8

Time: 30 minutes

Complexity: Easy—Adult assistance recommended

Ingredients:
- 2 cups whole almonds
- 2 8-ounce packages cream cheese
- 2 5-ounce jars favorite cheese spread (Cheddar, pimento, bacon)
- 1/4 cup chopped green onions
- 1 teaspoon Worcestershire sauce
- Breadsticks

What to Do:
1. Bake the whole almonds in a single layer in the jelly-roll pan for 10 minutes. Allow to cool.
2. With the electric mixer, mix the cream cheese and cheese spread together until smooth.
3. Stir in the green onions and Worcestershire sauce.
4. Shape the cheese into a turkey body (a round mound) and tail. Place on the platter.
5. Stick half a breadstick in one end of the cheese to form a turkey neck and several at the other end to form a tail.
6. Cut out a paper head from the construction paper and tape it onto the single breadstick.

Materials:
- Jelly-roll pan
- Oven, preheated to 375°
- Electric mixer
- Medium bowl
- Large spoon
- Platter
- Scissors
- Construction paper
- Tape

7. Cover the turkey body and tail with almonds to form feathers.
8. Cut out feet from brown construction paper (or use bread sticks). Place them at two points around the body.
9. Serve with crackers.

Variation: Use a variety of nuts and/or crackers instead of just almonds.

Practical Tip: Keep refrigerated until serving time.

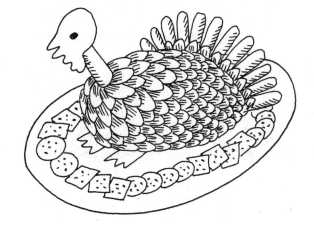

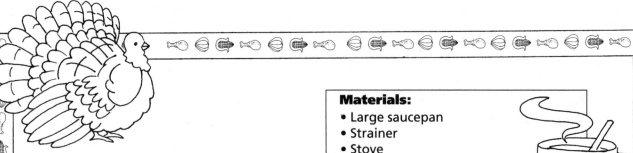

Cran-Apple Cider

Welcome your Thanksgiving Day guests with this hot drink. It's berry delicious!

Serves: 6–8

Time: 10 minutes

Complexity: Easy—Adult assistance recommended

Ingredients:
- 1 pint cranberry-juice cocktail
- 1 quart apple juice
- 1 cup water
- 6 whole cloves
- 2 cinnamon sticks
- 1 lemon, sliced thin

Materials:
- Large saucepan
- Strainer
- Stove
- Mugs

What to Do:
1. Mix the cranberry-juice cocktail, apple juice, water, cloves, cinnamon, and lemon together in a large saucepan.
2. Heat and strain.
3. Serve warm in mugs to cold guests.

Variations: Substitute other fruit drinks for apple juice.

Serve this drink cold.

Practical Tip: Keep the cider warm all day in a coffee warmer or Crockpot.

Ice-Cream Turkeys

They didn't have ice cream at the first Thanksgiving Day feast, but there's no reason you can't indulge in these ice-cream turkeys today!

Time: 15 minutes

Complexity: Easy—Adult assistance recommended

Ingredients:
- 1 cup flaked coconut
- Ice cream (chocolate, toffee, or toasted almond)
- Candy corn
- Raisins

Materials:
- Oven, preheated to 375°
- Cookie sheet
- Ice-cream scoop
- Small bowls
- Spoons

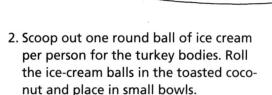

What to Do:
1. Spread out the coconut on the cookie sheet and toast in the oven until lightly brown. Allow to cool.

2. Scoop out one round ball of ice cream per person for the turkey bodies. Roll the ice-cream balls in the toasted coconut and place in small bowls.

3. Place two candy corns in the front of each ice-cream ball for beaks, two raisins for eyes, and form tails with candy corn. Serve immediately.

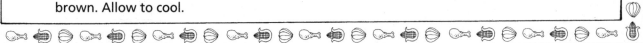

Pumpkin Ice-Cream Pie

Why not make a pumpkin ice-cream pie instead of the traditional pumpkin pie this year? It's easy, different, and refreshing.

Serves: 8

Time: 30 minutes

Complexity: Moderate—Adult assistance recommended

Ingredients:
- 1 cup plain canned pumpkin (not filling)
- 1/4 cup sugar
- 1/4 teaspoon cinnamon
- 1/4 teaspoon ginger
- 1 quart vanilla ice cream
- 1 graham-cracker pie crust
- **Optional:** whipped cream

What to Do:

1. In the medium bowl, mix the pumpkin, sugar, and spices together.

2. Soften the ice cream in the large bowl.

3. Add the pumpkin mixture to the ice cream and stir until well blended. Use an electric mixer, if desired.

4. Spoon the mixture into the pie crust and smooth the top. Place in a freezer for several hours, until firm.

Materials:
- Medium bowl
- Large spoon
- Large bowl
- Knife
- Plate or bowls
- **Optional:** electric mixer

5. Allow to thaw for a few minutes before serving. Add whipped cream to top, if desired. Serve on plates or in bowls.

Variation: Use eight mini pie crusts instead of one large one.

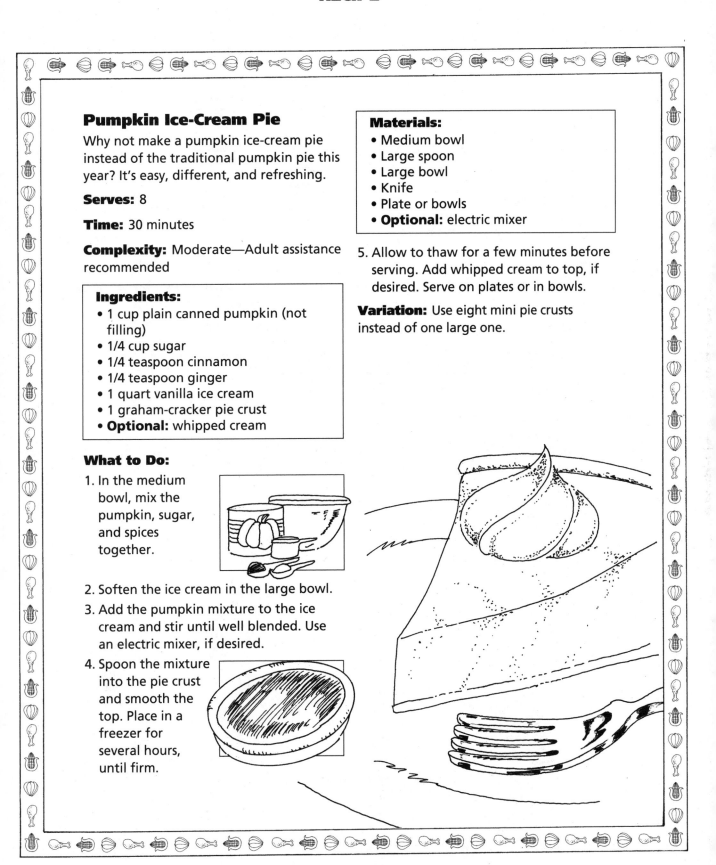

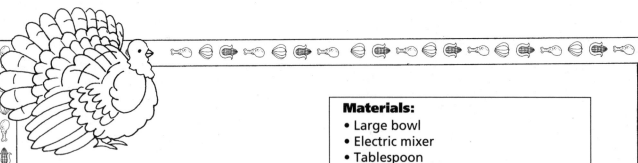

Pumpkin Cookies

These pumpkin cookies are sure to be a hit with pumpkin-pie lovers.

Yields: 3 dozen

Time: 20 minutes

Complexity: Moderate—Adult assistance recommended

Ingredients:
- 1/2 cup margarine, softened
- 3/4 cup brown sugar, packed
- 1 egg
- 1 teaspoon vanilla
- 1 cup canned pumpkin
- 2 cups flour
- 1 teaspoon baking soda
- 1 teaspoon cinnamon
- 1 teaspoon nutmeg
- 1/2 teaspoon ginger
- 1 cup raisins
- Vegetable-oil spray (such as Pam)

What to Do:

1. In the large bowl, mix the softened margarine and brown sugar. Beat at low speed until smooth.

2. Add the egg, vanilla, and pumpkin and beat until smooth.

3. Add the flour, baking soda, cinnamon, nutmeg, and ginger and mix well.

4. Stir in raisins.

Materials:
- Large bowl
- Electric mixer
- Tablespoon
- Cookie sheet
- Oven, preheated to 350°
- Spatula

5. Spray the cookie sheet with vegetable-oil spray.

6. Drop batter by tablespoons onto cookie sheet, about 1 inch apart.

7. Bake until edges begin to brown, about 15 minutes. Cool and serve.

Variations: Make cookies without raisins.

Decorate cookies with chocolate or yellow-tinted frosting.

Practical Tip: Make sure adults help with the mixer and oven for safety.

December

HANUKKAH
(Date Varies)

This eight-day celebration, often called the Festival of Lights, commemorates the victory of a small group of Jews led by Judah Maccabee over the Syrians and Greeks. It's also a celebration of the rededication of the Temple at Jerusalem, which was recovered by the Maccabees in 165 B.C. The holiday begins on the 25th day of Kislev, third month of the lunar year, which usually falls in December near the time of the winter solstice.

Hanukkah is a joyous celebration in both the home and in the synagogue. Each night one candle on the menorah—a lamp with eight candles, one for each day of the holiday, and one extra candle with which to light the others—is lit until all eight are burning brightly. This recalls the "miracle of the lamp" when the victorious Jews returned to worship in the damaged temple to find only enough oil for the "eternal light" to burn for one day. But instead it lasted for eight days. During the eight days of Hanukkah, families often play games, sing songs, and exchange gifts.

Hanukkah Greeting Card

Friends and family love receiving homemade cards, especially if they're made by kids. This one is simple to make.

Time: 30 minutes

Complexity: Easy

What to Do:

1. Fold a piece of the blue construction paper in half to form a card.
2. Drizzle white glue on the cover to form the six-pointed star of David.
3. Place white yarn over the glue. Allow the glue to dry.
4. Write a Hanukkah message inside.

Variation: Make potato-print cards featuring the Star of David by cutting a

Materials:
- Blue construction paper
- White glue
- White yarn
- Pen or marker

potato in half. Pin on a paper pattern of a six-pointed star, then trace around the pattern with the point of a knife, not too deeply. Remove pattern and cut away the area until the star stands out 1/4 inch. Dip the potato star in white paint and print on blue paper or vice versa.

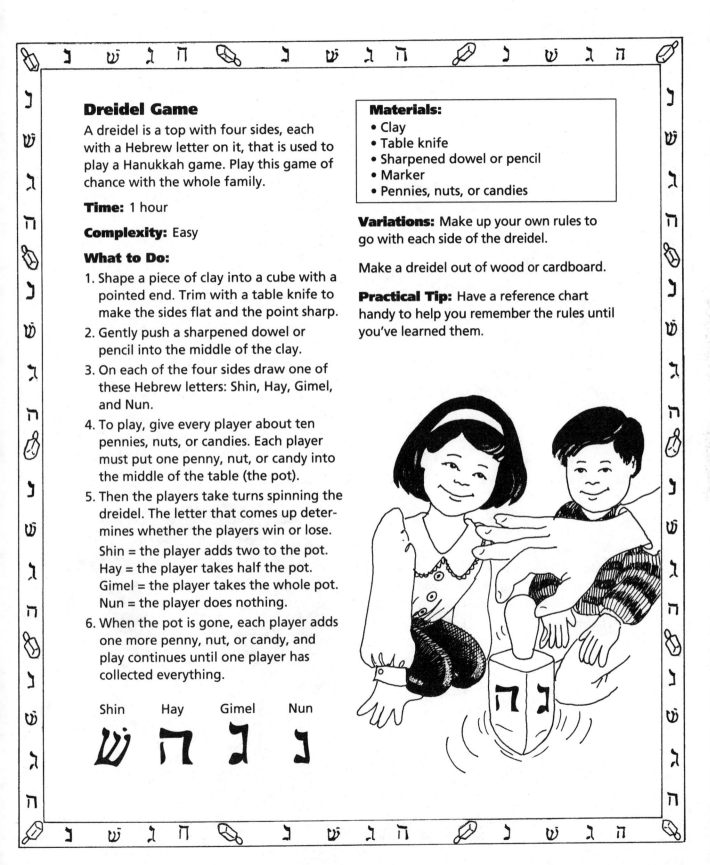

Dreidel Game

A dreidel is a top with four sides, each with a Hebrew letter on it, that is used to play a Hanukkah game. Play this game of chance with the whole family.

Time: 1 hour

Complexity: Easy

What to Do:

1. Shape a piece of clay into a cube with a pointed end. Trim with a table knife to make the sides flat and the point sharp.

2. Gently push a sharpened dowel or pencil into the middle of the clay.

3. On each of the four sides draw one of these Hebrew letters: Shin, Hay, Gimel, and Nun.

4. To play, give every player about ten pennies, nuts, or candies. Each player must put one penny, nut, or candy into the middle of the table (the pot).

5. Then the players take turns spinning the dreidel. The letter that comes up determines whether the players win or lose.

   Shin = the player adds two to the pot.
   Hay = the player takes half the pot.
   Gimel = the player takes the whole pot.
   Nun = the player does nothing.

6. When the pot is gone, each player adds one more penny, nut, or candy, and play continues until one player has collected everything.

Shin	Hay	Gimel	Nun
שׁ	ה	ג	נ

Materials:
- Clay
- Table knife
- Sharpened dowel or pencil
- Marker
- Pennies, nuts, or candies

Variations: Make up your own rules to go with each side of the dreidel.

Make a dreidel out of wood or cardboard.

Practical Tip: Have a reference chart handy to help you remember the rules until you've learned them.

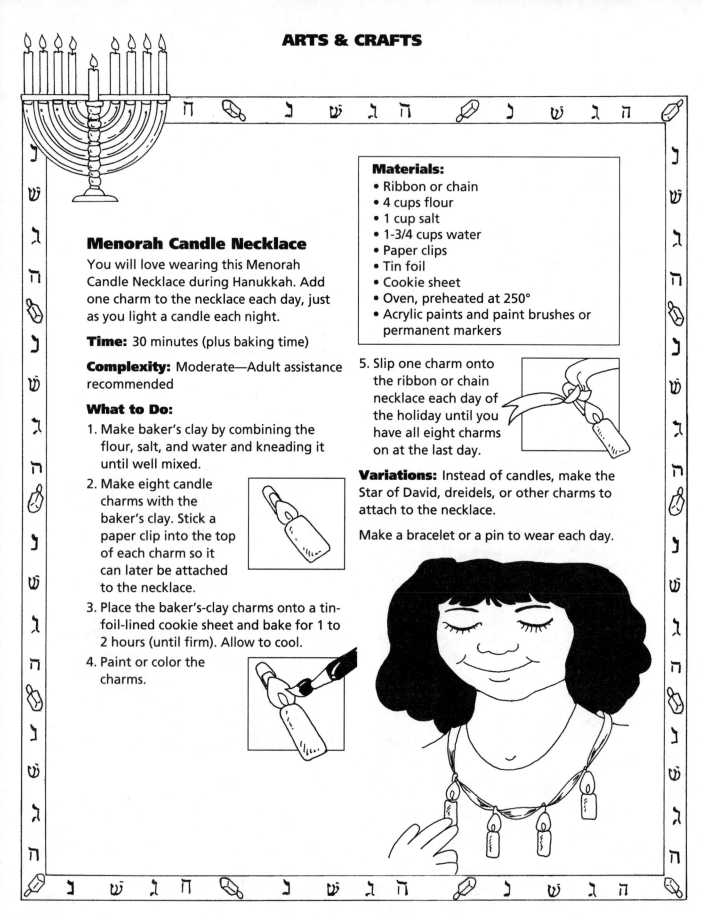

Menorah Candle Necklace

You will love wearing this Menorah Candle Necklace during Hanukkah. Add one charm to the necklace each day, just as you light a candle each night.

Time: 30 minutes (plus baking time)

Complexity: Moderate—Adult assistance recommended

What to Do:

1. Make baker's clay by combining the flour, salt, and water and kneading it until well mixed.

2. Make eight candle charms with the baker's clay. Stick a paper clip into the top of each charm so it can later be attached to the necklace.

3. Place the baker's-clay charms onto a tin-foil-lined cookie sheet and bake for 1 to 2 hours (until firm). Allow to cool.

4. Paint or color the charms.

Materials:
- Ribbon or chain
- 4 cups flour
- 1 cup salt
- 1-3/4 cups water
- Paper clips
- Tin foil
- Cookie sheet
- Oven, preheated at 250°
- Acrylic paints and paint brushes or permanent markers

5. Slip one charm onto the ribbon or chain necklace each day of the holiday until you have all eight charms on at the last day.

Variations: Instead of candles, make the Star of David, dreidels, or other charms to attach to the necklace.

Make a bracelet or a pin to wear each day.

Star of David

Symbolizing Judaism, this Star of David is a creative decoration for Hanukkah. Set it on a table or hang it from the ceiling.

Time: 45 minutes

Complexity: Moderate

What to Do:

1. Out of the posterboard cut two equal-sided (equilateral) triangles with 8-inch sides.

2. Place one triangle upside down on top of the other so they make a star shape.

3. Glue the triangles together.

4. Outline the star with glue and stick on toothpicks for a border.

5. Fill one section of the triangle with glue, and then with the macaroni noodles. Repeat with the other sections until the star is filled with noodles. Allow to dry.

6. Paint with blue paint.

Materials:

- Posterboard (white or blue)
- Ruler
- Pencil
- Scissors
- Glue
- Toothpicks
- Macaroni noodles
- Paint (blue)
- Paint brush

Variation: Use a variety of materials to fill the star, such as tissue paper, glitter, beads, seeds, or pictures of family members in a collage.

Practical Tip: Allow to dry completely before painting.

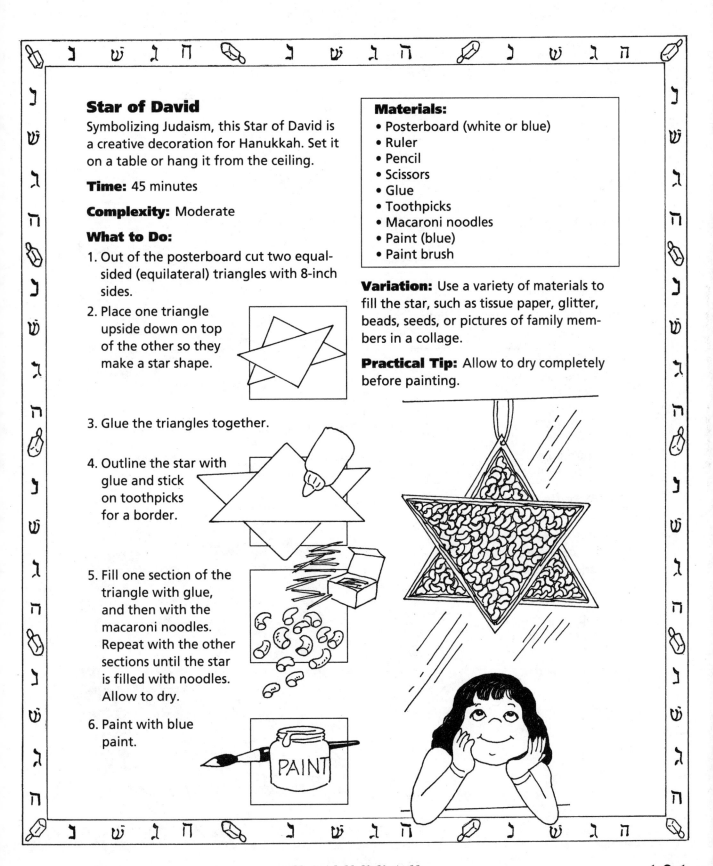

Potato Latkes

No Hanukkah meal is complete without Potato Latkes. They're delicious and fun to make, too.

Serves: 4

Time: 30 minutes

Complexity: Moderate—Adult assistance recommended

Ingredients:
- 4 potatoes, grated
- 1 egg
- 1 small onion, chopped
- Dash of salt
- 1 tablespoon flour
- Margarine
- Sour cream or applesauce

What to Do:

1. Mix the grated potatoes, egg, onion, salt, and flour in the medium bowl.

2. Drop large rounded spoonfuls onto the hot frying pan, greased with margarine.

Materials:
- Medium bowl
- Spoon
- Frying pan
- Stove
- Spatula

3. Fry on both sides until brown.

4. Serve hot with sour cream or applesauce.

Variation: Add shredded cheese.

Practical Tip: Serve immediately for best taste.

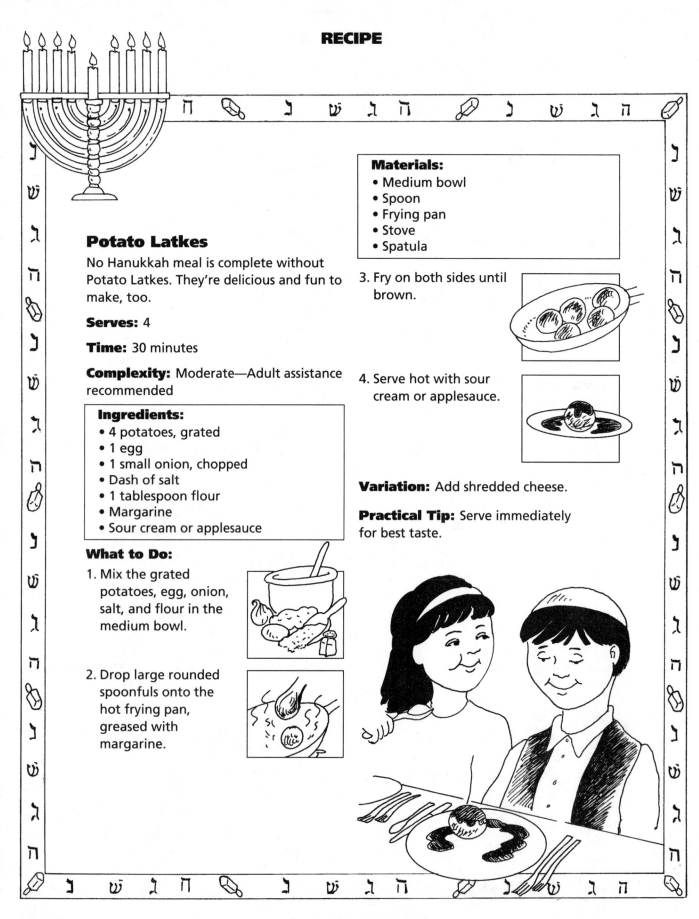

Sufganiyyot (Orange Donuts)

Israelis celebrate Hanukkah by making and eating orange-flavored donuts. They're fun and easy to make, but require adult supervision while cooking.

Yields: 1-1/2 dozen (depending on size of donuts)

Time: 30 minutes (plus 1 hour rising time)

Complexity: Easy—Adult assistance recommended

Ingredients:
- 3/4 cup orange juice
- 1/4 pound margarine, melted
- 1/4 cup granulated sugar
- 2 packages dry yeast
- 3 cups flour
- 2 eggs, beaten
- Dash of salt
- Vegetable oil for cooking
- Powdered sugar for dusting

What to Do:

1. Mix the orange juice, melted margarine, and granulated sugar together in the medium saucepan and heat until luke-warm. Sprinkle in the yeast and stir until it's dissolved.

2. Add the flour, eggs, and salt, and mix to a smooth dough.

3. On a lightly floured cutting board or counter, knead the dough until it is springy.

Materials:
- Medium saucepan
- Large spoon
- Large cutting board or large surface to knead on
- Medium bowl, greased
- Large frying pan
- Stove
- Spatula or tongs
- Paper towels
- Paper bag

4. Place the dough in the medium greased bowl, cover with a paper towel, and let rise for half an hour.

5. Knead again, shape into donut rings, and let rise for half an hour more.

6. In the large frying pan, fry the donuts in 2 inches of hot oil until golden brown, turning once with a spatula or tongs.

7. Drain on paper towels.

8. Put some powdered sugar in a paper bag, add donuts, and shake to cover with the sugar.

Variations: Although not traditional, substitute lemonade for the orange juice to make lemon donuts.

Frost the donuts with orange frosting or eat plain.

Practical Tips: If the dough gets sticky, add a little more flour.

Use caution around hot oil. Turn pan handles inward and use a back burner.

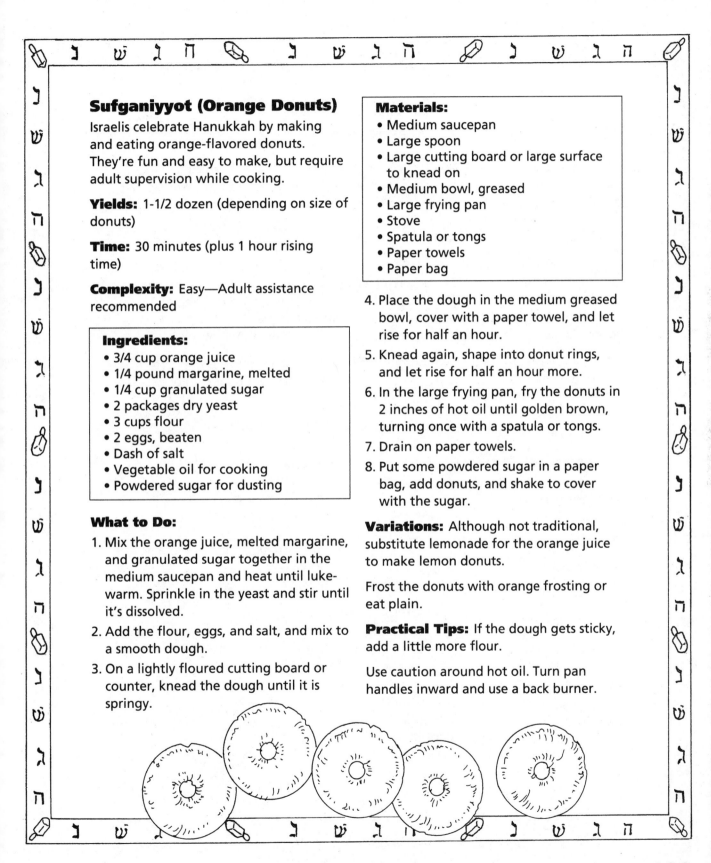

CHRISTMAS
December 25

Kids of all ages love this Christian holiday that commemorates the birth of Jesus Christ. Many Christmas customs come from the story of Christ's birth. People give each other gifts because the Three Wise Men, or Three Kings, brought gifts to the baby Jesus. Other customs come from older holidays. Burning the Yule log, for example, comes from a northern European holiday called Yule. And the tradition of the Christmas tree began in Germany from Druid tree worship.

Did you know that Santa Claus was a real person? He began as a kind bishop named St. Nicholas who lived in the fourth century. He passed out gifts to children and poor people in secret. Only with the poem "A Visit from St. Nicholas," by Clement Clarke Moore, did Santa Claus acquire reindeer, a red suit, and a sleigh full of toys.

No matter which Christmas traditions your family follows, Christmas is the perfect season for the whole family to gather together. It's also a great opportunity to create your own family traditions.

Snow-Storm Jar

Capture winter in a jar. This easy-to-make snow-storm jar is a gift anyone will appreciate.

Time: 15 minutes

Complexity: Easy

What to Do:

1. Fill the jar with baby oil or corn syrup, and a little water.
2. Add glitter, star sparkles, metallic confetti, or other decorations to act as snow.
3. Glue the tiny Christmas figurine to the inside of the lid with glue, and then put glue around the lid and seal it shut.

Materials:
- Small glass jar with lid, such as a baby-food jar
- Baby oil or corn syrup
- Water
- Glitter, star sparkles, or metallic confetti
- Glue
- Tiny Christmas figurine

4. When dry, turn the jar upside down and give it a shake. Then watch the "snow" fall on the tiny figurine.

GIFT WRAP

Wrap up your gifts with love using materials you already have at home.

Tin Foil

Materials:
- Tin foil
- Tape
- Permanent felt-tip pens (various colors)
- Scissors

What to Do:

1. Crinkle and then smooth out the tin foil.
2. Wrap the gift, then color in the smooth areas with colored permanent felt-tip pens. Leave some of the fold lines uncolored for a stained-glass look.

Practical Tips: Allow the ink to dry thoroughly before handling.

Wrap the top and bottom of gift boxes separately so each box can be opened without ripping the paper.

Construction Paper

Materials:
- Construction paper
- Tape
- Glue
- Scissors

What to Do:

1. Wrap the gift with construction paper.
2. Cut out "clues" to the gift and glue them onto the construction paper. For example, if the present is some fish hooks for Dad, cut out some colorful fish. If the present is perfume for Mom, cut out a picture of a skunk or a flower.

Variation: Draw the clues on the construction paper with felt-tip pens or crayons.

Brown Paper Bags

Materials:
- Brown paper bags
- Scissors
- Construction paper
- Tape

What to Do:

1. Place the gift inside a brown paper bag, fold over the top, and cut along the edge to give it a curved look.
2. Top the bag with construction paper eyes and place a bow under the cut edge to make a "Christmas Frog." Try other animals using this technique.

Other Ideas:

- Decorate gift boxes with pompoms, glitter, sequins, magazine pictures, wiggly plastic eyes, funny faces, stickers, or bows.
- Make "curls" for the top of boxes by cutting wrapping paper into 8-inch strips and pulling scissors along the unprinted side, gently but firmly, to make the ribbon "curl," much as you would curling ribbon. Tape a bunch of curls onto the packages.
- Find attractive pictures from Christmas cards or wrapping-paper designs and re-create the designs with construction paper or felt. Top the boxes with your creations. (If you make it from felt it can be used as an ornament later.)

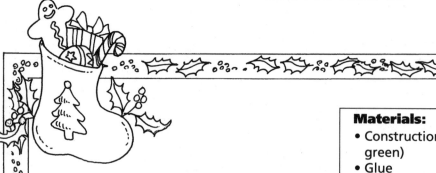

Santa Countdown

Here comes Santa Claus! Count down the days until Santa arrives with this Santa chain. Each link in the chain represents one day—cut one off each day until Christmas.

Time: 30–45 minutes

Complexity: Easy

What to Do:

1. Roll a sheet of white construction paper into a cone. Glue or tape it together. Trim the bottom of the cone so it will stand up straight and even.

2. With a red marker or felt-tip pen color the top third of the cone for Santa's hat.

3. With markers or felt-tip pens draw eyes, a nose, and a mouth on one side of the cone under the hat.

4. Glue on cotton balls for eyebrows, sideburns, a beard, and hair.

5. Glue a cotton ball to the top of the cone.

6. Out of red, green, and white construction paper cut twenty-four strips, each about 1-1/2 inches wide by 6- or 7-inches long. Number the strips from one to twenty-four.

7. Make a paper chain by gluing one strip into a circle and then linking another strip through it and gluing it together. Continue until all twenty-four strips are linked together.

Materials:
- Construction paper (white, red, and green)
- Glue
- Tape
- Scissors
- Markers or felt-tip pens (red, green, and black)
- Cotton balls

8. Glue or tape one end of the paper chain to the top or bottom of Santa's hat.

9. Cut off one link each day until Christmas.

Variation: Make a Christmas tree out of a piece of green construction paper rolled into a cone. Cut out circles from construction paper to make ornaments for the tree. Number the ornaments from one to twenty-four, and then tape them to the tree. Attach a cut-out star to the top. Pull off an ornament each day until Christmas.

Practical Tips: Make this at the beginning of December so you will have twenty-four days to cut the chain links apart. Or only attach as many links to your chain as you have days left until Christmas.

Cut the links off at the same time each day.

Advent Calendar

Waiting for Christmas is hard. This Advent Calendar provides something to look forward to during the countdown.

Time: 30 minutes

Complexity: Easy

What to Do:

1. Cut twenty-five "doors" in one piece of tagboard and glue it on top of the other piece.

2. Inside the doors attach small candies or notes, each telling where a small treat is hidden. Or write down a special activity you plan to do with a friend or family member, such as "Visit Santa," "Read *The Night Before Christmas*," "Sing Christmas Carols," "Go Gift Shopping," and so on.

3. Close the doors and seal them shut with stickers.

4. Number the doors on the outside from one to twenty-five.

Materials:
- 1 sheet red tagboard
- 1 sheet green tagboard
- Scissors
- Glue
- 25 candies or notes
- 25 stickers
- Felt-tip pen

5. Open a door in numerical order each day to find a treat, message, or something to do.

Variation: Have a series of Advent books and read a new story each day.

Practical Tip: Make sure the candies are wrapped so insects won't get into them.

DECORATION

Candy-Cane Sleigh

Santa is not the only one who rides in a sleigh. This decoration features a cute mouse. It will last for years—unless someone eats the runners off the sleigh.

Time: 30 minutes

Complexity: Easy

What to Do:

1. Wrap the lidless box with Christmas wrapping paper, or decorate it with felt-tip pens and ribbons.

2. Set the box open-side up on the table. Glue the candy canes to opposite sides of the box for the runners of the sleigh.

3. Make a mouse by gluing the wiggly plastic eyes to the gray pompom.

4. Glue the small black pompom on the gray pompom for a nose.

5. Cut ears out of the pink felt and glue them onto the top of the gray pompom.

6. Glue yarn to the bottom of the gray pompom for a tail.

Materials:
- Small box (without lid)
- Christmas wrapping paper or felt-tip pens and ribbons
- Tape
- 2 candy canes
- Glue
- Large gray pompom, approximately 1-1/2"–2" in diameter
- 1 tiny black pompom
- 2 wiggly plastic eyes
- Pink felt
- Yarn (pink, black, or gray)
- Scissors

7. Set the mouse in the sleigh, with its tail hanging over the edge of the box.

8. Use as a table or tree decoration.

Variation: Make lots of different kinds of animals to set in the sleigh. Or fill the sleigh with tiny Christmas candies.

Practical Tip: When gluing the candy canes onto the box, hold each one in place for a few seconds to make sure the glue has taken hold. Allow to dry thoroughly before handling.

198   DECEMBER

Yule-Log Centerpiece

This traditional Christmas decoration makes a great centerpiece for all of your holiday meals.

Time: 30 minutes

Complexity: Easy—Adult assistance recommended

What to Do:

1. Brush or spray a thin coat of glue on the log and sprinkle with glitter.
2. Melt wax in the center of the log and set the large round candle on the melted wax so it will stick to the log.
3. Glue small fir cones or other small decorations around the candle.

Materials:
- Log, about 20" long and 4" high
- Glue
- Glitter
- Wax
- Large round candle
- Small fir cones or other small decorations
- Ribbons
- Tree ornaments

4. Add ribbons and tree ornaments to the log. Place in center of the table.

Practical Tip: Be careful not to burn yourself with the hot wax.

Christmas Candles

People used candles to adorn Christmas trees before the days of electricity. Use these paper candles to give your Christmas tree an "old-fashioned" look.

Time: 30–45 minutes

Complexity: Easy

What to Do:

1. If you're using paper-towel tubes, cut them in half.
2. Glue or tape red construction paper around each tube.
3. Wrinkle the gold foil into flame shapes, one for each tube, and glue them to the inside of the tubes, but make sure the top of each flame sticks out.
4. Set the "candles" on the tree by placing them over upturned branches.

Materials:
- Paper-towel or toilet-paper tubes
- Red construction paper
- Glue
- Tape
- Scissors
- Gold foil gift wrap

Variation: Make the candles as decorations instead of tree trimmers. Set them on colorful plastic lids. Add glitter, lace, ribbon, or holly.

Practical Tip: If your tree does not have many upturned branches or the candles seem insecure on the tree, use florist wire to secure.

Santa Pencil

Have fun using this Santa pencil when you're writing your Christmas wish list. Make a few extra pencils to give to teachers or friends.

Time: 30 minutes

Complexity: Easy

What to Do:

1. Stick the pointed end of the pencil halfway into the Styrofoam ball.

2. Remove the ball, add a little glue to the eraser end of the pencil, and insert the eraser end of the pencil into the ball.

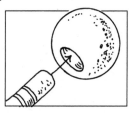

3. Cut the red felt into a square, and then fold or roll it into a cone shape for a hat.

4. Glue the hat together, and then glue it onto the Styrofoam ball.

5. Using the felt-tip pens, draw a face on the ball.

6. Glue cotton balls onto the Styrofoam ball for a beard, hat trim, and hat topper.

7. Allow to dry.

Materials:
- Pencil (red or green)
- Styrofoam ball, approximately 1"–1-1/2" in diameter
- Red felt
- Cotton balls
- Felt-tips pens (red and black)
- Glue
- Scissors

Variations: Personalize the pencils by portraying family members and friends instead of Santa. Decorate to suit their features, then place the pencils on the tree or give them as Christmas gifts.

Add wiggly plastic eyes and cheeks colored with a pink felt-tip pen. Write the name of friends or family members along the side of the pencil.

Practical Tip: Separate the cotton balls into smaller pieces to make eyebrows and other smaller details.

Twelve Days of Christmas Gifts

"On the first day of Christmas . . ." Act out this popular Christmas song by giving your true love (or best friend) a gift on each day of Christmas, beginning on Christmas Day and ending on January 5, the day before Epiphany.

What to Do:

1. Using "The Twelve Days of Christmas" as a guide, write down your own version of the song on index cards. Change each stanza to fit a small gift you plan to give someone special. For example, you might write, "On the first day of Christmas my true love gave to me—a sweet-smelling candle made of fresh bayberry."

2. Choose two things to give your true love for the second day, three for the third, and so on, until you have twelve. You might include such things as two matching socks, three shiny apples, four scented soaps, five candy bars, a six-pack of soda, seven stickers, eight chocolate gold coins, nine bath beads, ten sticks of gum, eleven colorful pencils, and a dozen blueberry muffins.

3. Decorate each index card with Christmas stickers or markers, and set one card with a gift on the doorstep of your special friend each night of the twelve days of Christmas, then ring the bell and run away.

4. Sign the card on the last day.

Materials:
- 12 index cards
- Christmas stickers or markers
- Pen or pencil
- 12 small gifts

Picture-Frame Ornament

Here's a way to decorate the tree with a familiar smiling face year after year!

What to Do:

1. Make baker's clay by combining the flour, salt, and water and kneading it until well mixed.

2. Make several shapes, such as Christmas trees, stars, or stockings.

3. Cut out the centers of the shapes, leaving a 1/2-inch frame. Stick a paper clip or other metal hanger in the top of each frame and bake for 1 to 2 hours (until firm). Allow to cool.

4. Paint and then glue a piece of felt to the back to hold photos, leaving a gap at the top to slip them in. Slip in family photos and hang the ornaments on the tree.

Materials:
- 4 cups flour
- 1 cup salt
- 1-3/4 cups water
- Knife
- Paper clips or metal picture hangers
- Cookie sheet
- Oven, preheated to 250°
- Acrylic paints
- Paint brush
- Glue
- Felt
- Photos

No-Bake Clay Ornaments

These ornaments look like Christmas cookies—but don't eat them, they're for your Christmas tree.

Time: 30–45 minutes (plus drying time)

Complexity: Easy—Adult assistance recommended

What to Do:

1. In the medium saucepan, bring water to a boil, then remove from heat.

2. Stir in the salt and cornstarch.

3. Return to low heat and cook until dough becomes difficult to stir.

4. Pour dough onto waxed paper. Allow to cool.

5. Knead until smooth, then roll dough to 1/8-inch thickness and cut with Christmas cookie cutters.

6. Poke a hole in the top of each ornament with a toothpick. Allow to dry for 2 to 3 days. Store the leftover dough in an airtight container.

7. Paint with acrylic paint.

8. Attach string through the hole in the top of the ornaments and hang on the tree.

Materials:
- 1-1/2 cups water
- Medium saucepan
- Stove
- 2 cups salt
- 1 cup cornstarch
- Large spoon
- Waxed paper
- Roller
- Christmas cookie cutters
- Toothpick
- Acrylic paint
- Paint brush
- String

CHRISTMAS CAROLING

Get into the holiday spirit. Gather your family and friends together and go caroling through the neighborhood, local hospital, or retirement community.

Jolly Old Saint Nicholas

Jolly Old Saint Nicholas,
　　Lean your ear this way!
　　　　Don't you tell a single soul
　　　　What I'm going to say;
　　Christmas Eve is coming soon;
　　　　Now you dear old man,
　　Whisper what you'll bring to me;
　　　　Tell me, if you can.

Johnny wants a pair of skates;
　　Susy wants a sled;
　　　　Nellie wants a picture book,
　　　　Yellow, blue, and red;
　　Now I think I'll leave to you
　　　　What to give the rest;
　　Choose for me, dear Santa Claus;
　　　　You will know the best.

Up on the House-Top

Up on the house-top reindeer pause,
　　Out jumps good old Santa Claus;
　　Down through the chimney
　　　　with lots of toys,
　　All for the little ones' Christmas joys.

First comes the stocking of little Nell;
　　Oh, dear Santa, fill it well;
Give her a dolly that laughs and cries,
　　One that will open and shut her eyes.

Refrain:
Ho, ho, ho! Who wouldn't go!
Ho, ho, ho! Who wouldn't go!
Up on the house-top click, click, click,
Down through the chimney with good
　　Saint Nick.

We Wish You a Merry Christmas

We wish you a Merry Christmas,
We wish you a Merry Christmas,
We wish you a Merry Christmas,
And a happy New Year.

Good tidings we bring to you and your kin,
Good tidings for Christmas and a happy
　　New Year.

We all know that Santa's coming,
We all know that Santa's coming,
We all know that Santa's coming,
And soon will be here.

Good tidings we bring to you and your kin.
Good tidings for Christmas and a happy
　　New Year.

We wish you a Merry Christmas,
We wish you a Merry Christmas,
We wish you a Merry Christmas,
And a happy New Year.

Practical Tips:

- Bring along hot apple cider to keep the group warm between songs.
- Carry candles to light while you are singing.
- Wear red, white, and green clothes.

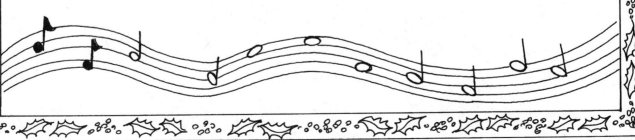

Cookie House

Work together to build this cookie house. Remember to set aside a few extra cookies for your hardworking construction workers to nibble on.

Time: 1 hour

Complexity: Moderate

What to Do:

1. From the cardboard cut out a roof to fit the box.
2. Glue, tape, or staple it onto the box.
3. Frost the cardboard box with royal icing (see recipe below), and then cover the box with cookies.
4. With the cookies make doors, windows, shingles, and designs for the outside of the house.

Variations: Make a candy house, using the same technique, or make it a combination of both.

Use graham crackers instead of cardboard for house walls and roof. "Glue" together with royal icing.

Practical Tip: Use up leftover Halloween candy as house decorations. Also make candy fences, flowers, paths, and trees. Put it all on a large Christmas tray.

Materials:

- Cardboard box about the size you want your "house" to be
- Cardboard scrap
- Scissors
- Glue, tape, or stapler
- Cookies
- Mixer
- Large bowl
- Damp towel

Royal Icing Recipe

Ingredients:

- 1 egg white
- 1/2 teaspoon cream of tartar
- 1 16-ounce package powdered sugar

What to do:

1. Beat the egg white with the cream of tartar until foamy.
2. Add powdered sugar, then beat until stiff peaks form, about 7 minutes.
3. Keep the bowl covered with the damp towel when not using—it dries fast and hard.

Taffy Candy Canes

Be a little daffy, pull some taffy! Everyone will enjoy working on this project, especially when it's time to taste the results.

Yields: 2 dozen

Time: 45 minutes

Complexity: Moderate—Adult assistance recommended

Ingredients:
- 1-1/4 cups sugar
- 1/4 cup water
- 2 tablespoons white distilled vinegar
- 1-1/2 teaspoons butter
- 1/2 teaspoon peppermint extract
- Red food coloring

What to Do:

1. Combine the sugar, water, vinegar, and butter in the medium saucepan.

2. Cook over medium heat until sugar is dissolved, stirring constantly.

3. Lower the heat and continue to cook without stirring, to 260° on the candy thermometer (or until a small amount of syrup forms a firm ball when dropped in very cold water).

4. Remove from heat and stir in the peppermint extract.

5. Pour half the mixture into the buttered pan.

6. Color the remaining half with red food coloring. Allow to cool a few minutes.

7. With clean, lightly buttered hands, pull the taffy until it becomes a satiny opaque look and begins to feel a little stiff (about 6 to 8 minutes).

Materials:
- Medium saucepan
- Stove
- Candy thermometer
- Large spoon
- Buttered pan, such as a cookie sheet with a lip
- Waxed paper

8. Take one strand of white and one of red and twist together, then form into candy-cane shapes. Allow to cool on waxed paper.

Variation: Use a variety of food coloring to make the taffy, then make all sorts of shapes and designs for the holiday.

Practical Tip: Be sure the taffy has cooled enough before you pull it so you won't burn your hands.

Rice Krispy Christmas Trees

Make Rice Krispy Christmas Trees to decorate your home or gobble up during those special Christmas TV programs.

Serves: 6–8

Time: 20 minutes

Complexity: Moderate—Adult assistance recommended

Ingredients:
- 1/4 cup butter
- 40 marshmallows
- Green food coloring
- 5–6 cups Rice Krispies
- Red-hot candies
- Powdered sugar

Materials:
- Large saucepan
- Stove
- Large spoon
- Large plate or cookie sheet

What to Do:

1. Melt the butter and marshmallows in the large saucepan over low heat.
2. Add a few drops of green food coloring.
3. Stir in the Rice Krispies.
4. Quickly shape into trees, then add the red hots for ornaments. Place on a plate or cookie sheet.
5. Sift a small amount of powdered sugar over the top for "snow."

Variation: Make other shapes or designs with cookie cutters.

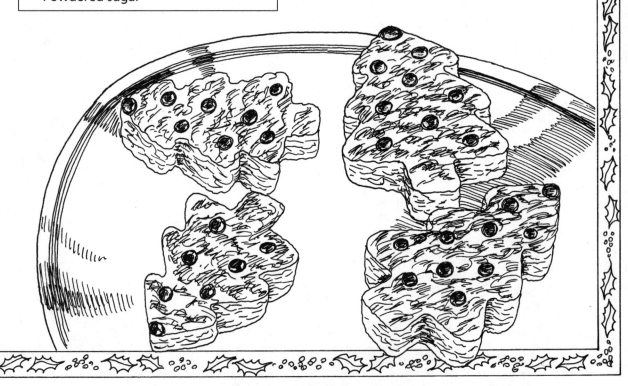

Red-Nosed Reindeer Drink

Here's a warm drink for cold winter nights. Named after our favorite reindeer, this drink is popular around the Pole and might turn your nose red.

Serves: 6–8

Time: 10 minutes

Complexity: Easy—Adult assistance recommended

Ingredients:
- 1 16-ounce bottle apple juice
- 1 16-ounce bottle cranberry juice
- 1 16-ounce bottle lemon-line soda
- 3 cinnamon sticks
- Tiny candy-cane stirrers

Materials:
- Large saucepan
- Stove
- Mugs

What to Do:
1. In the large saucepan mix the apple juice, cranberry juice, and lemon-lime soda with the cinnamon sticks.
2. Heat, and then serve in mugs with tiny candy-cane stirrers.

Variation: Mix together a variety of drink flavors to create your own recipe.

EXTRA IDEAS
A Time of Giving

The true meaning of Christmas is about giving of yourself. Spend some of the holiday time giving to others as a family.

- Make gifts and donate them to charitable organizations. Check first to see what they need and can accept.
- Prepare extra goodies to give to the local senior citizens' center or nursing home.
- Invite a single person to Christmas dinner—an elderly neighbor, a college student away from home, or a soldier.
- Ask that one gift be made in your name to a charitable organization.
- Join in a walkathon that benefits a needy group.
- Adopt a hungry child in another part of the world. Remember that this is a year-round commitment.
- Collect toys and clothes from the neighborhood and donate them to a local homeless shelter. (Check first to see if they can accept second-hand goods.)

KWANZAA
December 26–January 1

Kwanzaa is an African-American holiday based on the traditional African winter harvest festival. The holiday was created by Dr. Maulana Karenga in 1966. Kwanzaa, which means "first fruit" in Swahili, focuses on seven principles that contribute to the unity of the black family. It also focuses on developing community with a sense of African-American cultural heritage.

Each night families talk about one of the seven principles and how it can be applied to their daily lives. The seven principles are "umoja" (unity), "kujichagulia" (self-determination), "ujima" (collective work and responsibility), "ujamaa" (cooperative economics), "nia" (purpose), "kuumba" (creativity), and "imani" (faith). Children play a central role in this celebration. They light the Kinara (a seven-place candle holder), recite and explain the principles, help prepare special foods, and make music and dance presentations. Gifts are traditionally exchanged on the last day of Kwanzaa.

Karamu Feast Tabbouleh

A high point of Kwanzaa is the Karamu or feast. Karamu foods, like this recipe, incorporate the Kwanzaa colors of black, red, and green.

Serves: 4

Time: 1-1/2 hours

Complexity: Easy—Adult assistance recommended

Ingredients:
- 2 cups boiling water
- 1 cup bulgur wheat
- 1 cup fresh parsley, finely chopped
- 1/2 cup mint, finely chopped
- 1/2 pound tofu, finely chopped
- 2 tomatoes, finely chopped
- 1/2 cup black olives
- 1/4 cup lemon juice
- 1/4 cup green onions, chopped
- 2 tablespoons olive oil
- 1/2 teaspoon salt
- 1/2 teaspoon black pepper
- Leaf lettuce

Materials:
- Medium saucepan
- Stove
- Strainer
- Medium bowl

What to Do:
1. Pour boiling water over the bulgur wheat and soak for 1 hour.
2. Pour off water and drain well.
3. In the medium bowl combine the bulgar wheat with the remaining ingredients. Serve with leaf lettuce.

African Animal Necklace

Jewelry is an important part of African dress. Wear this necklace during Kwanzaa or anytime.

Time: 30 minutes (plus baking time)

Complexity: Easy—Adult assistance recommended

What to Do:

1. Make baker's clay by combining the flour, salt, and water and kneading it until well mixed.

2. Shape the dough into African animals, such as an elephant, a lion, a zebra, and a giraffe, or use animal cookie cutters.

3. Poke a hole at the top of each animal, then bake for 1 to 2 hours, until firm.

4. Paint your animals appropriate colors, allow to dry, then string one animal onto a black satin cord and tie a knot so it will stay in one place.

Materials:
- 4 cups flour
- 1 cup salt
- 1-3/4 cups water
- Medium bowl
- Animal cookie cutters
- Cookie sheet
- Oven, preheated to 250°
- Spatula
- Paint
- Paint brush
- Black satin cord

5. Add a second animal and repeat, until your necklace is complete.

Variation: Make a beaded necklace from red, black, and green baker's clay, by making tiny little balls of the three colors, poking a hole through the center, baking, and stringing through strong thread to make a necklace.

Practical Tip: Don't make the animals too big.

Kwanzaa Candles

On each night of Kwanzaa, one of seven candles in a holder (a Kinara) is lit. Three red candles on the right represent struggle, three green candles on the left represent the future, and a black one in the middle is for African people everywhere. Kinaras are usually homemade—make this one for your home.

Time: 30–45 minutes

Complexity: Easy

What to Do:

1. Wash and dry the cans or jars.
2. Spread newspaper out on your work area and paint the cans or jars red, green, and black. Paint them solid colors or with designs.
3. Place a candle in each can or jar.
4. Place the candles on a table or mantel. Light one candle each night of the holiday.

Materials:
- 7 small cans or jars, empty, without sharp edges
- 7 small votive candles (3 red, 3 green, and 1 black)
- Enamel paint (red, green, and black)
- Paint brushes
- Newspaper

5. After lighting the candle, talk about the principle honored on that day and how it applies to you.

Variations: Decorate the jars or cans with colorful cloth or paper, torn tissue paper, or wide ribbons.

Glue the jars onto a candelabra made of wood or posterboard.

Practical Tip: Be careful around the lit candles. Place a juice-can lid or dish under the candle to protect furniture from leaking wax.

Sweet-Potato Cookies

These yummy, African-style cookies have an unusual cookie ingredient—sweet potatoes. The cookies turn out bright orange and cakelike, with good nutrition along with good taste.

Yields: 2-1/2 dozen

Time: 30 minutes

Complexity: Easy—Adult assistance recommended

Cookie Dough Ingredients:
- 5 tablespoons margarine
- 1/8 cup sugar
- 1/2 teaspoon lemon juice
- 1/2 teaspoon nutmeg
- 1/8 cup honey
- 1 egg
- 1/2 cup raw sweet potato, finely grated
- 1-1/4 cups flour
- 3/4 teaspoon baking powder
- 1/4 teaspoon baking soda
- 1/4 teaspoon salt

Lemon Glaze Ingredients:
- 1/2 teaspoon margarine
- 1 tablespoon lemon juice
- 3/4 cup powdered sugar
- 1/2 tablespoon water

Materials:
- Large bowl
- Electric mixer
- Large spoon
- Teaspoon
- Cookie sheet
- Oven, preheated to 350°
- Medium bowl
- Spatula

What to Do:

1. With the electric mixer, combine the margarine and sugar in the large bowl until creamy.

2. Blend in the lemon juice, nutmeg, honey, and egg.

3. Fold in the sweet potato.

4. Add the flour, baking powder, baking soda, and salt. Stir until well blended.

5. Place rounded teaspoons onto the ungreased cookie sheet.

6. Bake for 6 to 8 minutes.

7. Make the glaze by combining ingredients in the medium bowl and stirring until smooth. Add water by the drop until the glaze is easy to spread on cooled cookies.

8. Spread glaze on cooled cookies.

Variation: Decorate the cookies with frosting and sprinkles in Kwanzaa colors. Use chocolate for black.

INDEX

INDEX

INDEX

Order Form

Qty.	Title	Author	Order No.	Unit Cost (US $)	Total
	Bad Case of the Giggles	Lansky, B.	2411	$15.00	
	Free Stuff for Kids	Free Stuff Editors	2190	$5.00	
	Girls to the Rescue	Lansky, B.	2215	$3.95	
	Girls to the Rescue, Book #2	Lansky, B.	2216	$3.95	
	Kids' Holiday Fun	Warner, P.	6000	$12.00	
	Kids' Party Cookbook	Warner, P.	2435	$12.00	
	Kids' Party Games and Activities	Warner, P.	6095	$12.00	
	Kids' Pick the Funniest Poems	Lansky, B.	2410	$15.00	
	New Adventures of Mother Goose	Lansky, B.	2420	$15.00	
	Poetry Party	Lansky, B.	2430	$12.00	
				Subtotal	
				Shipping and Handling (see below)	
				MN residents add 6.5% sales tax	
				Total	

YES! Please send me the books indicated above. Add $2.00 shipping and handling for the first book and 50¢ for each additional book. Add $2.50 to total for books shipped to Canada. Overseas postage will be billed. Allow up to four weeks for delivery. Send check or money order payable to Meadowbrook Press. No cash or C.O.D's, please. Prices subject to change without notice. **Quantity discounts available upon request.**

Send book(s) to:

Name _____ Address _____

City _____ State _____ Zip_____ Telephone (_____) _____ P.O.# (if ness.)_____

Payment via: ❑ Check or money order payable to Meadowbrook Press (No cash or C.O.D.'s, please)

Amount enclosed $ _____ ❑ Visa (for orders over $10.00 only) ❑ MasterCard (for orders over $10.00 only)

Account # _____ Signature _____ Exp. Date _____

A FREE Meadowbrook Press catalog is available upon request.
You can also phone us for orders of $10.00 or more at **1-800-338-2232.**
Meadowbrook, Inc., 18318 Minnetonka Boulevard, Deephaven, MN 55391

Mail to:
Phone (612) 473-5400   Toll-Free 1-800-338-2232   Fax (612) 475-0736